D1784759

Transport
Yearbook
2008

*A joint venture between
the Transport Statistics Users Group (TSUG)
and The Stationery Office*

London: TSO

information & publishing solutions

Published by TSO (The Stationery Office) and available from:

Online
www.tsoshop.co.uk

Mail, Telephone, Fax & E-mail
TSO
PO Box 29, Norwich, NR3 1GN
Telephone orders/General enquiries: 0870 600 5522
Fax orders: 0870 600 5533
E-mail: customer.services@tso.co.uk
Textphone 0870 240 3701

TSO Shops
16 Arthur Street, Belfast BT1 4GD
028 9023 8451 Fax 028 9023 5401
71 Lothian Road, Edinburgh EH3 9AZ
0870 606 5566 Fax 0870 606 5588

TSO@Blackwell and other Accredited Agents

To note that after the information was collected for this yearbook, Scottish Ministers formally
adopted the title 'Scottish Government' to replace the term 'Scottish Executive' as an expression of
corporate identity.

ISBN 978 0 11 703786 1

Printed in the United Kingdom by The Stationery Office
N5670808   C8   12/07

Contents

SECTION 1

Selected UK Transport Information and Statistics

SECTION 2

Directory of Government Organisations

SECTION 3

Directory of Non-Government Organisations

SECTION 4

Sources of Transport Statistics

SECTION 5

Educational Establishments

SECTION 6

Directory of Media, Publications and Research Companies

SECTION 7

Index of Organisations

Introduction

The Transport Yearbook is a comprehensive paperback guide to sources of transport statistics available in Britain and elsewhere. The development of the Transport Yearbook is a joint venture between the Transport Statistics Users Group (TSUG) and The Stationery Office, bringing together a wealth of knowledge and experience in the publication and use of transport statistics. Assistance in compilation of the Yearbook is provided by IRN Research.

The successful development of the Yearbook has come through the considerable efforts of the editorial board:

Ivan Coutinho	The Stationery Office
Fred Hitchins	IRN Research
Dr Jock Robertson	TSUG representative

The aim of the Yearbook is to provide an authoritative overview of transport in the UK and a quick but comprehensive reference guide to major UK transport organisations, sources of transport statistics and other important contacts. The guide is divided into six main sections:

Section 1	Selected UK Transport Information and Statistics
Section 2	Directory of Government Organisations
Section 3	Directory of Non-Government Organisations
Section 4	Sources of Transport Statistics
Section 5	Educational Establishments
Section 6	Directory of Media and Publications

Sections 2-6 have been cross-referenced to make it easier to find contacts and information. The (*) icon attached to organisations listed in the directory sections indicates that the organisation provides or publishes transport statistics found in Section 4. The entries in sections 3 and 4 have been characterised into UK and International entries and Non-UK entries. They have also been ordered by mode of transport to effect quick reference.

The TSUG would like to hear from anyone who has any suggestions to improve the Yearbook or would like to notify any corrections or omissions that should be made before the next edition. Please feel free to do so by sending an email to fhitchins@irn-research.com or robertson@rtclincs.co.uk

Transport Statistics Users Group (TSUG)

The TSUG was formed in 1985, following an initiative by The Institute of Logistics and Transport (then known as the Chartered Institute of Transport) and the Statistics Users Council.

The Aims of TSUG:

- to identify problems in the provision and understanding of transport statistics and to discuss solutions with the responsible authorities,

- to provide a forum for the exchange of views and information between users and providers,

- to encourage the use of transport statistics through publicity and education.

The Main Activities of TSUG:

The production of a regular newsletter containing reviews of recently published transport statistics, TSUG seminars and other information relating to transport statistics. The newsletter is distributed to members approximately four times per year.

The production of this Transport Yearbook. The aim of the Yearbook is to provide an easy-to-use but comprehensive reference guide to major UK transport organisations, sources of transport statistics, and other important UK and international contacts.

The organisation of ten or more seminars per year addressing contemporary issues in the field of transport statistics (see below). Most seminars are held in London, but there is an annual seminar held in Scotland and other ad hoc regional seminars.

The Membership of TSUG:

The Membership of TSUG includes a wide range of corporate organisations - including environmental agencies, government departments, local authorities, planning and development agencies, trade associations, transport consultants, transport operators and universities - as well as individual professionals. A management committee drawn from the membership runs the TSUG on a voluntary basis. More information is available on the TSUG website at www.tsug.org.uk. Applications for corporate, individual and student TSUG membership can be made through the web site.

The TSUG Seminar Programme:

The seminar programme organised by TSUG covers a wide range of topics both by area and by mode. In general, the aim of TSUG seminars is to engage in a dialogue between and among the users of transport statistics and the providers. Sometimes this is very direct as in the consultation on Department for Transport (DfT) reviews. In others, an explanation of how the data is currently being used will give providers more insight into the quality required of the data and important directions for improving its value. A topic which frequently arises is the opportunities that the adoption of new technology offers in the collection of statistics

One of the highlights of the 2006/07 programme was a seminar on bus and light rail statistics, which showed the wide range of sources that are now being consulted in producing DfT's bus and light rail statistical publications. Not only are data collected from bus operators, but details on punctuality, attitudes to crime on buses, and bus reliability are also consulted. Another new survey is the bus satisfaction survey which is already being modified to take on a 'mystery traveller' element, something DfT has borrowed from Transport for London. This shows how much of a learning process is involved in developing new statistics, and also highlights the potential that smart cards have for improving the detail available.

Another seminar from the 2006/07 programme covered maritime statistics and highlighted the reach of statistics that is now required for policy development. While the movement of goods and people through ports will remain important, it is necessary to cover topics such as port employment and accidents in ports in order to provide a better picture of the industry for policy makers.

The changing needs of policy makers in respect of statistics were highlighted by a seminar on transport and social inclusion – the best attended of the year's programme. It discussed the relevance of the indicators proposed by DfT guidance on accessibility planning, the types of journeys undertaken by people who are considered to be socially excluded, and the relationship between the risk of road injury and levels of deprivation.

The Links between TSUG and Government:

Transport Statistics Division in the Department for Transport is keen to maintain and improve its links with users, and it regards the Transport Statistics Users Group as an important forum in this context. TSUG seminars provide the Department with opportunities to present specific aspects of its statistical activity to those outside the Department, to engage users in the National Statistics quality reviews, and to seek feedback on its outputs. The more representative TSUG is of all users of transport statistics, the more valuable the Group is to the Department.

TSUG has also developed an excellent working relationship with the Scottish Executive Transport Statistics Branch.

SECTION 1

Selected UK Transport Information and Statistics

This first section of the Transport Yearbook provides a compendium of selected published information and statistics on UK transport activity. It is intended to document some of the key features of transport use and ownership in the UK, and to illustrate the wide range of statistics which are publicly available. The latest available statistics will usually be found on the websites of the source organisations.

The information and statistics are grouped under the following headings:

The major provider of published UK transport statistics is the **Department for Transport** (DfT), and many of the tables provided on the following pages are drawn from their publications. The prime source for obtaining DfT statistics is their website at www.dft.gov.uk/transtat. A number of statistics reports are published by the DfT annually or on an ad hoc basis. Chief amongst these are 'Transport Statistics Great Britain' and 'Transport Trends'. All the tables of statistics

published by the DfT are made available on their website.

Transport statistics for Scotland, Wales and Northern Ireland are published by the statistics branches of the **devolved administrations**. Each publishes an annual report on transport statistics for their area. A summary table of key transport statistics for each of the three administrations is presented in Section 1.10. The relevant websites are:

www.scotland.gov.uk/transtat
www.wales.gov.uk
http://csrb.drdni.gov.uk

The chief provider of statistics on **air transport** is the Civil Aviation Authority (CAA). The CAA publishes annual reports on statistics for both UK Airports and UK Airlines. Section 1.6 presents some statistics drawn from the CAA publications. Their website is at www.caa.co.uk and their statistics can be found on the Economic Regulation pages of the website.

A key source of statistics on **rail transport** is the Office of Rail Regulation (ORR), which has taken over many of the statistics responsibilities of the former Strategic Rail Authority. Their main annual publication is the National Rail Trends Yearbook. Their website is at www.rail-reg.gov.uk and their statistics can be found on the ORR website at: http://www.rail-reg.gov.uk/server/show/nav.1527

Further contact details for all these sources of transport statistics can be found in Section 2 of this Yearbook.

1.1 Transport by All Modes

Statistics on the total volumes of domestic passenger and freight transport in the UK are compiled by DfT from a variety of sources, including the National Travel Survey (NTS). The following tables show the long-term trends in volumes of passenger and freight transport, and in the shares handled by different modes.

Both passenger and freight transport have increased substantially over the longer term. The shares of both passenger and freight transport by different modes have remained little changed since 1990.

Passenger Transport, 1955-2005

	1955	1975	1990	1995	2000	2005
Total Billion Passenger Km.	239	438	690	712	749	798
Percentage by:						
Rail	16	8	6	5	6	6
Bus and Coach	38	14	7	6	6	6
Cars, Vans and Taxis	35	76	85	86	85	85
Other	11	2	2	3	3	3
Total	100	100	100	100	100	100

Source: Department for Transport

Freight Transport, 1955-2005

	1955	1975	1990	1995	2000	2005
Total Billion Tonne Km.	93	147	219	227	256	257
Percentage by:						
Rail	38	14	7	6	7	9
Road	41	63	62	66	62	63
Other	21	23	31	28	31	28
Total	100	100	100	100	100	100

Source: Department for Transport

1.2 Personal Travel

A key source of statistics on personal travel is the National Travel Survey, which currently collects information from the travel diaries of more than 8,000 households each year, representing the journeys of more than 20,000 people.

The NTS results for 2005 show that each person makes on average just over one thousand trips each year, where a trip is defined as a one-way course of travel for a single main purpose - so that a journey to and from work counts as two trips. The number of trips per person has increased only slightly in recent years, with NTS results for the period 1999–2001 having reported an average of 1,019 trips per year compared with the 2005 figure of 1,044. Nearly two thirds of all trips are made by car, either as drivers or passengers. The average one-way distance per trip is just less than seven miles.

The high proportion of trips made by car reflects the high levels of car ownership now prevailing. The following table shows how the availability of cars has increased steadily over the last 50 years. In 1955 only about 20% of households had regular use of a car, whereas by 2005 that figure had risen to about 75%. About 30% of households now have the regular use of two or more cars.

Household Car Availability, 1995-2005

	Percentage of Households with regular use of:		
	No car	*One car*	*Two or more cars*
1955	80	19	2
1965	59	43	6
1975	44	45	11
1980	41	44	15
1985	38	45	18
1990	33	44	23
1995	30	45	25
2000	27	45	28
2005	25	43	32

Source: Department for Transport

Annual Number of Trips and Mileage per Person, 2005

	Walk	Pedal Cycle	Car	Bus & Rail	Other Modes	All Modes	Total miles	Average miles per trip
				Number of Trips				
Commuting/Business	20	5	141	26	6	198	2,114	10.8
Education (incl. escorts)	48	1	48	13	4	114	305	2.7
Shopping	51	2	131	19	3	206	879	4.3
Leisure	49	5	193	19	11	277	2,848	10.3
Other Purposes	77	1	157	10	2	248	1,062	4.3
All Purposes	245	14	671	86	28	1,044	7,208	6.9

Source: Department for Transport

1.3 Road Transport

The DfT compiles extensive information on roads and traffic from various sources. Data on road lengths is obtained from the Highways Agency, the devolved administrations, local authorities and the Ordnance Survey. The main source of information on vehicle numbers is the Driver and Vehicle Licensing Agency which has a database holding records for over 80 million vehicles, past and present. The estimation of road traffic volumes is a major exercise which employs data obtained from 250 automatic traffic counters and around 10,000 manual counters located across the road network. Some key statistics on roads and traffic are shown below

Road Lengths, 2005

(kilometres)	All roads (Including motorways)	Trunk Roads	Motorways
England	297,911	7,322	2,992*
Wales	33,233	1,688	141
Scotland	56,864	3,192	386
Northern Ireland	24,931	1,209	114

* includes 54km of non-trunk road motorways

Source: Department for Transport and Northern Ireland Roads Service

Licensed Vehicles in Great Britain, 2005

(thousands)

Private and light goods	29,227
Motor cycles, scooters, mopeds	1,075
Buses	103
Goods vehicles	433
Exempt	1,978
Others	82
Total	32,897

Source: Department for Transport

Road Traffic by Vehicle Type, 1995-2005

	1995	2000	2005	Increase on 2000
(billion vehicle kilometres)				
Cars	351.1	377.4	397.2	+5%
Motor cycles	3.7	4.6	5.4	+17%
Light vans	44.5	52.3	62.6	+20%
Goods vehicles	25.4	28.2	29.0	+3%
Larger buses and coaches	4.9	5.2	5.2	–
All motor vehicles	429.7	467.1	499.4	+7%
Pedal cycles	4.1	4.2	4.4	+5%

Source: Department for Transport

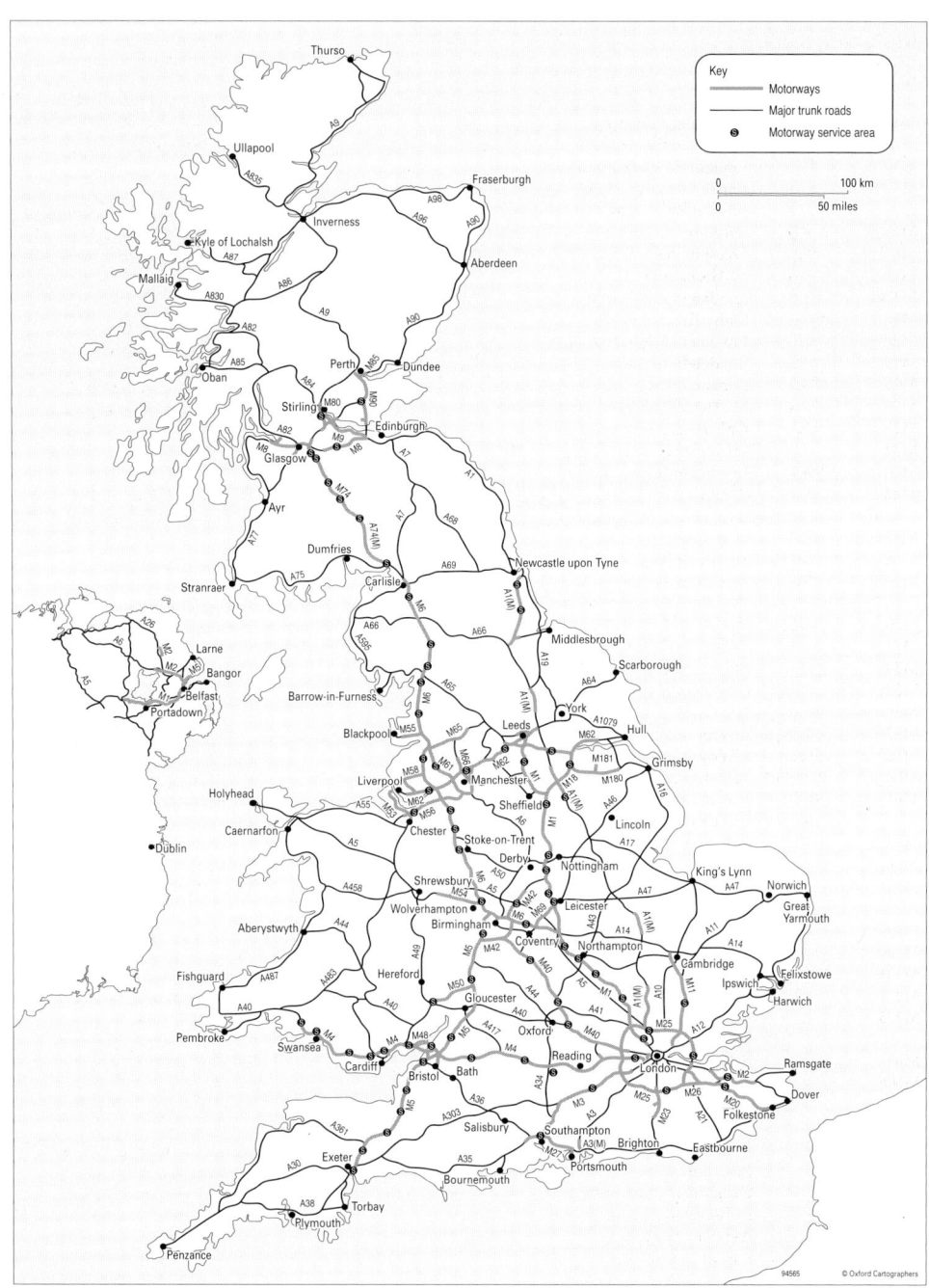

MAP 1: Motorways and major trunk roads

Motorways 2007

ENGLAND AND WALES:

	kms	
M1	318.5	London to Yorkshire
M2	43.2	London to Faversham
M3	99.0	London to Southampton
M4	315.3	London to South Wales
M5	269.7	Birmingham to Exeter
M6	378.0	Catthorpe to Carlisle
M6 Toll	39.9	Coleshill to Cannock
M10	4.6	St Albans spur
M11	83.9	London to Cambridge
M18	48.1	Rotherham to Goole
M20	82.7	London to Folkestone
M23	27.8	London to Crawley
M25	188.5	London orbital route
M26	15.8	M20 to M25 link
M27	51.1	Cadnam to Portsmouth
M32	7.3	M4 to Bristol spur
M40	146.1	London to Birmingham
M42	67.7	Southwest of Birmingham to Measham
M45	13.2	Dunchurch spur
M48	20.4	Severn Bridge
M49	9.3	Link from M5 to 2nd Severn Crossing
M50	34.6	Ross spur
M53	34.4	Chester to Birkenhead
M54	36.7	M6 to Telford
M55	20.2	Preston to Blackpool
M56	61.4	Manchester to Chester
M57	17.1	Liverpool Outer Ring Road
M58	20.6	Liverpool to Wigan
M60	60.0	Manchester Ring Road
M61	40.2	Manchester to Preston
M62	160.9	Liverpool to Hull
M65	44.1	Calder Valley route
M66	14.0	Bury by-pass
M67	7.6	Manchester Hyde to Denton
M69	28.0	Coventry to Leicester
M180	41.1	South Humberside route
M181	4.3	Scunthorpe M180(J3) to A18
M271	4.1	A35 Southampton to M27(J3)
M275	4.5	A3 Portsmouth to M27(J12)
M602	6.5	Salford M62(J12) to A5063
M606	3.8	M62(J26) Hunsworth to A6177 Bradford
M621	16.7	Leeds southern road
A1(M)	212.0	London to Newcastle (not continuous)
A3(M)	9.3	Catherington to Havant
A38(M)	4.3	Birmingham Centre A4540 to M6(J6)
A48(M)	3.9	Cardiff to Castleton

	kms	
A57(M)	2.6	Manchester Mancunian Way elevated road
A58(M)	1.9	Leeds Inner Ring Road
A64(M)	1.6	Leeds Inner Ring Road
A66(M)	3.2	A1 (J57) to Blackwell
A74(M)	0.8	Gretna Green, A74 to Border
A167(M)	2.4	Newcastle Inner Ring Rd
A194(M)	5.9	Birtley to Wardley
A308(M)	1.1	A4 J8/9 to Bray Wick
A329(M)	8.2	Bracknell to Wokingham
A404(M)	4.0	M4(J8) to Maidenhead
A601(M)	2.1	Carnforth M6(J35) to Warton
A627(M)	6.9	Chadderton to Rochdale
A6144(M)	2.0	Trafford to M60(J8)

SCOTLAND:

	kms	
M8	88.2	Edinburgh by-pass to Newhouse/Baillieston-West Ferry Interchange
M9	52.3	Newbridge (M8) to Dunblane
M73	10.2	Maryville to Mollinsburn
M74	41.0	Junction 12(A70) to Junction 1 (West of Fullerton Road) Glasgow (A763/A74)
M77	27.3	Glasgow (M8) to Fenwick (N of Kilmarnock)
M80	19.9	Stirling to Haggs/ Glasgow (M8) to Stepps
M90	54.5	Inverkeithing to Perth
M876	12.5	Dennyloanhead (M80) to Kincardine Bridge
M898	1.6	M8(J30) Erskine to A726
A74(M)	90.0	Border to Junction12 (A70)
A823(M)	1.5	A823/B980 Nr Rosyth to M90(J2)

NORTHERN IRELAND:

	kms	
M1	61.7	Belfast to Dungannon
M2	34.7	Belfast to Antrim/ Ballymena by-pass
M3	1.8	Belfast Cross Harbour Bridge
M5	2.8	Junction with M2 to Greencastle
M12	4.1	Junction with M1 to Craivagon
M22	7.7	Antrim to Randalstown
A8(M)	1.5	Sandyknowes to Cors Corner roundabout

Source: Department for Transport, Transport Scotland, and Northern Ireland Roads Service

1.4 Rail Transport

Comprehensive statistics about the national rail network and its use are collected by the Office of Rail Regulation, and a compendium of these is published annually as the National Rail Trends Yearbook. Information is obtained from Network Rail, DfT and the train operating companies. Estimates of passenger journeys and kilometres are obtained from the rail industry's central ticketing system. The key statistics presented in the table below show how use of the national rail network has increased significantly in recent years. Passenger journey numbers increased by 13% in the five years to 2005/06.

Figures compiled by the DfT show that the number of journeys made on the London Underground (970 million) is only about 10% less than the number of journeys on the National Rail network. Nine other much smaller urban rail or light rail networks carried a total of 175 million passengers in 2005/06.

Some Key Statistics for National Rail, 2005/06

	2005/06	Increase on 2000/01
Route length of national passenger network	14,356 km	
Number of passenger stations	2,510	
Total train kilometres timetabled	463.2 million	8%
Total number of passenger journeys	1,082 million	13%
Total passenger kilometres	43.2 billion	13%
Total passenger revenue	£4,493 million	32%
Total freight lifted (tonnes)	103.9 million	9%
Total freight tonne kilometres	22.1 billion	22%

Sources: Department for Transport and Office of Rail Regulation

Passengers carried by UK Rail Systems, 2005/06

	millions
National Rail	1,082
London Underground	970
Docklands Light Railway	52
Tyne & Wear Metro	36
Croydon Tramlink	23
Manchester Metrolink	20
Glasgow Underground	13
Sheffield Supertram	13
Nottingham Transit	10
West Midlands Metro	5
Blackpool Trams	4

Source: Department for Transport

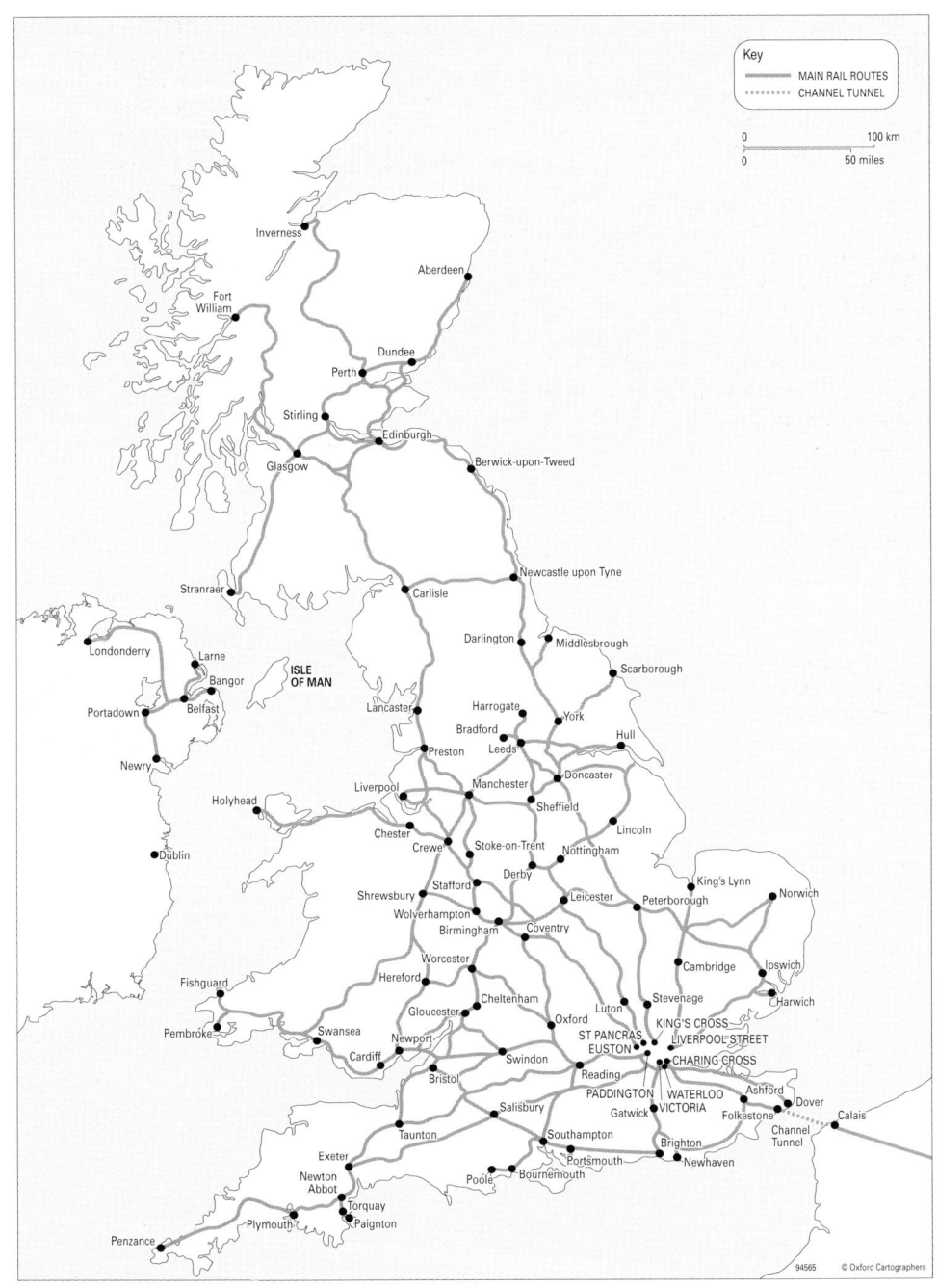

MAP 2: Main rail routes

National rail passenger operations are divided into 21 rail franchises, each run by a Train Operating Company. The following table indicates the main features of these franchises as they existed in 2006/07.

Train Operating Company	Franchisee	Passenger kms (millions)	Train kms (millions)
Arriva Trains Wales	Arriva Trains Ltd	846	21.2
c2c	National Express Group plc	844	6.2
Central Trains	National Express Group plc	1,567	30.4
Chiltern Railways	M40 Trains Ltd (Laing Investments)	817	9.1
First Capital Connect	First Group plc	3,020	23.2
First Great Western	First Group plc	4,736	44.8
First ScotRail	First ScotRail Ltd	2,406	38.6
Gatwick Express	National Express Group plc	219	2.5
Great North Eastern Railways	GNER Holdings Ltd (Sea Containers Ltd)	4,302	18.8
Island Line	Stagecoach Group	7	0.3
Merseyrail*	Serco Group/Ned Railways	334	5.9
Midland Mainline	National Express Group plc	1,380	11.5
Northern Rail	Northern Rail Limited (Serco Group/Ned Railways)	1,766	47.0
One Railway	London Eastern Railway Limited (National Express Group plc)	3,667	31.7
Silverlink	National Express Group plc	1,157	9.1
Southern	GOVIA Ltd (Go-Ahead Group/Keolis SA)	3,161	27.9
Southeastern	GOVIA Ltd (Go-Ahead Group/Keolis SA)	3,357	28.5
South West Trains	Stagecoach Group	4,898	37.8
TransPennine Express	First/Keolis TransPennine Holdings	942	14.0
Virgin CrossCountry	Virgin Rail Group Ltd	2,925	30.0
Virgin West Coast	Virgin Rail Group Ltd	3,747	22.4

Train Operating Companies/Franchisees, Great Britain, 2006-07

* Merseyrail concession managed by Merseytravel (PTE)

Source: Train Operating Companies

Changes are being made to a number of franchises late in 2007. These will see the operations of the existing Central Trains franchise transferred to a number of other new or modified franchises. The main changes are as follows:

- A new East Midlands franchise will incorporate the existing Midland Mainline franchise and the eastern services of Central Trains, and has been awarded to Stagecoach Midland Rail Ltd.

- A new West Midlands franchise will incorporate the existing Silverlink franchise and the West Midlands services of Central Trains, and has been awarded to London and Birmingham Railway Ltd (a subsidiary of GOVIA Ltd).

- A modified Cross-Country franchise will incorporate the Nottingham-Cardiff and Birmingham-Stansted Airport services of Central Trains, and has been awarded to Arriva plc.

The Great North Eastern Railways (or Inter City East Coast) franchise has been re-let and awarded to NXEC trains Ltd (a subsidiary of National Express Group). It has also been announced that the Gatwick Express franchise is to terminate in June 2008 and will be integrated into the Southern franchise.

1.5 Bus and Coach Transport

The Department for Transport collects statistics on bus and coach services, chiefly through an annual sample survey of operators and from Transport for London. Some key statistics are presented below. Passenger journey statistics refer to boardings, so that a journey which requires a change of bus will count twice.

Key Bus and Coach Statistics (Great Britain), 2005	
Number of vehicles (December 2005)	80,800
Bus and coach services vehicle km (millions)	
– local bus services	2,570
– other (non-local) services	1,395
All services	3,965
Local bus Journeys (millions)	4,719
Passenger receipts (£million)*	
– local bus services	3,594
– other (non-local) services	1,637
All services	5,231
*Includes concessionary fare reimbursement	
Source: Department for Transport	

The following table shows how the number of local bus journeys made in different parts of the country has changed over the last ten years. Journeys in London have increased substantially in numbers, while they have continued to decline in the rest of England.

Local Bus Journeys by Area, 1995/96-2005/06			
	1995/96	*2000/01*	*2005/06*
London	1,193	1,347	1,810
English metropolitan areas	1,358	1,203	1,117
Rest of England	1,303	1,292	1,198
Scotland	506	458	477
Wales	130	119	118
Great Britain	4,489	4,420	4,719
Source: Department for Transport			

1.6 Air Transport

The prime source of statistics on air transport in the UK is the Civil Aviation Authority. They collect information on a regular basis from all UK airlines and airports, and they also carry out passenger surveys annually at selected groups of airports.

The total number of passengers passing through UK airports has increased more than five-fold over the past thirty years and continues to grow.

Total UK Airport Passengers, 1975-2006		
	Passengers (000)	*Change over preceding 5 years*
1975	41,846	–
1980	57,823	38%
1985	70,434	22%
1990	102,418	45%
1995	129,369	26%
2000	179,885	39%
2005	228,214	27%
2006	235,139	–

The figures show total terminal passengers (scheduled and charter passengers)

Source: Civil Aviation Authority/Department for Transport

Some 29 UK airports are now handling more than 500,000 passengers per year. Seven of these are owned by BAA (now part of the Ferrovial Group, the Spanish infrastructure operator), and four of them are owned by the Manchester Airport Group (MAG).

Airport Terminal Passengers, 1995-2006

UK airports handling more than 500,000 passengers in 2006*

Airport	Passengers (000)				% Change	Ownership
	1995	2000	2005	2006	2006/2000	
Heathrow	54,125	64,277	67,683	67,339	5	BAA
Gatwick	22,379	31,948	32,693	34,080	7	BAA
Stansted	3,889	11,858	21,992	23,680	100	BAA
Manchester	14,514	18,349	22,083	22,124	21	MAG
Luton	1,806	6,164	9,135	9,415	53	
Birmingham	5,192	7,492	9,311	9,056	21	
Glasgow	5,420	6,920	8,775	8,820	27	BAA
Edinburgh	3,274	5,494	8,449	8,607	57	BAA
Bristol	1,430	2,124	5,199	5,710	169	
Newcastle	2,480	3,145	5,187	5,407	72	
Belfast International	2,344	3,127	4,820	5,015	60	
Liverpool	502	1,978	4,409	4,962	151	
Nottingham East Midlands	1,878	2,227	4,182	4,721	112	MAG
Aberdeen	2,179	2,454	2,852	3,163	29	BAA
Leeds Bradford	923	1,573	2,609	2,787	77	
Prestwick	313	905	2,405	2,395	165	
London City	553	1,581	1,996	2,358	49	
Belfast City	1,280	1,288	2,237	2,106	64	
Cardiff Wales	1,025	1,498	1,765	1,993	33	
Southampton	507	854	1,835	1,913	124	BAA
Exeter	180	317	842	971	206	
Bournemouth	92	271	829	961	255	MAG
Durham Tees Valley	413	740	898	900	22	
Doncaster Sheffield	-	-	601	899	-	
Isle of Man	512	698	801	783	12	
Norwich	250	365	545	745	104	
Inverness	271	337	589	671	99	
Coventry	1	2	719	610	-	
Blackpool	75	107	377	553	417	
Humberside	275	443	459	516	16	MAG

* The figures show total terminal passengers (scheduled and charter passengers)

Source: Civil Aviation Authority

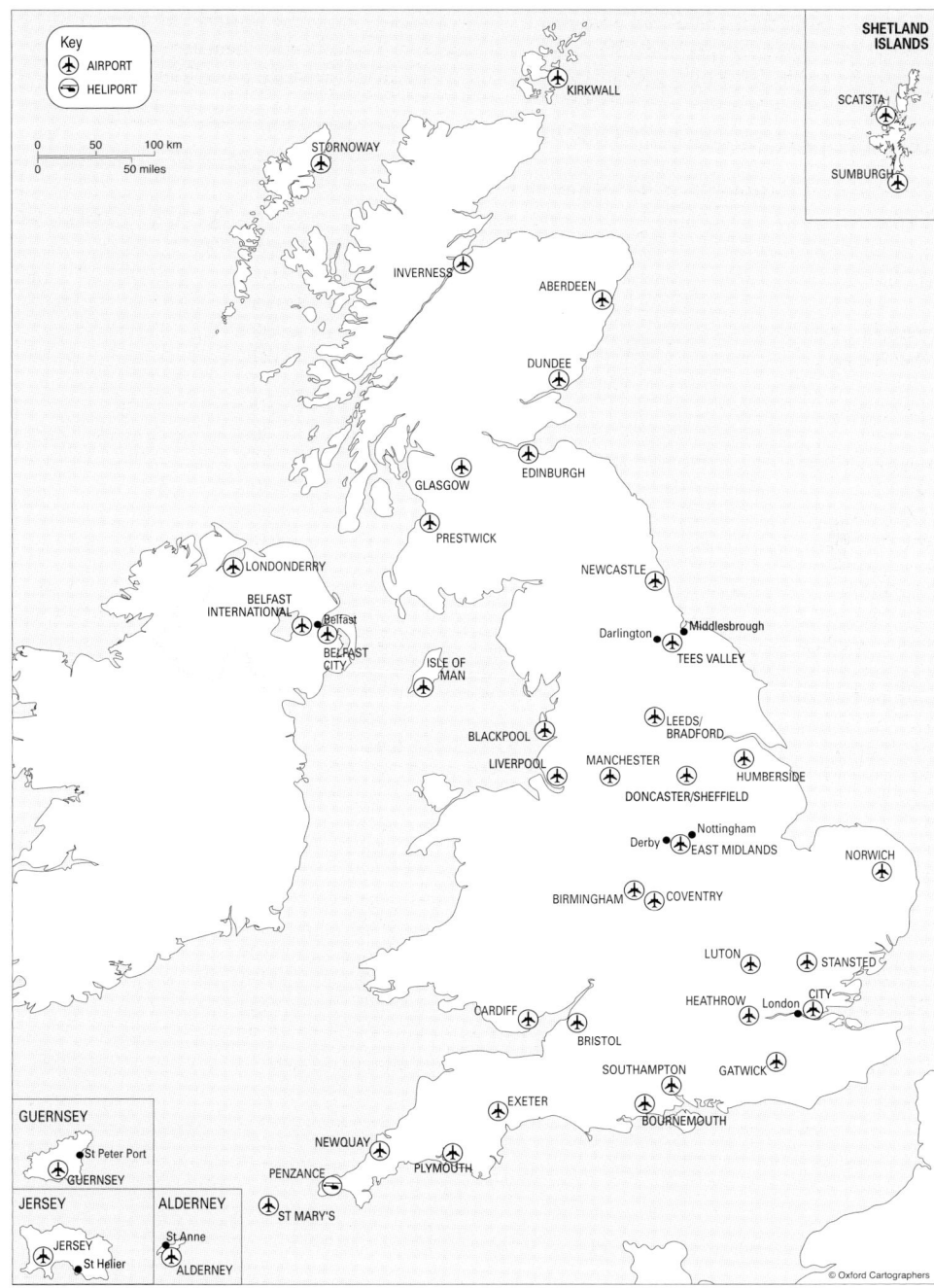

Key
✈ AIRPORT
⬡ HELIPORT

SHETLAND ISLANDS
SCATSTA
SUMBURGH

KIRKWALL
STORNOWAY
INVERNESS
ABERDEEN
DUNDEE
GLASGOW
EDINBURGH
PRESTWICK
NEWCASTLE
LONDONDERRY
BELFAST INTERNATIONAL
Belfast
BELFAST CITY
Darlington   Middlesbrough
TEES VALLEY
ISLE OF MAN
LEEDS/BRADFORD
BLACKPOOL
LIVERPOOL
MANCHESTER
HUMBERSIDE
DONCASTER/SHEFFIELD
Derby   Nottingham
EAST MIDLANDS
NORWICH
BIRMINGHAM   COVENTRY
LUTON
STANSTED
HEATHROW   London   CITY
CARDIFF
BRISTOL
GATWICK
SOUTHAMPTON
EXETER
BOURNEMOUTH
NEWQUAY
PENZANCE
PLYMOUTH
ST MARY'S

GUERNSEY
St Peter Port
GUERNSEY

JERSEY
JERSEY
St Helier

ALDERNEY
St Anne
ALDERNEY

© Oxford Cartographers

MAP 3: Main UK airports

Nearly 72% of all international passengers passing through UK airports in 2006 had origins or destinations at airports in Western Europe (including Ireland). The number of European passengers has grown by over 34% since 2000. The highest growth has been in passengers to and from North Africa and the Indian Sub-continent. The number of passengers to and from the USA has fallen over the same period.

UK airlines carried over 127 million passengers during 2006, at an average load factor of 78.9. Twelve major UK airlines or airline groups carried more than three million passengers each in the year.

International Air Passengers, 2000-2006

Country/Region	Passengers (000) 2000	2006	% Change 2006/2000
Spain	25,925	34,878	35
Ireland	9,295	12,357	33
France	8,237	11,571	40
Germany	8.718	11,503	32
Italy	7,033	10,573	50
Netherlands	7,097	8,258	16
Rest of Western Europe	31,890	42,912	35
USA	19,214	18,074	-6
Canada	3,302	3,634	10
Rest of America	3,216	3,617	12
Africa	4,184	7,065	69
Eastern Europe/ Middle East	4,683	8,199	75
Asia and the Far East	8,454	10,943	29

Source: Civil Aviation Authority

UK Airlines, 2006

Airline	Passengers (000)	Aircraft Km Flown (000)	Average Load Factor %	Number of Aircraft
British Airways Plc	32,724	614,195	76.7	234
EasyJet Airline Company Ltd	27,971	227,430	81.5	103
BMI Group	9,943	94,487	69.1	61
Thomsonfly Ltd	9,617	117,917	86.9	47
Monarch Airlines	5,788	71,630	82.0	28
First Choice Airways Ltd	5,517	78,515	90.7	31
Virgin Atlantic Airways	4,888	139,528	72.8	37
Thomas Cook Airlines Ltd	4,873	66,563	87.2	24
Flybe Ltd	4,537	41,228	63.3	41
My Travel Airways UK	3,568	54,625	91.2	25
BA Connect Ltd	3,303	55,483	58.9	49
XL Airways UK Ltd	3,194	47,272	85.4	19

Source: Civil Aviation Authority

1.7 Ports and Maritime Transport

Statistics on maritime transport are collected by the Department for Transport from port authorities, shipping lines or their UK agents, and other maritime agencies. Some key statistics on maritime transport are presented in the following tables.

Some Key Statistics of UK Maritime Transport, 2005

Total traffic through UK ports	585.7 m tonnes
Foreign Imports	262.3 m tonnes
Foreign Exports	164.1
Domestic Traffic *	159.3

* Domestic traffic refers to coastwise traffic between ports in the UK and with the Isle of Man and the Channel Islands, traffic to and from offshore installations, landing of sea-dredged aggregates, and material shipped for dumping at sea

Liquid Bulk	265.3 m tonnes
Dry Bulk	134.9
Container and roll-on traffic	154.7
Other modes of appearance	30.7
Total unit loads through UK ports	12.165 m
Containers	4.754 m
Road goods vehicles	3.906
Unaccompanied trailers	2.840
Other units	0.665
Accompanied passenger cars on:	
- overseas ferry routes	4.861 m
- coastwise ferry routes	1.444 m
International passengers through UK ports	23.7 m
UK-owned trading vessels	
- number	557
- gross tonnage	13.7 m tonnes

Source: Department for Transport

Some 20 UK ports or port groupings handled more than 5 million tonnes of traffic in 2005, and accounted for 85% of all the UK's seaport trade. The fortunes of different ports have varied greatly in recent years, in some cases linked to changing levels of activity in the offshore oil industry.

Traffic through Major UK Ports, 1990-2005

UK ports handling more than 5.0m tonnes, 2005

	Throughput (million tonnes)				% Change
	1990	*1995*	*2000*	*2005*	*2005 /2000*
Grimsby & Immingham	39.4	46.8	52.5	60.7	16
Tees & Hartlepool	40.2	46.1	51.5	55.8	8
London	58.1	51.4	47.9	53.8	12
Southampton	28.8	32.4	34.8	39.9	15
Milford Haven	32.2	32.5	33.8	37.5	11
Forth	25.4	47.1	41.1	34.2	-17
Liverpool	23.2	30.0	30.4	33.8	11
Felixstowe	16.4	24.1	29.7	23.1	-22
Dover	13.0	12.7	17.4	21.1	21
Sullom Voe	36.0	38.3	38.2	20.5	-46
Clyde	8.9	7.6	7.2	15.7	118
Medway	13.6	14.2	15.3	15.5	1
Orkneys	8.6	12.9	22.8	14.5	-36
Belfast	8.0	10.5	12.5	13.5	8
Hull	6.8	10.0	10.7	13.4	25
Bristol	4.9	7.3	9.6	11.2	16
Rivers Hull & Humber	7.6	6.4	9.0	9.8	9
Port Talbot	8.9	11.0	11.7	8.6	-27
Manchester	8.1	8.4	7.7	7.2	-6
Glensanda	3.3	4.9	5.9	5.4	-8
Other ports	100.6	93.6	83.4	90.5	9
Total	492.0	548.2	573.1	585.7	+2

Source: Department for Transport

Total traffic through UK ports is provisionally estimated to have been about 586 million tonnes. The following map shows the location and relative scale of traffic handled at the main UK ports.

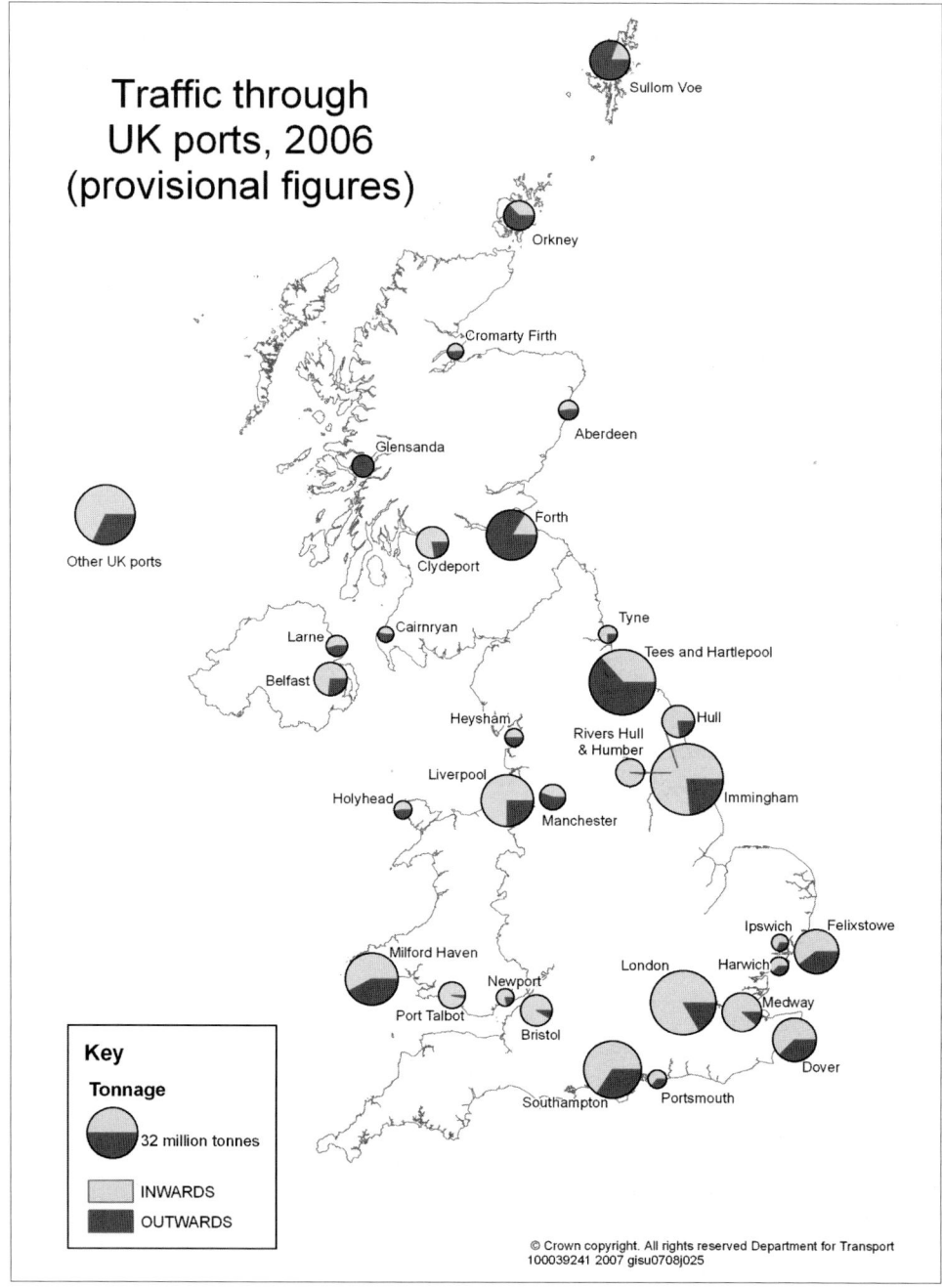

Traffic through UK ports, 2006 (provisional figures)

Sullom Voe

Orkney

Cromarty Firth

Aberdeen

Glensanda

Forth

Other UK ports

Clydeport

Tyne

Cairnryan

Tees and Hartlepool

Larne

Belfast

Hull

Heysham

Rivers Hull & Humber

Liverpool

Holyhead

Immingham

Manchester

Ipswich   Felixstowe

Milford Haven

London   Harwich

Newport

Medway

Port Talbot

Bristol

Southampton   Portsmouth

Dover

Key

Tonnage

32 million tonnes

INWARDS

OUTWARDS

MAP 4: Main UK seaports

Unitised traffic through UK ports has grown steadily for many years and increased by 15% over the five years to 2005. Some 16 ports handle nearly 90% of all unitised (container/ro-ro) traffic.

Nearly 23.7 million international passengers travelled to and from the UK on short-sea ferry routes in 2005, a further 2.3 million passengers travelled to and from Northern Ireland on Irish Sea ferry routes, and some 15.5 million passengers used the Channel Tunnel to cross to and from France.

Unitised Traffic through UK Ports, 1990-2005

(000 units)	1990	1995	2000	2005	% Change 2005 /2000
Dover	1,025	1,071	1,625	2,047	26
Felixstowe	1,206	1,677	2,330	1,945	-17
London	541	546	831	962	16
Southampton	264	486	713	857	20
Liverpool	231	483	737	837	14
Grimsby/ Immingham	305	330	478	732	53
Belfast	197	272	471	472	0
Medway	82	231	324	413	27
Harwich	308	220	246	408	66
Larne	333	375	301	385	28
Hull	221	325	324	376	16
Portsmouth	216	307	292	305	4
Holyhead	82	98	185	296	60
Heysham	98	177	259	250	-3
Tees & Hartlepool	122	282	234	232	-1
Cairnryan	94	126	157	231	47
Other Ports	1,382	1,298	1,039	1,317	27
All Ports	6,707	8,304	10,546	12,165	15

Source: Department for Transport

Main Ports for Sea Passenger Movements, 2005

	(000s)
Short Sea Ferry Routes:	
Dover	13,360
Portsmouth	2,631
Holyhead	2,174
Hull	964
Harwich	958
Tyne	699
Plymouth	634
Fishguard	590
Others	773
Total	23,693
Channel Tunnel	15,527
Great Britain to Northern Ireland	
Stranraer	1,235
Cairnryan	602
Others	455
Total	2,292

Source: Department for Transport

The inland waterways network of Great Britain extends to about 5,100 km of fully navigable canals and navigable rivers, of which British Waterways is responsible for the management and promotion of about 3,200 km. In 2004 the volume of goods moved internally on the waterways network was only about 150 million tonne-kilometres, but they have become a major national asset for leisure and recreation, and British Waterways estimate that over 400 million visits a year are made to their network.

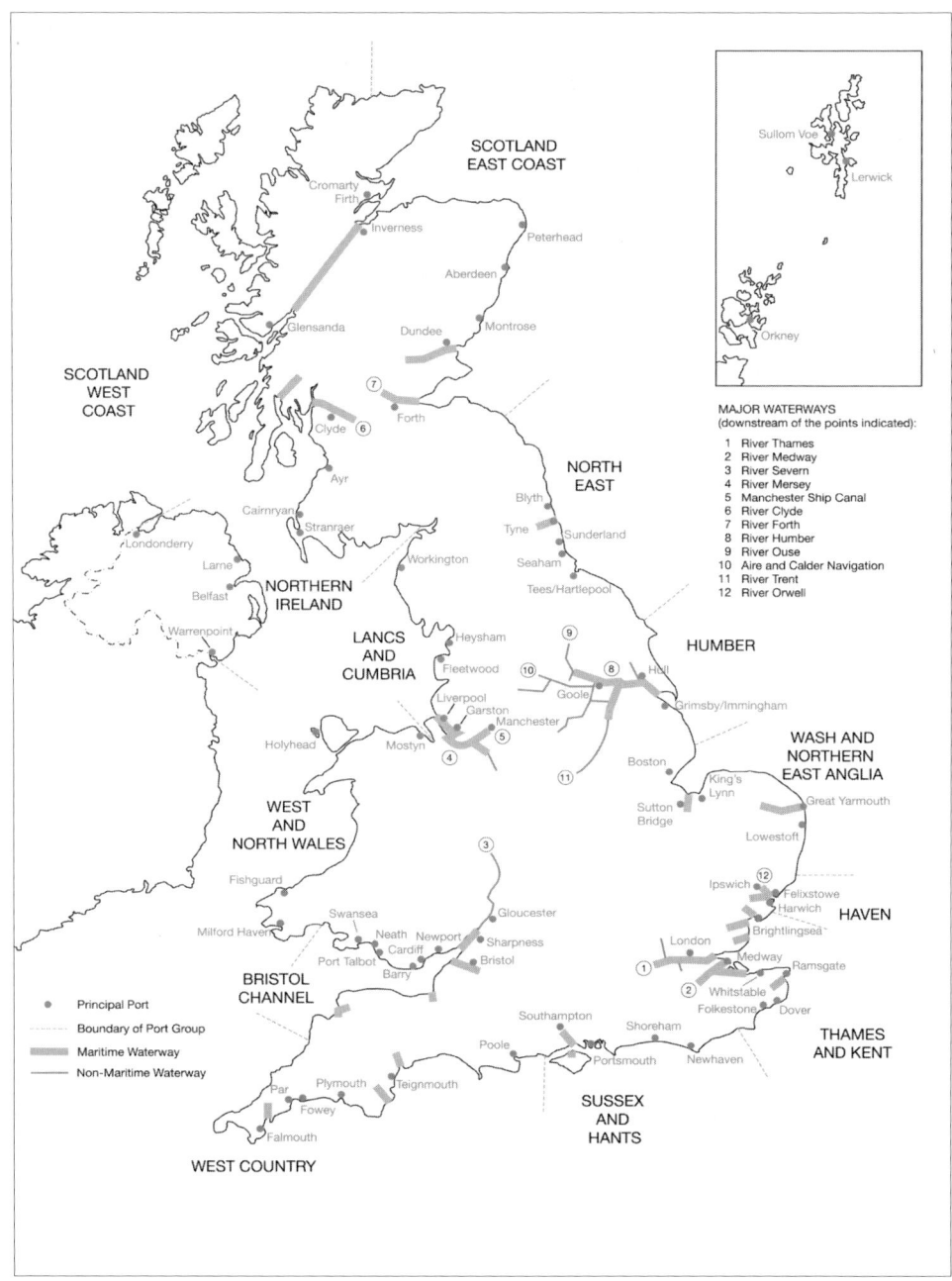

MAP 5: Commercial waterway network

1.8 Environment and Health

Emission figures for the UK are published by DEFRA in the Digest of Environmental Statistics and can be found at www.defra.gov.uk/environment/statistics/. Carbon dioxide is the most important greenhouse gas and is estimated to account for about two thirds of man-made global warming. Road transport is estimated to account for over 20% of all carbon dioxide emissions in the UK.

The National Travel Survey provides information on the amount of walking and cycling undertaken by residents of Great Britain for different purposes of travel. On average, each person makes nearly 250 (one-way) walking trips per year, or about one return journey on foot every three days. The average length of a (one-way) walking trip is just over two-thirds of a mile, whereas the average length of cycle trips is 2.5 miles.

Carbon Dioxide Emissions in the UK, 1995-2005

	Million tonnes of Carbon Dioxide		
	1995	*2000*	*2005*
Source:			
Passenger cars	69.2	72.3	69.9
Heavy goods vehicles	24.0	25.8	28.6
Other road transport	17.8	17.9	21.4
All road transport	110.9	116.0	119.9
Rail, air and other transport	6.7	7.2	9.1
All domestic transport	117.6	123.2	129.0
All sources of emissions	549.6	548.8	554.2
Proportion from transport	21.4%	22.4%	23.3%

Source: AEA Energy & Environment

Walking and Cycling, 2005

	Walk	*Bicycle*
Annual trips per person		
Commuting/business	20	5
Education/escort education	48	1
Shopping	51	2
Personal business	26	1
Leisure	49	5
Other purposes	51	–
All purposes	245	14
Annual mileage per person	169*	35
Average mileage per trip	0.7	2.5

*Total distance walked per person per year is 197 miles, including where walking is a subsidiary mode of travel.

Source: Department for Transport

1.9 Transport Safety

The Department for Transport compiles information on road accidents and casualties from returns made by police forces. The numbers killed and seriously injured on the roads has fallen substantially from the peaks reached in the 1960s and early 1970s.

Road Accidents, 2005

Road accidents (000s)			199
Total casualties (000s)			271
of which:			
– Pedestrians			32
– Pedal/Motor Cyclists			34

	Killed*	Injuries (000s)	
		Serious	Slight
1965	7,952	98	292
1970	7,499	93	262
1975	6,366	77	241
1980	6,010	79	243
1985	5,165	71	241
1990	5,217	60	275
1995	3,621	46	261
1996	3,598	44	272
1997	3,599	43	281
1998	3,421	41	281
1999	3,423	39	278
2000	3,409	38	279
2001	3,450	37	273
2002	3,431	36	263
2003	3,508	34	253
2004	3,221	31	246
2005	3,201	29	239

* Died within 30 days of accident

Source: Department for Transport

Statistics on safety for other transport modes are also collated by the DfT. The total number of fatalities on the railways in the ten years since 1996/97 is 393, or just over one percent of the number killed on the roads.

Other Transport Accidents, 2005

	Killed	Other Casualties
Railways		
Passengers	10	2,800
Staff	6	2,279
Others	17	60
Total	33	5,139
Aviation (UK airspace)	27	78
Maritime		
– UK registered merchant vessels	3	350
– where Coastguard assistance rendered	376	–

Source: Department for Transport

1.10 Transport in the Devolved Administrations

Each of the devolved administrations – for Northern Ireland, Scotland and Wales – collects and publishes information on transport within their regions. A table of key transport statistics for each of the three regions is presented below.

NORTHERN IRELAND – Key Statistics

	Latest year available	*Latest year*	*Ten years previously*	*Change over 10 years*
Number of vehicles licensed (000)	2006	959	639	+50%
Proportion of households with car	2006-07	76%	70%	…
Road traffic (million vehicle kms)	2006	19,397	14,245	+36%
Road accidents, all casualties	2006	9,173	12,575	-37%
Passenger journeys for Ulsterbus/Citybus (million boardings)	2006-07	67.5	78.2	-14%
Rail passenger journeys (millions)	2006-07	8.6	6.2	+38%
Air passengers (million terminal passengers)	2006	7.46	3.78	+98%
Road freight lifted (million tonnes)	2005	60	50	+21%
Freight through ports (million tonnes)	2005	24	20	+20%

Source: Central Statistics and Research Branch, Northern Ireland '

SCOTLAND – Key Statistics

	Latest year available	*Latest year*	*Ten years previously*	*Change over 10 years*
Number of vehicles licensed (million)	2006	2.59	1.96	+32%
Proportion of households with car	2004	69%	62%	…
Road traffic (million vehicle kms)	2006	43,880	37,777	+16%
Road accidents, all casualties	2006	17,165	21,716	-21%
Local bus passengers (million boardings)	2005-06	477	506	-6%
Rail passengers on ScotRail services (million)	2006-07	77.3	52.8	+46%
Air passengers (million terminal pass.)	2006	24.4	13.2	+85%
Road freight lifted (million tonnes)	2005	166	158	*
Rail freight lifted (million tonnes)	2005-06	14.0	5.4	+159%
Freight through ports (million tonnes)	2005	110	127	-14%

*Figures not comparable because of changes in measurement

Source: Transport Statistics Branch, Scottish Executive

WALES – Key Statistics

	Latest year available	*Latest year*	*Ten years previously*	*Change over 10 years*
Number of vehicles licensed (000)	2005	1,664	1,175	+42%
Proportion of households with car	2004	76%	67%	…
Road traffic (million vehicle kms)	2005	27,277	23,060	+18%
Road accidents, all casualties	2006	12,692	14,853	-15%
Local bus passengers (million boardings)	2005-06	118	130	-9%
Rail passenger journeys (millions)	2005-06	20.1	14.5	+39%
Air passengers (million terminal pass.)	2005	1.76	1.04	+70%
Road freight lifted (million tonnes)	2005	95	101	-6%
Freight through ports (million tonnes)	2005	59	57	+4%

Source: Transport Statistics, Welsh Assembly Government

1.11 International Comparisons

The Department for Transport prepares a number of broad international comparisons of transport statistics. However, such comparisons need to be interpreted with caution, because of the wide variety of sources involved and the scope that this provides for differences in statistical methods and definitions to distort the comparisons.

The following table compares three key transport indicators for a number of European countries and for Japan and the USA. Amongst the five major EU countries, Italy and Germany have the highest levels of car ownership, but the UK has a somewhat higher proportion of passenger travel being made by car. At the same time, the UK has the lowest rate of road deaths by far of the five major EU countries, bettered only slightly by the Netherlands and Sweden.

Some International Transport Statistics, 2003/4

	Cars per 1,000 population 2004	Proportion of passenger travel by car 2003	Road deaths per 100,000 population 2004
UK	465	89	5.5
France	494	87	9.2
Germany	546	86	7.1
Italy	587	83	9.7
Netherlands	429	87	4.9
Poland	313	78	15.0
Spain	462	83	11.0
Sweden	457	83	5.3
Japan	432	70	6.7
USA	465	97	14.5

Source: Compiled by DfT from international publications

SECTION 2

Directory of Government Organisations

Central Government

The Department for Transport (DfT) is responsible for formulating policies relating to land, sea and air transport in the UK. Its specific responsibilities include sponsorship of the rail and bus industries; overseeing road transport in Great Britain, including the registration, licensing, certification and inspection of vehicles, driver testing and licensing, bus and road freight licensing, regulation of taxis and private hire cars, and road safety; the construction, improvement and maintenance of motorways and other trunk roads in England (through the Highways Agency); overseeing English local authorities' transport planning; the shipping industry and ports; navigational lights, pilotage, the Maritime and Coastguard Agency (MCA), marine safety and marine pollution; airports; and domestic and international civil aviation.

With devolution, the responsibility for the implementation of transport policy, including the construction, improvement and maintenance of motorways and other trunk roads has been transferred to:

- The Scottish Executive

- The National Assembly for Wales

- The Northern Ireland Assembly

The (*) icon attached to organisations listed in the directory sections indicates that the organisation provides or publishes transport statistics found in Section 4.

Department for Transport (DfT)

Secretary of State for Transport
Rt Hon Ruth Kelly, MP
Private Secretary: Lara Sherwin
Tel: 020 7944 3011
Fax: 020 7944 4399

Minister of State
Rt Hon Rosie Winterton MP
Private Secretary: Richard Buckley
Tel: 020 7944 3082
Fax: 020 7944 4492

Parliamentary Under Secretary
Jim Fitzpatrick, MP
Private Secretary: Eamonn Beirne
Tel: 020 7944 2566
Fax: 020 7944 4309

Parliamentary Under Secretary
Tom Harris, MP
Private Secretary: Roy Cahill
Tel: 020 7944 3084
Fax: 020 7944 4521

Permanent Secretary
Robert Devereux
Private Secretary: Suzanne Roddie
Tel: 020 7944 3017
Fax: 020 7944 4389

DfT Contact Addresses

Great Minster House
76 Marsham Street
London
SW1P 4DR
Tel: 020 7944 8300

Ashdown House
123 Victoria Street
London
SW1E 6DE

Southside House
105 Victoria Street
London SW1E 6DT

*Transport Statistics Website:
Web: http://www.dft.gov.uk/transtat

City & Regional Networks (CRN)

Great Minster House
76 Marsham Street
London
SW1P 4DR

Director General: Bronwyn Hill
Tel: 020 7944 2667
Fax: 020 7944 2195

Road Pricing and Statistics (RPS)
Director: Steve Gooding
Tel: 020 7944 4080
Fax: 020 7944 2195

Regional and Local Transport Policy (RLTP)
Director: Bob Linnard
Tel: 020 7944 2970
Fax: 020 7944 2207

Regional and Local Transport Delivery (RLTD)
Director: Lucy Chadwick
Tel: 020 7944 6948
Fax: 020 7944 6011

Major Projects (MPD)
Director: Mike Fuhr
Tel: 020 7944 2918
Fax: 020 7944 2608

Accessibility & Equalities (AE)
Divisional Manager: Miranda Carter
Tel: 020 7944 4461
Fax: 020 7944 6102

Rail & National Networks (RNN)

Great Minster House
76 Marsham Street
London
SW1P 4DR

Director General: Mike Mitchell
Tel: 020 7944 4155
Fax: 020 7944 2158

Rail Projects (RPROJ)
Director: Graham Dalton
Tel: 020 7654 5093

Rail Service Delivery (RSERD)
Director: Graham Backler
55 Victoria Street
London SW1H 0EU
Tel: 020 7654 8031

Rail Strategy & Finance (RSF)
Director: Mark Lambirth
Tel: 020 7944 4250
Fax: 020 7944 2154

Rail Customer & Stakeholder Relations (RCSR)
Director: Peter McCarthy
Tel: 020 7944 2647
Fax: 020 7944 2158

Rail Procurement (RPRO)
Director: Jack Paine
Tel: 020 7944 3064
Fax: 020 7944 2177

Rail Technical & Professional (RTPRO)
Director: Clive Burrows
Tel: 020 7944 5214
Fax: 020 7944 2160

Strategic Roads, Planning & National Networks (SRNN)
Director: Brian Wadsworth
Tel: 020 7944 2750
Fax: 020 7944 2759

International Networks & Environmental Group (INE)

Great Minster House
76 Marsham Street
London
SW1P 4DR

Director General: Simon Webb
Tel: 020 7944 3240
Fax: 020 7944 2039

Maritime & Dangerous Goods (MDG)
Director: Ian Woodman
Tel: 020 7944 4872
Fax: 020 7944 2165

Aviation (AD)
Director: David McMillan
Tel: 020 7944 4740
Fax: 020 7944 2190

Director: Jonathan Moor
Tel: 020 7944 4597
Fax: 020 7944 2191

Transport Security and Contingencies (TRANSEC)
Director: Niki Tompkinson
Southside
105 Victoria Street
London SW1E 6DT
Tel: 020 7944 2850
Fax: 020 7944 2175

Environment & International (ENI)
Director: Graham Pendlebury
Tel: 020 7944 6050

Maritime & Coastguard Agency (MCA)
Spring Place
105 Commercial Street
Southampton
SO15 1EG
Director: John Astbury
Tel: 023 8032 9103
Fax: 023 8032 9105

Marine Accident Investigation Branch (MAIB)
Carlton House
Carlton Place
Southampton
SO15 2DZ
Chief Inspector: Stephen Meyer
Tel: 02380 395528
Fax: 02380 233459

Air Accident Investigation Branch (AAIB)
Berkshire Copse Road
Aldershot
Hants
GU11 2HH
Chief Inspector: David King
Tel: 01252 510300
Fax: 01252 376999

Rail Accident Investigation Branch (RAIB)
2A Dukes Court
Duke Street
Woking
Surrey
GU21 5BH
Chief Inspector: Carolyn Griffiths
Tel: 01932 440002
Fax: 01932 440001

Safety, Service Delivery & Logistics (SSDL)

Great Minster House
76 Marsham Street
London
SW1P 4DR

Director General: Stephen Hickey
Tel: 020 7944 5459
Fax: 020 7944 6523

Roads and Vehicle Safety and Standards (RVSSD)
Director: Tricia Hayes
Tel: 020 7944 5212
Fax: 020 7944 2196

Transformation, Licensing, Logistics & Sponsorship (TLLS)
Director: Vivien Bodnar
Tel: 020 7944 5990
Fax: 020 7944 6523

Driving Standards Agency (DSA)
Stanley House
56 Talbot Street
Nottingham NG1 5GU
Chief Executive: Rosemary Thew
Tel: 0115 901 2981
Fax: 0115 901 2510

Driver & Vehicle Licensing Agency (DVLA)
Longview Road
Morriston
Swansea
SA6 7JL
Chief Executive: Clive Bennett

Vehicle & Operator Services Agency (VOSA)
Berkeley House
Croydon Street
Bristol
B55 0DA
Chief Executive: Stephen Tetlow
Tel: 0117 954 3211
Fax: 0115 954 3309

Vehicle Certification Agency (VCA)
The Eastgate Office Centre
Eastgate Road
Bristol
B55 6XX
Chief Executive: Paul Markwick
Tel: 0117 952 4100
Fax: 0115 954 4104

Government Car & Despatch Agency (GCDA)
46 Ponton Road
London
SW8 5AX
Chief Executive: Roy Burke
Tel: 020 7217 3821
Fax: 020 7217 3875

Corporate Resources (CR)

Great Minster House
76 Marsham Street
London
SW1P 4DR

Director General: Barbara Moorhouse
Tel: 020 7944 2391
Fax: 020 7944 6969

Transport Finance (TFD)
Director: Ken Beeton
Tel: 020 7944 6960
Fax: 020 7944 6969

Human Resources Directorate (HRD)
Director: Julian Duxfield
Tel: 020 7944 6200
Fax: 020 7944 2214

Planning and Performance (DPP)
Director: Ian Woodman
Tel: 020 7944 4872
Fax: 020 7944 2664

Communications (CD)
Director: Jeremy Mooney
Tel: 020 7944 4650
Fax: 020 794 4679

Transport Analysis & Economics (TAE)
Director: David Thompson
Tel: 020 7944 3640
Fax: 020 7944 2664

Commercial Adviser (COM)
Andy Friend
Tel: 020 7944 6816
Fax: 020 7944 3086

Business Delivery Services (BDS)
Director: Michael Herron
Tel: 020 7944 6182
Fax: 020 7944 5064

Corporate Finance (CFD)
Director: Kate Mingay
Tel: 020 7944 6840
Fax: 020 7944 6969

Highways Agency

Highways Agency Corporate Centre
123 Buckingham Palace Road
London SW1W 9HA

Chief Executive: Archie Robertson
Tel: 020 7153 4700
Fax: 020 7153 4786

Information (ID)
Broadway
5 Broadway
Birmingham B15 1BL
Director: Denise Plumpton
Tel: 0121 678 4130
Fax: 0121 678 8406

Human Resource Services (HRSD)
Director: Steve Williams
Tel: 020 7153 4735
Fax: 020 7153 4818

Major Projects (MP)
Director: Keith Miller
Tel: 01234 796614

Traffic Operations (TO)
Broadway
5 Broadway
Birmingham B15 1BL
Director: Derek Turner
Tel: 0121 678 8403
Fax: 0121 678 8406

Safety Standards and Research (SSR)
Board Director: Ginny Clarke
Tel: 020 7153 4779
Fax: 020 7153 7664

Network Strategy (NS)
Board Director: Hilary Chipping
Tel: 020 7153 4764
Fax: 020 7153 4787

Finance Services (FS)
Director: Mel Zuydam
Tel: 020 7153 4743
Fax: 020 7153 4818

*Transport Statistics Divisions

Great Minster House
76 Marsham Street
London
SW1P 4DR

Statistics Logistics, Aviation and Maritime (SLAM)
Chief Statistician and Head of Profession:
Antonia Roberts
Tel: 020 7944 4280
Fax: 020 7944 2165

Statistics Travel (ST)
Chief Statistician: Anthony Boucher
Tel: 020 7944 3079
Fax: 020 7944 2166

Statistics Roads (SR)
Chief Statistician: Barbara Noble
Tel: 020 7944 4270
Fax: 020 7944 2164

Scottish Executive

First Minister: Alex Salmond MSP
St Andrews House, Regent Road
Edinburgh, EH1 3DG
Tel Private Secretary: 0131 244 5218

Cabinet Secretary for Finance & Sustainable Growth: John Swinney MSP
St Andrew's House, Regent Road
Edinburgh EH1 3DG
Tel Private Secretary: 0131 244 5227

Minister for Transport, Infrastructure & Climate Change: Stewart Stevenson MSP
Victoria Quay
Edinburgh EH6 6QQ
Tel Private Secretary: 0131 244 5027

Director General – Economy: Dr Andrew Goudie
Room 3H05
Victoria Quay
Edinburgh
EH6 6QQ
Tel: 0131 244 7937

Transport Directorate

Director
John Ewing
Email: John.Ewing@scotland.gsi.gov.uk
Tel: 0131 244 0629
Fax: 0131 244 1554

Deputy Director – Transport Strategy
Diane McLafferty
Email: Diane.Mclafferty@scotland.gsi.gov.uk
Tel: 0131 244 7269
Fax: 0131 244 7281

Responsible for National Transport Strategy and Planning, Policy Co-ordination, Performance Monitoring, Regional Transport Strategy and Policy, Environment and Sustainable Transport, Modal Shift, Cycling and Walking, Safer Route to School/Home Zones, Transport User Committees, Analytical Services Team, Transport Legislation and Regional Transport Partnership Liaison – East, West and North.

Deputy Director – Transport Bus, Freight and Roads
David Patel
Email: David.Patel@scotland.gsi.gov.uk
Tel: 0131 244 0147
Fax: 0131 244 7281

Responsible for Bus and Taxi Policy, Freight Policy and Roads, Road Safety Policy, Traffic Management Roads Casework, Local Roads Policy and Finance, Tolled Bridges, Road Pricing and Congestion Charging

Deputy Director – Transport Aviation, Ports and Mobility
Alastair Wilson
Email: Alastair.Wilson@scotland.gsi.gov.uk
Tel: 0131 244 7187
Fax: 0131 244 0871

Responsible for Aviation Policy, Highlands and Islands Airports Ltd Sponsorship, Air Route Development Fund, Ports and Harbours Policy, Inland Waterways, International Ferry Links, Rural Transport, Accessibility, Equality/Disability Issues, European Transport Liaison and Concessionary Fares Policy.

Deputy Director – Transport Ferries
David Hart
Email: David.Hart@scotland.gsi.gov.uk
Tel: 0131 244 7277
Fax: 0131 244 7444

Responsible for Ferry Operations, Piers and Harbours Grant, Caledonian MacBrayne Tendering, Northern Isles Tendering, Campbeltown – Ballycastle Tendering

Transport Scotland

Chief Executive
Malcolm Reed
Email:
chiefexecutive@transportscotland.gsi.gov.uk
Tel: 0141 272 7112
Fax: 0141 272 7111

Director of Finance & Corporate Services
Guy Houston
Email:
Guy.Houston@transportscotland.gsi.gov.uk
Tel: 0141 272 7131
Fax: 0141 272 7111

Responsible for corporate and business planning, performance monitoring for Transport Scotland as a whole, management of the concessionary fare schemes, support services such as ICT, HR and legal and financial management of Transport Scotland, including internal audit and secretariat support to the Chief Executive

Director of Rail Delivery
Bill Reeve
Email: Bill.Reeve@transportscotland.gsi.gov.uk
Tel: 0141 272 7421
Fax: 0141 272 7111

Responsible for Rail performance, managing and overseeing the ScotRail franchise, monitoring Network Rail's delivery responsibilities and financial performance, major project expenditure, sponsorship of small projects delivery, technical support and co-ordinating rail devolution transition

Director of Strategy & Investment
Frances Duffy
Email:
Frances.Duffy@transportscotland.gsi.gov.uk
Tel: 0141 272 7562
Fax: 0141 272 7111

Responsible for leading policy development on all modes of transport within the agency's remit, project appraisal guidance (STAG) and analysis, developing the Transport Model for Scotland (TMfS), advising on rail, public transport and trunk road policy within the strategic priorities set out by Scottish Ministers and the National Transport Strategy, advising on the investment priorities for rail and trunk road networks for the next ten years and managing Scotland's first strategic projects review covering all modes of transport.

Director of Trunk Roads: Infrastructure & Professional Services
Ainslie McLaughlin
Email:
Ainslie.Mclaughlin@transportscotland.gsi.gov.uk
Tel: 0141 272 7215
Fax: 0141 272 7111

Responsible for delivering improvements to the network which meet today's needs and future challenges, organising the design and build of major road schemes in Scotland and designing, procuring and overseeing enhancements to current trunk roads and the construction of new ones.

Director of Trunk Roads: Network Management
Jim Barton
Email:
Jim.Barton@transportscotland.gsi.gov.uk
Tel: 0141 272 7321
Fax: 0141 272 7537

Responsible for managing the efficient operation of the trunk roads network, procuring and managing network maintenance contracts, major maintenance projects, maintenance policy and finance, managing real-time information services (such as Traffic Scotland) and integration of these services between modes, planning applications and accident investigation and prevention.

*Transport Statistics branch

Transport Statistician
Frank Dixon
Email: transtat@scotland.gsi.gov.uk
Web: www.scotland.gov.uk/transtat
Transport Statistics branch
Scottish Executive
Victoria Quay
Edinburgh
EH6 6QQ
Enquiry point:- *Tel:* 0131 244 7256
Fax: 0131 244 7281

National Assembly for Wales

Cardiff Bay
Cardiff CF99 1NA
Tel: 029 2082 5111
Email: assembly.info@wales.gsi.gov.uk
Web: www.wales.gov.uk

First Minister for Wales: The Rt Hon Rhodri
Morgan AM
Email: Rhodri.Morgan@wales.gsi.gov.uk
Tel: 029 2089 8764

Deputy First Minister for the Economy and
Transport: Ieuan Wyn Jones AM
Email: Ieuan.Wynjones@wales.gsi.gov.uk
Tel: 029 2089 8790

Welsh Assembly Government

Cathays Park
Cardiff CF10 3NQ
Tel: 029 2082 5111

*Group Director – Department for the Economy
and Transport*
Gareth Hall
Email: Gareth.Hall@wales.gsi.gov.uk
Tel: 029 2082 6646
Fax: 029 2082 5524

Director of Transport
Robin Shaw
Email: Robin.Shaw@wales.gsi.gov.uk
Tel: 029 2082 6242
Fax: 029 2082 6241

*Chief Highways Engineer and Head of Rail and
New Roads Division*
Tony Parker
Email: Tony.Parker@wales.gsi.gov.uk
Tel: 029 2082 6252
Fax: 029 2082 3712

Deputy Head of Rail and New Roads Division
Russell Bennett
Email: Russell.Bennett@wales.gsi.gov.uk
Tel: 029 2082 6565
Fax: 029 2082 3712

Director of Roads, Network Management Division
Robert Cone
Email: Robert.Cone@wales.gsi.gov.uk
Tel: 029 2082 6249
Fax: 029 2082 3712

*Director of Transport Policy and Administration
Division*
Simon Shouler
Email: Simon.Shouler@ wales.gsi.gov.uk
Tel: 029 2082 3839
Fax: 029 2082 3712

Head of Transport Planning
Tim Griffin
Email: Tim.Griffin@wales.gsi.gov.uk
Tel: 029 2082 6520
Fax: 029 2082 3748

***National Assembly for Wales (Transport
Statistics)**
Henry Small
Address: Cathays Park
Cardiff CF10 3NQ
Tel: 029 2082 6960
Fax: 029 2082 5350
Email: stats.pubs@wales.gsi.gov.uk
Web: www.wales.gov.uk

Northern Ireland Assembly

The Department for Regional Development
(DRD) is responsible for Transportation in
Northern Ireland. Further information about
the Department can be found at
www.drdni.gov.uk

Minister for Regional Development
Mr Connor Murphy, MP, MLA
Clarence Court
10–18 Adelaide Street
Belfast BT2 8GB
Tel: 028 9054 0105
Fax: 028 9054 0028

Roads Service
Mr Geoff Allister
Acting Chief Executive
Clarence Court
10–18 Adelaide Court
Belfast BT2 8GB
Tel: 028 9054 0511
Fax: 028 9054 0531

Ports and Public Transport Division
Mr Brian White
Director
Clarence Court
10–18 Adelaide Court
Belfast BT2 8GB
Tel: 028 9054 0651
Fax: 028 9054 0593

Public Transport Performance Division
Mr David Carson
Director
Clarence Court
10–18 Adelaide Street
Belfast BT2 8GB
Tel: 028 9054 0358
Fax: 028 9054 0662

Regional Planning and Transportation Division
Mr Mike Thompson
Director
Clarence Court
10–18 Adelaide Street
Belfast BT2 8GB
Tel: 028 9054 0794
Fax: 028 9054 0604

Central Statistics and Research Branch
Clarence Court
10–18 Adelaide Street
Belfast BT2 8GB
Tel: 028 9054 0800
Fax: 028 9054 0782

*Northern Ireland Statistics and Research Agency
Address: Mc Auley House, 2–14 Castle Street
Belfast BT1 1SA
Tel: 028 9034 8100
Fax: 028 9034 8106
Web: www.nisra.gov.uk

Government Offices for the Regions

The Government Offices for the regions were
originally established in 1994. They now bring
together the English regional services for ten
government departments, including the
Department for Transport. A Regional Co-
ordination Centre was set up in 2000 as the
corporate centre of the Government Office
network.

Regional Co-ordination Unit
Riverwalk House
157–161 Millbank
London SW1P 4RR
Tel: 020 7217 3595
Fax: n.a.
Email: rcuenquiries@rcu.gsi.gov.uk
Web: www.gos.gov.uk

East of England
Eastbrook ,Shaftesbury Road
Cambridge CB2 8DF
Tel: 01223 372500
Fax: 01223 372501
Email: enquiries.go-east@go-regions.gsi.gov.uk
Web: www.go-east.gov.uk

East Midlands
The Belgrave Centre, Stanley Place
Talbot Street, Nottingham NG1 5GG
Tel: 0115 971 9971
Fax: 0115 971 2404
Email: enquiries.goem@go-regions.gsi.gov.uk
Web: www.goem.gov.uk

London
Riverwalk House
157-161 Millbank
London SW1P 4RR
Tel: 020 7217 3111
Fax: 020 7217 3450
Email: enquiries@gol.gsi.gov.uk
Web: www.gos.gov.uk/gol/

North East
Citygate, Gallowgate
Newcastle-upon-Tyne NE1 4WH
Tel: 0191 201 3300
Fax: 0191 202 3398
Email: general.enquiries @gone.gsi.gov.uk
Web: www.go-ne.gov.uk

North West
City Tower, Piccadilly Plaza
Manchester M1 4BE
Telephone: 0161 952 4000
Fax: 0161 952 4099
Email: gowmmailbox@gonw.gsi.gov.uk
Web: www.gonw.gov.uk

South East
Bridge House, 1 Walnut Tree Close
Guildford, Surrey GU1 4GA
Tel: 01483 882255
Fax: 01483 882259
Email: info@gose.gsi.gov.uk
Web: www.gose.gov.uk

South West
Rivergate, Temple Quay
Bristol BS1 6EH
Tel: 0117 900 1700
Fax: 0117 900 1900
Email: swcontactus@gosw.gsi.gov.uk
Web: www.gosw.gov.uk

West Midlands
5 St Philip's Place, Colmore Row
Birmingham B3 2PW
Tel: 0121 235 5050
Fax: 0121 235 1010
Email: transport.team@gowm.gsi.gov.uk
Web: www.go-wm.gov.uk

Yorkshire and The Humber
Lateral, 8 City Walk
Leeds LS11 9AT
Tel: 0113 341 3000
Fax: 0113 341 3066
Email: yhenquiries@goyh.gsi.gov.uk
Web: www.goyh.gov.uk

Local Government

The following contact details have all been
confirmed by the local authorities themselves as
the appropriate first points of contact for
enquiries related to transport matters.

English County Councils

Bedfordshire County Council
Address: Highways and Transport
            County Hall, Cauldwell Street
            Bedford MK42 9AP
Tel: 01234 228601
Fax: 01234 228232
Email: ltp@bedscc.gov.uk
Web: www.bedfordshire.gov.uk

Buckinghamshire County Council

Address: County Hall, Walton Street
Aylesbury HP20 1UY
Tel: 01296 382053
Fax: 01296 383990
Email: transportps@buckscc.gov.uk
Web: www.buckscc.gov.uk

Cambridgeshire County Council

Address: Shire Hall, Castle Hill
Cambridge CB3 0AP
Tel: 08450 455200
Fax: 01223 717201
Email: cambridgeshire.direct@
cambridgeshire.gov.uk
Web: www.cambridgeshire.gov.uk

Cheshire County Council

Address: County Hall
Chester CH1 1SF
Tel: 08451 133311
Fax: n.a.
Email: info@cheshire.gov.uk
Web: www.cheshire.gov.uk

*Cornwall County Council

Address: Western Group Centre
Radnor Road, Scorrier
Redruth TR16 5EH
Tel: 01872 222000
Fax: 01209 821151
Email: highways@cornwall.gov.uk
Web: www.cornwall.gov.uk

Cumbria County Council

Address: The Courts, Carlisle
Cumbria, CA3 8NA
Tel: 01228 606060
Fax: 01228 606327
Email: information@cumbriacc.gov.uk
Web: www.cumbria.gov.uk

Derbyshire County Council

Address: Environmental Services,
County Hall, Matlock
Derbyshire DE4 3AG
Tel: 01629 580000, ext. 7064
Fax: 01629 585740
Email: integrated.transport@
derbyshire.gov.uk
Web: www.derbyshire.gov.uk

Devon County Council

Address: County Hall, Topsham Road
Exeter, Devon EX2 4QD
Tel: 08451 551004
Fax: n.a.
Email: info@devon.gov.uk
Web: www.devon.gov.uk

Dorset County Council

Address: Environment Directorate
County Hall, Colliton Park
Dorchester DT1 1XJ
Tel: 01305 224258
Fax: n.a.
Email: n.a.
Web: www.dorsetforyou.com

Durham County Council

Address: County Hall
Durham DH1 5UL
Tel: 0191 383 3337
Fax: 0191 383 4096
Email: transinfo@durham.gov.uk
Web: www.durham.gov.uk

East Sussex County Council

Address: County Hall, St Anne's Crescent
Lewes BN7 1UN
Tel: 01273 481000
Fax: 01273 481261
Email: transenv@eastsussexcc.gov.uk
Web: www.eastsussexcc.gov.uk

Essex County Council

Address: County Hall, Market Road
Chelmsford CM1 1LX
Tel: 0845 743 0430
Fax: 01245 251601
Email: highways.helpline@essexcc.gov.uk
Web: www.essexcc.gov.uk

Gloucestershire County Council

Address: Shire Hall, Westgate Street
Gloucester GL1 2TG
Tel: 01452 425000
Fax: n.a.
Email: speakout@gloucestershire.gov.uk
Web: www.gloucestershire.gov.uk

*Hampshire County Council
Address: The Castle
Winchester SO23 8UJ
Tel: 01962 870500
Fax: 01962 847055
Email: env.enquiries@hants.gov.uk
Web: www.hants.gov.uk

*Hertfordshire County Council
Address: County Hall, Pegs Lane
Hertford SG13 8DE
Tel: 01992 555555
Fax: 01992 555644
Email: hertsdirect@hertscc.gov.uk
Web: www.hertsdirect.org

*Kent County Council
Address: Kent Highway Services, Invicta
House
Maidstone, Kent ME14 1XX
Tel: 0845 824 7247
Fax: n.a.
Email: county.hall@kent.gov.uk
Web: www.kent.gov.uk

Lancashire County Council
Address: Environment Directorate
PO Box 9, County Hall
Preston, Lancashire PR1 8RD
Tel: 01772 533718
Fax: 01772 533937
Email: environmentmail@env.lancscc.gov.uk
Web: www.lancashire.gov.uk

Leicestershire County Council
Address: Highways, Transportation & Waste
Management
County Hall, Glenfield
Leicester LE3 8RJ
Tel: 0116 265 7127
Fax: 0116 265 7014
Email: tpp@leics.gov.uk
Web: www.leics.gov.uk

Lincolnshire County Council
Address: Transport Service Group,
Development
4th Floor, City Hall
Lincoln LN1 1DN
Tel: 01522 782070
Fax: 01522 568735
Email: transport_services@
lincolnshire.gov.uk
Web: www.lincolnshire.gov.uk

Norfolk County Council
Address: County Hall, Martineau Lane
Norwich NR1 2SG
Tel: 01603 223288 or 224225
Fax: 01603 223128
Email: information@norfolk.gov.uk
Web: www.norfolk.gov.uk

North Yorkshire County Council
Address: Highways & Transportation, Business
and Environmental Services
County Hall
Northallerton DL7 8AH
Tel: 0845 872 7374
Fax: 01609 779838
Email: highways.northyorkshire@
northyorks.gov.uk
Web: www.northyorks.gov.uk

Northamptonshire County Council
Address: County Hall
Northampton NN1 1DN
Tel: 01604 236236
Fax: n.a.
Email: citizensfirst@
northamptonshire.gov.uk
Web: www.northamptonshire.gov.uk

Northumberland County Council
Address: County Hall, Morpeth
Northumberland NE61 2EF
Tel: 01670 533000
Fax: 01670 533253
Email: contactcentre@
northumberland.gov.uk
Web: www.northumberland.gov.uk

Nottinghamshire County Council

Address: County Hall, West Bridgford
Nottingham NG2 7QP
Tel: 0115 982 3823
Fax: 0115 981 7945
Email: enquiries@nottscc.gov.uk
Web: www.nottscc.gov.uk

*Oxfordshire County Council

Address: Environment & Economy
Speedwell House
Speedwell Street, Oxford OX1 1NE
Tel: 01865 815700
Fax: 01865 815085
Email: environment.economy@
oxfordshire.gov.uk
Web: www.oxfordshire.gov.uk

Shropshire County Council

Address: The Shirehall
Abbey Foregate
Shrewsbury SY2 6ND
Tel: 0845 678 9018
Fax: 01743 253003
Email: transport@shropshire-cc.gov.uk
Web: www.shropshire.gov.uk

Somerset County Council

Address: County Hall
Taunton TA1 4DY
Tel: 0845 345 9155
Fax: 01823 356936
Email: roads&transport@somerset.gov.uk
Web: www.somerset.gov.uk

Staffordshire County Council

Address: County Buildings, Martin Street
Stafford, ST16 2LH
Tel: 01785 223121
Fax: 01785 215153
Email: webmaster@staffordshire.gov.uk
Web: www.staffordshire.gov.uk

Suffolk County Council

Address: Endeavour House, Russell Road
Ipswich IP1 2BX
Tel: 0845 606 6067
Fax: n.a.
Email: customerservice@ csduk.com
Web: www.suffolkcc.gov.uk

*Surrey County Council

Address: County Hall, Penhryn Road
Kingston upon Thames
Surrey KT1 2DN
Tel: 08456 009009
Fax: 020 8541 9004
Email: contact.centre@surreycc.gov.uk
Web: www.surreycc.gov.uk

Warwickshire County Council

Address: Shire Hall, Market Square
Warwick CV34 4RA
Tel: 01926 410410
Fax: 01926 412377
Email: feedback@warwickshire.gov.uk
Web: www.warwickshire.gov.uk

*West Sussex County Council

Address: Highways and Transport
The Grange, Tower Street
Chichester PO19 1RH
Tel: 01243 642105
Fax: 01243 777257
Email: highwaysandtransporthq@
westsussex.gov.uk
Web: www.westsussex.gov.uk

Wiltshire County Council

Address: County Hall, Bythesea Road
Trowbridge, Wiltshire BA14 8JN
Tel: 01225 713000
Fax: 01225 713999
Email: communications@wiltshire.gov.uk
Web: www.wiltshire.gov.uk

Worcestershire County Council

Address: Passenger Transport Group
PO Box 82, Pershore Lane
Worcester WR4 0AA
Tel: 01905 768411
Fax: 01905 453754
Email: sharelink@worcestershire.gov.uk
Web: www.worcestershire.gov.uk

English Metropolitan Councils

Barnsley Metropolitan Borough Council
Address: Town Hall
        Barnsley S70 2TA
Tel: 01226 770770
Fax: 01226 773099
Email: townhall@barnsley.gov.uk
Web: www.barnsley.gov.uk

Birmingham City Council
Address: Transportation Strategy
        1 Lancaster Circus, Queensway
        Birmingham B4 7DQ
Tel: 0121 303 7454
Fax: 0121 303 6379
Email: transportpolicy@birmingham.gov.uk
Web: www.birmingham.gov.uk

Bolton Council
Address: Town Hall, Victoria Square
        Bolton BL1 1RU
Tel: 01204 333 333
Fax: n.a.
Email: bolton@bolton.gov.uk
Web: www.bolton.gov.uk

City of Bradford Metropolitan District Council
Address: 1 City Road,
        Bradford BD8 8UR
Tel: 01274 757418
Fax: 01274 390313
Email: bdirectmail@bradford.gov.uk
Web: www.bradford.gov.uk

Bury Metropolitan Borough Council
Address: Town Hall, Knowsley Street
        Bury BL9 0SW
Tel: 0161 253 5000
Fax: 0161 253 5119
Email: info@bury.gov.uk
Web: www.bury.gov.uk

Calderdale Metropolitan Borough Council
Address: Town Hall, Crossley Street
        Halifax HX1 1UJ
Tel: 01422 357257
Fax: 01422 393102
Email: engineeringservices@
        calderdale.gov.uk
Web: www.calderdale.gov.uk

Coventry City Council
Address: Council House, Earl Street
        Coventry CV1 5RR
Tel: 024 7683 3333
Fax: 024 7683 3680
Email: coventrydirect@coventry.gov.uk
Web: www.coventry.gov.uk

Doncaster Metropolitan Borough Council
Address: 2 Priory Place
        Doncaster DN1 1BN
Tel: 01302 734444
Fax: 01302 734040
Email: askus@doncaster.gov.uk
Web: www.doncaster.gov.uk

Dudley Metropolitan Borough Council
Address: Council House, Priory Road
        Dudley DY1 1HF
Tel: 01384 812345
Fax: n.a.
Email: dudleycouncilplus@dudley.gov.uk
Web: www.dudley.gov.uk

Gateshead Metropolitan Borough Council
Address: Civic Centre, Regent Street
        Gateshead NE8 1HH
Tel: 0191 433 3000
Fax: 0191 477 5855
Email: enquiries@gateshead.gov.uk
Web: www.gateshead.gov.uk

Kirklees Council
Address: Civic Centre 3, Market Street
        Huddersfield HD1 1WG
Tel: 01484 221000
Fax: 01484 223330
Email: performance.communication@
        kirklees.gov.uk
Web: www.kirkleesmc.gov.uk

Knowsley Metropolitan Borough Council
Address: Transportation, Highways &
Engineering
Yorkon Building, PO Box 26
Archway Road
Huyton, Liverpool L36 9FB
Tel: 0151 443 2228
Fax: 0151 443 2370
Email: transport.policy@knowsley.gov.uk
Web: www.knowsley.gov.uk

*Leeds City Council
Address: Civic Hall
Leeds LS1 1UR
Tel: 0113 234 8080
Fax: n.a.
Email: onestop@leeds.gov.uk
Web: www.leeds.gov.uk

Liverpool City Council
Address: PO Box 88, Municipal Buildings
Dale Street, Liverpool L69 2DH
Tel: 0151 233 3000
Fax: n.a.
Email: liverpool.direct@liverpool.gov.uk
Web: www.liverpool.gov.uk

Manchester City Council
Address: Town Hall, Albert Square
Manchester M60 2LA
Tel: 0161 234 5000
Fax: 0161 234 3760
Email: city.council@ manchester.gov.uk
Web: www.manchester.gov.uk

Newcastle City Council
Address: Civic Centre, Barras Bridge
Newcastle-upon-Tyne NE99 2BN
Tel: 0191 232 8520
Fax: 0191 211 4843
Email: plantransport@newcastle.gov.uk
Web: www.newcastle.gov.uk

North Tyneside Metropolitan Borough Council
Address: Town Hall,
Wallsend NE28 7RR
Tel: 0191 200 5000
Fax: 0191 200 7272
Email: call.centre@northtyneside.gov.uk
Web: www.northtyneside.gov.uk

Oldham Metropolitan Borough Council
Address: PO Box 160, Civic Centre
West Street, Oldham OL1 1UG
Tel: 0161 770 4300
Fax: n.a.
Email: transport@oldham.gov.uk
Web: www.oldham.gov.uk

Rochdale Metropolitan Borough Council
Address: Environmental Management Services
H.Q.
Green Lane, Heywood, Lancs.
OL10 2DY
Tel: 01706 647474
Fax: 01706 693026
Email: environmental.management@
rochdale.gov.uk
Web: www.rochdale.gov.uk

Rotherham Metropolitan Borough Council
Address: Transportation Unit, Planning and
Transportation
Bailey House, Rawmarsh Road
Rotherham S60 1TD
Tel: 01709 382 121
Fax: 01709 822 139
Email: transportation@rotherham.gov.uk
Web: www.rotherham.gov.uk

Salford City Council
Address: Salford Civic Centre, Chorley Road
Swinton, Salford M27 5AP
Tel: 0161 794 4711
Fax: 0161 794 6595
Email: information.centre@salford.gov.uk
Web: www.salford.gov.uk

Sandwell Metropolitan Borough Council
Address: Sandwell Council House,
Oldbury B69 3DE
Tel: 0845 358 2200
Fax: 0121 569 3722
Email: smbc@sandwell.gov.uk
Web: www.sandwell.gov.uk

Sefton Metropolitan Borough Council
Address: Technical Services, Magdalene House
30 Trinity Road, Bootle L20 3NJ
Tel: 0845 140 0845
Fax: 0151 934 4532
Email: transport.planning@
technical.sefton.gov.uk
Web: www.sefton.gov.uk

Sheffield City Council
Address: Transport and Highways
Howden House, 1 Union Street
Sheffield S1 2SH
Tel: 0114 272 6444
Fax: n.a.
Email: firstpoint@sheffield.gov.uk
Web: www.sheffield.gov.uk

Solihull Metropolitan Borough Council
Address: PO Box 18, Council House
Solihull B91 3QS
Tel: 0121 704 6000
Fax: 0121 704 6114
Email: customer@solihull.gov.uk
Web: www.solihull.gov.uk

South Tyneside Metropolitan Borough Council
Address: Town Hall, Westoe Road
South Shields NE33 2RL
Tel: 0191 427 1717
Fax: 0191 454 5678
Email: n.a.
Web: www.s-tyneside-mbc.gov.uk

St Helens Metropolitan Borough Council
Address: Victoria Square, Corporation Street
St.Helens WA10 1HP
Tel: 01744 456000
Fax: 01744 733337
Email: n.a.
Web: www.sthelens.gov.uk

Stockport Metropolitan Borough Council
Address: Stockport Town Hall, Edward Street
Stockport SK1 3XE
Tel: 0161 480 4949
Fax: 0161 477 9530
Email: stockport.council@stockport.gov.uk
Web: www.stockport.gov.uk

Sunderland City Council
Address: PO Box 100, Civic Centre
Burdon Road, Sunderland SR2 7DN
Tel: 0191 520 5555
Fax: 0191 553 1020
Email: Enquiries@sunderland.gov.uk
Web: www.sunderland.gov.uk

Tameside Metropolitan Borough Council
Address: Wellington Road,
Ashton-Under-Lyne OL6 6DL
Tel: 0161 342 8355
Fax: 0161 342 3070
Email: envform@tameside.gov.uk
Web: www.tameside.gov.uk

Trafford Metropolitan Borough Council
Address: Trafford Town Hall, Talbot Road
Stretford, Manchester M32 0YX
Tel: 0161 912 4399
Fax: 0161 912 4430
Email: trafford.direct@trafford.gov.uk
Web: www.trafford.gov.uk

Wakefield Metropolitan District Council
Address: County Hall, Bond Street
Wakefield WF1 2QL
Tel: 01924 306090
Fax: 01924 303450
Email: internet@wakefield.gov.uk
Web: www.wakefield.gov.uk

Walsall Metropolitan Borough Council
Address: Civic Centre,
Walsall WS1 1TP
Tel: 01922 650000
Fax: 01922 720885
Email: info@walsall.gov.uk
Web: www.walsall.gov.uk

Wigan Borough Council
Address: Town Hall, Library Street
Wigan WN1 1YN
Tel: 01942 244991
Fax: 01942 827451
Email: ce@wigan.gov.uk
Web: www.wigan.gov.uk

Metropolitan Borough Council of Wirral

Address: Transport Section, 250 Cleveland
Street
Birkenhead CH41 3QL
Tel: 0151 647 8002
Fax: 0151 666 1997
Email: technicalservices@wirral.gov.uk
Web: www.wirral.gov.uk

Wolverhampton City Council

Address: Transport Strategy, Regeneration &
Environment
Heantun House, Salop Street,
Wolverhampton WV3 0SQ
Tel: 01902 551155
Fax: n.a.
Email: transport.strategy@
wolverhampton.gov.uk
Web: www.wolverhampton.gov.uk

English Unitary Councils

Bath and North East Somerset Council

Address: Guildhall, High Street
Bath BA1 5AW
Tel: 01225 477000
Fax: n.a.
Email: enquiries@bathnes.gov.uk
Web: www.bathnes.gov.uk

Blackburn with Darwen Borough Council

Address: Castleway House, 17 Preston New
Road
Blackburn BB2 1AU
Tel: 01254 273838
Fax: 01254 273559
Email: info@blackburn.gov.uk
Web: www.blackburn.gov.uk

Blackpool Council

Address: Transportation Division
Layton Depot, Plymouth Road
Blackpool FY3 7HW
Tel: 01253 477477
Fax: 01253 476198
Email: transport.policy@blackpool.gov.uk
Web: www.blackpool.gov.uk

Bournemouth Borough Council

Address: Town Hall, Bourne Avenue
Bournemouth BH2 6DY
Tel: 01202 451451
Fax: 01202 451000
Email: enquiries@bournemouth.gov.uk
Web: www.bournemouth.gov.uk

Bracknell Forest Borough Council

Address: Time Square, Market Street
Bracknell RG12 1JD
Tel: 01344 352000
Fax: 01344 352810
Email: customer.services@bracknell-
forest.gov.uk
Web: www.bracknell-forest.gov.uk

Brighton & Hove City Council

Address: King's House, Grand Avenue
Hove BN3 2LS
Tel: 01273 290000
Fax: 01273 291003
Email: local.transport@brighton-hove.gov.uk
Web: www.brighton-hove.gov.uk

Bristol City Council

Address: The Council House, College Green
Bristol BS1 5TR
Tel: 0117 922 2000
Fax: n.a.
Email: n.a.
Web: www.bristol-city.gov.uk

Darlington Borough Council

Address: Town Hall, Feethams
Darlington DL1 5QT
Tel: 01325 380651
Fax: 01325 388290
Email: enquiries@darlington.gov.uk
Web: www.darlington.gov.uk

Derby City Council

Address: The Council House, Corporation
Street
Derby DE1 2FS
Tel: 01332 293111
Fax: 01332 255500
Email: enquiries@derby.gov.uk
Web: www.derby.gov.uk

East Riding of Yorkshire Council
Address: County Hall
Beverley HU17 9BA
Tel: 01482 393939
Fax: 01482 393375
Email: customer.services@eastriding.gov.uk
Web: www.eastriding.gov.uk

Halton Borough Council
Address: Municipal Building, Kingsway
Widnes, Cheshire WA8 7QF
Tel: 0151 907 8300
Fax: 0151 471 7301
Email: transportco-ordination@
halton.gov.uk
Web: www.halton.gov.uk

Hartlepool Borough Council
Address: Bryan Hanson House, Hanson Square
Hartlepool TS24 7BT
Tel: 01429 523004
Fax: 01429 860830
Email: transport@hartlepool.gov.uk
Web: www.hartlepool.gov.uk

Herefordshire Council
Address: Brockington, 35 Hafod Road
Hereford HR1 1SH
Tel: 01432 260000
Fax: n.a.
Email: info@herefordshire.gov.uk
Web: www.herefordshire.gov.uk

Kingston Upon Hull City Council
Address: Streetscene Services
Kingston House, Bond Street
Hull HU1 3ER
Tel: 01482 300300
Fax: 01482 612012
Email: Info@hullcc.gov.uk
Web: www.hullcc.gov.uk

Isle of Wight Council
Address: Engineering Services
Enterprise House, Monks Brook
Newport PO30 5WB
Tel: 01983 821000
Fax: 01983 823545
Email: highways@iow.gov.uk
Web: www.iwight.com

Leicester City Council
Address: New Walk Centre, Welford Place
Leicester LE1 6ZG
Tel: 0116 254 9922
Fax: 0116 254 8954
Email: customer.services@leicester.gov.uk
Web: www.leicester.gov.uk

Luton Borough Council
Address: Town Hall, George Street
Luton LU1 2BQ
Tel: 01582 546000
Fax: 01582 547143
Email: feedback@luton.gov.uk
Web: www.lutonline.gov.uk

Medway Council
Address: Compass Centre, Chatham Maritime
Chatham, Kent ME4 4YH
Tel: 01634 331505
Fax: 01634 331125
Email: transport.planning@medway.gov.uk
Web: www.medway.gov.uk

Middlesbrough Borough Council
Address: Transport and Design
Vancouver House, Gurney Street
Middlesbrough TS1 1QP
Tel: 01642 728100
Fax: 01642 728962
Email: n.a.
Web: www.middlesbrough.gov.uk

*Milton Keynes Council
Address: Civic Offices, I Saxon Gate East
Central Milton Keynes MK9 3HQ
Tel: 01908 691691
Fax: 01908 252302
Email: transport.policy@milton-
keynes.gov.uk
Web: www.mkweb.co.uk/mkcouncil

North East Lincolnshire Council
Address: Transport Strategy Team, Origin One
1 Origin Way, Europarc
Grimsby DN37 9TZ
Tel: 01472 313131
Fax: 01472 324702
Email: transport@nelincs.gov.uk
Web: www.nelincs.gov.uk

North Lincolnshire Council

Address: Pittwood House, Ashby Road
Scunthorpe DN16 1AB
Tel: 01724 296296
Fax: 01724 281705
Email: customerservice@northlincs.gov.uk
Web: www.northlincs.gov.uk

North Somerset Council

Address: Transport Planning, Somerset House,
Oxford Street
Weston-Super-Mare BS23 1TR
Tel: 01934 888888
Fax: 01275 888569
Email: transport.policy@n-somerset.gov.uk
Web: www.n-somerset.gov.uk

Nottingham City Council

Address: City Development, Planning
Transport & Intelligence Strategy
Exchange Buildings North, Smithy
Row
Nottingham NG1 2BS
Tel: 0115 915 5555
Fax: 0115 915 5483
Email:: customer.services@
nottinghamcity.gov.uk
Web: www.nottinghamcity.gov.uk

Peterborough City Council

Address: Town Hall, Bridge Street
Peterborough PE1 1PJ
Tel: 01733 747474
Fax: 01733 345090
Email: ask@peterborough.gov.uk
Web: www.peterborough.gov.uk

Plymouth City Council

Address: Civic Centre,
Plymouth PL1 2EW
Tel: 01752 668000
Fax: 01752 304819
Email: info@plymouth.gov.uk
Web: www.plymouth.gov.uk

Borough of Poole

Address: Transportation Services, St Johns
House,
Serpentine Road, Poole BH15 2DX
Tel: 01202 262000
Fax: 01202 262091
Email: transportationhelpdesk@poole.gov.uk
Web: www.boroughofpoole.com

Portsmouth City Council

Address: Directorate of Environment &
Transport
Civic Offices, Guildhall Square
Portsmouth PO1 2NE
Tel: 023 9283 4092
Fax: 023 9283 4655
Email: general@portsmouthcc.gov.uk
Web: www.portsmouth.gov.uk

Reading Borough Council

Address: Civic Centre
Reading RG1 7TD
Tel: 0118 939 0900
Fax: 0118 958 9770
Email: customer.services@reading.gov.uk
Web: www.reading.gov.uk

Redcar and Cleveland Borough Council

Address: Town Hall, Fabian Road
South Bank, Middlesbrough
TS6 9AR
Tel: 0845 612 6126
Fax: 01642 444588
Email: n.a.
Web: www.redcar-cleveland.gov.uk

Rutland County Council

Address: Catmose
Oakham LE15 6HP
Tel: 01572 722577
Fax: 01572 758307
Email: enquiries@rutland.gov.uk
Web: www.rutland.gov.uk

Slough Borough Council

Address: Town Hall, Bath Road, Slough
Berkshire SL1 3UQ
Tel: 01753 475111
Fax: 01753 692499
Email: enquiries@slough.gov.uk
Web: www.slough.gov.uk

South Gloucestershire Council

Address: Planning, Transportation & Strategic
Environment
The Council Offices, Castle Street
Thornbury BS35 1HF
Tel: 01454 868004
Fax: 01454 863855
Email: transport.policy@southglos.gov.uk
Web: www.southglos.gov.uk

Southampton City Council

Address: Travel & Transport Policy
Civic Centre, Southampton
SO14 7LY
Tel: 023 8022 3855
Fax: 023 8083 2607
Email: gateway@southampton.gov.uk
Web: www.southampton.gov.uk

Southend-on-Sea Borough Council

Address: Enterprise, Tourism & the
Environment
Civic Centre, Victoria Avenue
Southend on Sea SS2 6QZ
Tel: 01702 215321
Fax: 01702 339607
Email: doete@southend.gov.uk
Web: www.southend.gov.uk

Stockton-on-Tees Council

Address: PO Box 11, Municipal Buildings
Church Road
Stockton on Tees TS18 1LD
Tel: 01642 393939
Fax: 01642 393092
Email: member.services@stockton.gov.uk
Web: www.stockton.gov.uk

Stoke-on-Trent City Council

Address: Regeneration and Heritage
PO Box 630, Civic Centre,
Glebe Street
Stoke on Trent ST4 1RF
Tel: 01782 236178
Fax: 01782 232171
Email: transportation@stoke.gov.uk
Web: www.stoke.gov.uk

Swindon Borough Council

Address: Civic Offices, Euclid Street
Swindon SN1 2JH
Tel: 01793 463000
Fax: 01793 463930
Email: customerservices@swindon.gov.uk
Web: www.swindon.gov.uk

Telford and Wrekin Council

Address: Transport Policy and Management
Environment and Regeneration
PO Box 212, 3B Darby House
Telford TF3 4LB
Tel: 01952 384602
Fax: 01952 384634
Email: transport.policy@telford.gov.uk
Web: www.telford.gov.uk

Thurrock Borough Council

Address: Civic Offices, New Road
Grays RM17 6SL
Tel: 01375 652652
Fax: 01375 652359
Email: general.enquiries@thurrock.gov.uk
Web: www.thurrock.gov.uk

Torbay Council

Address: Town Hall, Castle Circus
Torquay TQ1 3DR
Tel: 01803 201201
Fax: 01803 292677
Email: fss@torbay.gov.uk
Web: www.torbay.gov.uk

Warrington Borough Council

Address: Town Hall, Sankey Street
Warrington WA1 1UH
Tel: 01925 444400
Fax: 01925 442138
Email: contact@warrington.gov.uk
Web: www.warrington.gov.uk

West Berkshire Council

Address: Transport Policy
Market Street, Newbury
Berkshire RG14 5LD
Tel: 01635 424000
Fax: 01635 519408
Email: LTP@westberks.gov.uk
Web: www.westberks.gov.uk

Royal Borough of Windsor and Maidenhead

Address: Town Hall, St Ives Road
Maidenhead SL6 1RF
Tel: 01628 683800
Fax: 01628 796474
Email: info@rbwm.gov.uk
Web: www.rbwm.gov.uk

Wokingham District Council

Address: Civic Offices, Shute End
Wokingham
Berkshire RG40 1BN
Tel: 0118 974 6000
Fax: 0118 978 9078
Email: wokinghamdc@wokingham.gov.uk
Web: www.wokingham.gov.uk

City of York Council

Address: The Guildhall,
York YO1 9QN
Tel: 01904 613161
Fax: 01904 551090
Email: comments@york.gov.uk
Web: www.york.gov.uk

London Authorities

City of London

Address: PO Box 270, Guildhall
London EC2P 2EJ
Tel: 020 7606 3030
Fax: 020 7332 1119
Email: plans@cityoflondon.gov.uk
Web: www.cityoflondon.gov.uk

Greater London Authority

Address: City Hall, The Queen's Walk
London SE1 2AA
Tel: 020 7983 4000
Fax: 020 7983 4057
Email: mayor@london.gov.uk
Web: www.london.gov.uk

London Borough of Barking & Dagenham

Address: Civic Centre, Rainham Road North
Dagenham RM10 7BN
Tel: 020 8215 3000
Fax: 020 8227 5184
Email: 3000direct@lbbd.gov.uk
Web: www.barking-dagenham.gov.uk

London Borough of Barnet

Address: Building 4, North London Business
Park
Oakleigh Road South N11 1NP
Tel: 020 8359 2000
Fax: 020 8359 2480
Email: first.contact@barnet.gov.uk
Web: www.barnet.gov.uk

London Borough of Bexley

Address: Transportation and Traffic
Department
Wyncham House,
207 Longlands Road
Sidcup, Kent DA15 7JH
Tel: 020 8308 7794
Fax: 020 8308 7845
Email: transportandtraffic@bexley.gov.uk
Web: www.bexley.gov.uk

London Borough of Brent

Address: Brent Town Hall, Forty Lane
Wembley HA9 9HD
Tel: 020 8937 1234
Fax: 020 8937 1444
Email: customer.services@brent.gov.uk
Web: www.brent.gov.uk

London Borough of Bromley

Address: Bromley Civic Centre, Stockwell
Close
Bromley BR1 3UH
Tel: 020 8464 3333
Fax: 020 8313 0095
Email: traffic@bromley.gov.uk
Web: www.bromley.gov.uk

London Borough of Camden

Address: Camden Town Hall Ext.
Argyle Street
London WC1H 8EQ
Tel: 020 7278 4444
Fax: 020 7974 2706
Email: info@camden.gov.uk
Web: www.camden.gov.uk

London Borough of Croydon

Address: Planning & Transportation
Department
Taberner House, Park Lane
Croydon CR9 1JT
Tel: 020 8726 6000
Fax: n.a.
Email: contact.thecouncil@croydon.gov.uk
Web: www.croydon.gov.uk

London Borough of Ealing

Address: Perceval House, 14-16 Uxbridge Road
Ealing, London W5 2HL
Tel: 020 8825 6000
Fax: n.a.
Email   transportandplanningpolicy@
ealing.gov.uk
Web: www.ealing.gov.uk

London Borough of Enfield

Address: Traffic & Transportation Service
Civic Centre, Silver Street
Enfield EN1 3XY
Tel: 020 8379 3554
Fax: 020 8379 3475
Email: transportation@enfield.gov.uk
Web: www.enfield.gov.uk

London Borough of Greenwich

Address: Woolwich Town Hall, Wellington
Street
Woolwich, London SE18 6PW
Tel: 020 8854 8888
Fax: 020 8855 9818
Email: n.a.
Web: www.greenwich.gov.uk

London Borough of Hackney

Address: Neigbourhoods and Regeneration
Town Hall, Mare Street
Hackney, London E8 1EA
Tel: 020 8356 8404
Fax: n.a.
Email: info@hackney.gov.uk
Web: www.hackney.gov.uk

London Borough of Hammersmith & Fulham

Address: Town Hall, King Street
London W6 9JU
Tel: 020 8748 3020
Fax: n.a.
Email: information@lbhf.gov.uk
Web: www.lbhf.gov.uk

London Borough of Haringey

Address: River Park House, 225 High Road
Wood Green, London N22 8LE
Tel: 020 8489 0000
Fax: n.a.
Email: customer.services@haringey.gov.uk
Web: www.haringey.gov.uk

London Borough of Harrow

Address: PO Box 57, Civic Centre
Harrow HA1 2XF
Tel: 020 8863 5611
Fax: 020 8424 7662
Email: transportation@harrow.gov.uk
Web: www.harrow.gov.uk

London Borough of Havering

Address: Transport Planning
9th Floor, Mercury House
Mercury Gardens
Romford RM1 3SL
Tel: 01708 434343
Fax: 01708 432428
Email: dtp@ havering.gov.uk
Web: www.havering.gov.uk

London Borough of Hillingdon

Address: Civic Centre, High Street
Uxbridge UB8 1UW
Tel: 01895 250111
Fax: 01895 273636
Email: transportstrategy@hillingdon.gov.uk
Web: www.hillingdon.gov.uk

London Borough of Hounslow

Address: The Civic Centre, Lampton Road
Hounslow TW3 4DN
Tel: 020 8583 2000
Fax: 020 8583 2598
Email: information@hounslow.gov.uk
Web: www.hounslow.gov.uk

London Borough of Islington

Address: Town Hall, Upper Street
London N1 2UD
Tel: 020 7527 2000
Fax: n.a.
Email: contact@islington.gov.uk
Web: www.islington.gov.uk

Royal Borough of Kensington & Chelsea

Address: Town Hall, Hornton Street
London W8 7NX
Tel: 020 7937 5464
Fax: 020 7938 1445
Email: traffic@rbkc.gov.uk
Web: www.rbkc.gov.uk

Royal Borough of Kingston upon Thames

Address: High Street
Kingston KT1 1EU
Tel: 020 8546 2121
Fax: n.a.
Email: n.a.
Web: www.kingston.gov.uk

London Borough of Lambeth

Address: Lambeth Environment – Street
Management
Floor 3, Blue Star House
243-244 Stockwell Road
London SW9 9SP
Tel: 020 7926 9000
Fax: 020 7926 2357
Email: DESTranCPZ3@lambeth.gov.uk
Web: www.lambeth.gov.uk

London Borough of Lewisham

Address: Lewisham Town Hall, Catford
London SE6 4RU
Tel: 020 8314 6000
Fax: 020 8314 5659
Email: transport@lewisham.gov.uk
Web: www.lewisham.gov.uk

London Borough of Merton

Address: Merton Civic Centre, London Road
Morden SM4 5DX
Tel: 020 8274 4901
Fax: 020 8543 7126
Email: postroom@merton.gov.uk
Web: www.merton.gov.uk

London Borough of Newham

Address: Town Hall, Barking Road
East Ham, London E6 2RP
Tel: 020 8430 2000
Fax: 020 8472 0293
Email: Customer.Services@newham.gov.uk
Web: www.newham.gov.uk

London Borough of Redbridge

Address: Engineering and Building Services
Lynton House, 255-259 High Road
Ilford, Ilford Essex 1G1 1NY
Tel: 020 8708 5050
Fax: n.a.
Email: streetscene@redbridge.gov.uk
Web: www.redbridge.gov.uk

London Borough of Richmond upon Thames

Address: Transport Planning, Civic Centre
44 York Street
Twickenham TW1 3BZ
Tel: 020 8891 7310
Fax: 020 8487 5010
Email: tps@richmond.gov.uk
Web: www.richmond.gov.uk

London Borough of Southwark

Address: Chiltern House, Portland Street
Walworth, London SE17 2ES
Tel: 020 7525 5317
Fax: 020 7525 5683
Email: transport@southwark.gov.uk
Web: www.southwark.gov.uk

London Borough of Sutton

Address: Environment and Leisure
24 Denmark Road, Carshalton
Surrey SM5 2JG
Tel: 020 8770 5000
Fax: 020 8770 6298
Email: traffic.postbook@sutton.gov.uk
Web: www.sutton.gov.uk/environment

London Borough of Tower Hamlets

Address: Mulberry Place, 5 Clove Crescent
London E14 2BG
Tel: 020 7364 5000
Fax: 020 7364 4296
Email: webteam@towerhamlets.gov.uk
Web: www.towerhamlets.gov.uk

London Borough of Waltham Forest

Address: Transport Planning
Town Hall, Forest Road
London E17 4JF
Tel: 020 8496 3000
Fax: 020 8527 8313
Email: wfdirect@walthamforest.gov.uk
Web: www.walthamforest.gov.uk

Wandsworth Borough Council

Address: Town Hall, Wandsworth High Street
London SW18 2PU
Tel: 020 8871 6000
Fax: 020 8871 7560
Email: enquiries@wandsworth.gov.uk
Web: www.wandsworth.gov.uk

Westminster City Council

Address: City Hall
64 Victoria Street
London SW1E 6QP
Tel: 020 7641 6000
Fax: 020 7641 3776
Email: n.a.
Web: www.westminster.gov.uk

Scottish Councils

Aberdeen City Council

Address: Planning & Infrastructure
Broad Street, Aberdeen AB10 1BW
Tel: 01224 522000
Fax: 01224 636181
Email: PI@aberdeencity.gov.uk
Web: www.aberdeencity.gov.uk

Aberdeenshire Council

Address: Woodhill House, Westburn Road
Aberdeen AB16 5GB
Tel: 0845 608 1207
Fax: 01224 662005
Email: transportation@aberdeenshire.gov.uk
Web: www.aberdeenshire.gov.uk

Angus Council

Address: Angus House
Orchardbank Business Park
Forfar DD8 1AN
Tel: 0845 277 7778
Fax: 01307 476299
Email: accessline@angus.gov.uk
Web: www.angus.gov.uk

Argyll & Bute Council

Address: Transportation and Infrastructure
Kilmory
Lochgilphead PA31 8RT
Tel: 01546 602127
Fax: 01546 604291
Email: enquiries@argyll-bute.gov.uk
Web: www.argyll-bute.gov.uk

Clackmannanshire Council

Address: Roads and Transportation, Kilncraigs
Greenside Street, Alloa FK10 1EB
Tel: 01259 450000
Fax: 01259 727451
Email: roads@clacks.gov.uk
Web: www.clacksweb.org.uk

Dumfries & Galloway Council

Address: Militia House, English Street
Dumfries DG1 2HR
Tel: 01387 260000
Fax: 01387 260111
Email: CIS@dumgal.gov.uk
Web: www.dumgal.gov.uk

Dundee City Council

Address: Planning & Transportation
Tayside House, Crighton Street
Dundee DD1 3RB
Tel: 01382 433191
Fax: 01382 433313
Email: n.a.
Web: www.dundeecity.gov.uk

East Ayrshire Council

Address: Roads & Transportation,
          Council Offices, Greenholm Street
          Kilmarnock KA1 4DJ
Tel: 01563 576310
Fax: 01563 576312
Email: roads@east-ayrshire.gov.uk
Web: www.east-ayrshire.gov.uk

East Dunbartonshire Council

Address: The Triangle, Kirkintilloch Road
          Bishopriggs, Glasgow G64 2TR
Tel: 0141 578 8600
Fax: 0141 578 8575
Email: transportation@eastdunbarton.gov.uk
Web: www.eastdunbarton.gov.uk

East Lothian Council

Address: John Muir House
          Haddington EH41 3HA
Tel: 01620 827827
Fax: 01620 827888
Email: jmhreception@eastlothian.gov.uk
Web: www.eastlothian.gov.uk

East Renfrewshire Council

Address: Eastwood Park, Rouken Glen Road
          Glasgow G46 6UG
Tel: 0141 577 3001
Fax: 0141 620 0884
Email: customerservices@
          eastrenfrewshire. gov.uk
Web: www.eastrenfrewshire.gov.uk

City of Edinburgh Council

Address: City Chambers, High Street
          Edinburgh EH1 1YJ
Tel: 0131 200 2000
Fax: n.a.
Email: transport-edinburgh
          @edinburgh.gov.uk
Web: www.edinburgh.gov.uk

Falkirk Council

Address: Municipal Buildings
          Falkirk FK1 5RS
Tel: 01324 506070
Fax: 01324 506061
Email: info@falkirk.gov.uk
Web: www.falkirk.gov.uk

Fife Council

Address: Transportation Services
          Rothesay House, Rothesay Place
          Glenrothes KY7 5PQ
Tel: 01592 583330
Fax: 01592 413111
Email: transportation.services@fife.gov.uk
Web: www.fifedirect.org.uk

Glasgow City Council

Address: Land and Environmental Services
          Richmond Exchange,
          20 Cadogan Street
          Glasgow G2 7AD
Tel: 0141 287 9100
Fax: 0141 287 9103
Email: land@glasgow.gov.uk
Web: www.glasgow.gov.uk

The Highland Council

Address: Council Headquarters
          Glenurquhart Road
          Inverness IV3 5NX
Tel: 01463 702000
Fax: 01463 702111
Email: service.point@highland.gov.uk
Web: www.highland.gov.uk

Inverclyde Council

Address: Municipal Buildings
          Greenock PA15 1LY
Tel: 01475 717171
Fax: 01475 712777
Email: n.a.
Web: www.inverclyde.gov.uk

Midlothian Council

Address: Midlothian House, Buccleuch Street
          Dalkeith EH22 1DN
Tel: 0131 270 7500
Fax: 0131 271 3050
Email: enquiries@midlothian.gov.uk
Web: www.midlothian.gov.uk

Moray Council

Address: Council Offices, High Street
          Elgin IV30 1BX
Tel: 01343 543451
Fax: 01343 540183
Email: hotline@moray.gov.uk
Web: www.moray.gov.uk

North Ayrshire Council

Address: Cunninghame House
Irvine KA12 8EE
Tel: 01294 324100
Fax: 01294 324144
Email: contactus@north-ayrshire.gov.uk
Web: www.north-ayrshire.gov.uk

North Lanarkshire Council

Address: Environmental Services
PO Box 14, Civic Centre
Motherwell ML1 1TW
Tel: 01698 506235
Fax: 01698 844063
Email: transport@northlan.gov.uk
Web: www.northlan.gov.uk

Orkney Islands Council

Address: Council Offices, School Place
Kirkwall KW15 1NY
Tel: 01856 873535
Fax: 01856 874615
Email: customerservices@orkney.gov.uk
Web: www.orkney.gov.uk

Perth & Kinross Council

Address: 2 High Street
Perth PH1 5PH
Tel: 01738 475000
Fax: 01738 475005
Email: enquiries@pkc.gov.uk
Web: www.pkc.gov.uk

Renfrewshire Council

Address: Planning & Transport
HQ, South Building
Cotton Street, Paisley PA1 1LL
Tel: 0141 842 5811/5822
Fax: 0141 840 5040
Email: pt@renfrewshire.gov.uk
Web: www.renfrewshire.gov.uk

Scottish Borders Council

Address: Council Headquarters
Newtown St. Boswells
Melrose TD6 0SA
Tel: 01835 824000
Fax: 01835 825142
Email: enquiries@scotborders.gov.uk.
Web: www.scotborders.gov.uk

Shetland Islands Council

Address: 20 Commercial Road
Lerwick
Shetland ZE1 0HB
Tel: 01595 744868
Fax: 01595 744880
Email: sic@sic.shetland.gov.uk
Web: www.shetland.gov.uk

South Ayrshire Council

Address: Roads & Transportation Department
Burns House, Burns Statue Square
Ayr KA7 1UT
Tel: 01292 612000
Fax: 01292 612143?
Email: cst@south-ayrshire.gov.uk
Web: www.south-ayrshire.gov.uk

South Lanarkshire Council

Address: Council Offices, Almada Street
Hamilton ML3 0AA
Tel: 01698 454444
Fax: 01698 454275
Email: customer.services@
southlanarkshire. gov.uk
Web: www.southlanarkshire.gov.uk

Stirling Council

Address: Council Offices, Viewforth
Stirling FK8 2ET
Tel: 0845 2777000
Fax: 01786 443474
Email: info@stirling.gov.uk
Web: www.stirling.gov.uk

West Dunbartonshire Council

Address: Council Offices, Garshake Road
Dumbarton G82 3PU
Tel: 01389 737000
Fax: 01389 737293
Email: webmaster@west-dunbarton.gov.uk
Web: www.wdcweb.info

West Lothian Council

Address: West Lothian House
Almondvale Boulevard
Livingston EH54 6QG
Tel: 01506 775000
Fax: 01506 777102
Email: customer.service@westlothian.gov.uk
Web: www.westlothian.gov.uk

Western Isles Council / Comhairle nan Eilean Siar

Address: Council Offices, Sandwick Road
Stornoway, Isle of Lewis HS1 2BW
Tel: 01851 703773
Fax: 01851 705349
Email: enquiries@cne-siar.gov.uk
Web: www.w-isles.gov.uk

Welsh Councils

Blaenau Gwent County Borough Council

Address: Municipal Offices, Civic Centre
Ebbw Vale NP23 6XB
Tel: 01495 350555
Fax: 01495 301255
Email: info@blaenau-gwent.gov.uk
Web: www.blaenau-gwent.gov.uk

Bridgend County Borough Council

Address: Civic Offices, Angel Street
Bridgend CF31 4WB
Tel: 01656 643643
Fax: 01656 668126
Email: talktous@bridgend.gov.uk
Web: www.bridgend.gov.uk

Caerphilly County Borough Council

Address: Nelson Road, Tredomen, Hengoed
Ystrad Mynach, CF82 7WF
Tel: 01443 815588
Fax: 01443 864211
Email: info@caerphilly.gov.uk
Web: www.caerphilly.gov.uk

Cardiff Council

Address: County Hall, Atlantic Wharf
Cardiff CF10 4UW
Tel: 029 2087 2087
Fax: 029 2087 2086
Email: C2C@cardiff.gov.uk
Web: www.cardiff.gov.uk

Carmarthenshire County Council

Address: County Hall
Carmarthen SA31 1JP
Tel: 01267 234567
Fax: 01267 221737
Email: information@carmarthenshire.gov.uk
Web: www.carmarthenshire.gov.uk

Ceredigion County Council

Address: County Hall, Market Street
Aberaeron SA46 0AT
Tel: 01545 570881
Fax: 01545 572589
Email: hpw@ceredigion.gov.uk
Web: www.ceredigion.gov.uk

Conwy County Borough Council

Address: Bodlondeb
Conwy LL32 8DU
Tel: 01492 574000
Fax: 01492 592114
Email: information@conwy.gov.uk
Web: www.conwy.gov.uk

Denbighshire County Council

Address: Transport & Infrastructure,
Caledfryn,
Smithfield Road, Denbigh
Tel: 01824 706800
Fax: 01824 706970
Email: publictransport@denbighshire.gov.uk
Web: www.denbighshire.gov.uk

Flintshire County Council

Address: County Hall
Mold CH7 6NB
Tel: 01352 752121
Fax: 01352 758240
Email: info@flintshire.gov.uk
Web: www.flintshire.gov.uk

Gwynedd Council

Address: Council Offices
Caernarfon LL55 1SH
Tel: 01286 679535
Fax: 01286 673324
Email: bwsgwynedd@gwynedd.gov.uk
Web: www.gwynedd.gov.uk

Isle of Anglesey County Council / Cyngor Sir Ynys Môn

Address: Council Offices, Llangefni
Anglesey LL77 7TW
Tel: 01248 750057
Fax: 01248 750839
Email: communications@anglesey.gov.uk
Web: www.anglesey.gov.uk

Merthyr Tydfil County Borough Council

Address: Civic Centre, Castle Street
        Merthyr Tydfil CF47 8AN
Tel: 01685 725000
Fax: 01685 722146
Email: customer.care@merthyr.gov.uk
Web: www.merthyr.gov.uk

Monmouthshire County Council

Address: County Hall
        Cwmbran NP44 2XN
Tel: 01633 644748
Fax: 01633 644666
Email: highways@monmouthshire.gov.uk
Web: www.monmouthshire.gov.uk

Neath Port Talbot County Borough Council

Address: Civic Centre
        Port Talbot SA13 1PJ
Tel: 01639 763333
Fax: 01639 763444
Email: environment@npt.gov.uk
Web: www.neath-porttalbot.gov.uk

Newport City Council

Address: Civic Centre
        Newport NP20 4UR
Tel: 01633 656656
Fax: 01633 244721
Email: info@newport.gov.uk
Web: www.newport.gov.uk

Pembrokeshire County Council

Address: County Hall
        Haverfordwest SA61 1TP
Tel: 01437 764551
Fax: 01437 775303
Email: enquiries@pembrokeshire.gov.uk
Web: www.pembrokeshire.gov.uk

Powys County Council

Address: County Hall
        Llandrindod Wells LD1 5LG
Tel: 01597 826000
Fax: 01597 826220
Email: customer@powys.gov.uk
Web: www.powys.gov.uk

Rhondda Cynon Taff County Borough Council

Address: Sardis House, Sardis Road
        Pontypridd, CF37 1DU
Tel: 01443 494700
Fax: 01443 494888
Email: n.a.
Web: www.rhondda-cynon-taff.gov.uk

City and County Council of Swansea

Address: Transportation and Engineering
        County Hall, Oystermouth Road
        Swansea SA1 3SN
Tel: 01792 636000
Fax: 01792 636340
Email: transportation.engineering@
        swansea.gov.uk
Web: www.swansea.gov.uk

Torfaen County Borough Council

Address: Civic Centre
        Pontypool NP4 6YB
Tel: 01495 762200
Fax: 01495 755513
Email: your.call@torfaen.gov.uk
Web: www.torfaen.gov.uk

Vale of Glamorgan Council

Address: Civic Offices, Holton Road
        Barry CF63 4RU
Tel: 01446 700111
Fax: 01446 421479
Email: enquiries@valeofglamorgan.gov.uk
Web: www.valeofglamorgan.gov.uk

Wrexham County Borough Council

Address: Transportation & Asset Management
        Dept.
        Crown Buildings, 31 Chester Street
        Wrexham LL13 8BG
Tel: 01978 297102
Fax: 01978 297103
Email: transport.policy@wrexham.gov.uk
Web: www.wrexham.gov.uk

Other Governments

Isle of Man Government

Address: Department of Transport
           Sea Terminal Building
           Douglas, Isle of Man IM1 2RF
Tel: 01624 686600
Fax: n.a.
Email: enquiries@dot.gov.im
Web: www.gov.im/transport

Council of The Isles of Scilly

Address: Town Hall, St Mary's
           Isles of Scilly TR21 0LW
Tel: 01720 422537
Fax: 01720 422202
Email: enquiries@scilly.gov.uk
Web: www.scilly.gov.uk

The States of Guernsey

Address: Sir Charles Frossard House
           PO Box 43, La Charroterie
           St Peter Port, Guernsey GY1 1FH
Tel: 01481 717000
Fax: n.a.
Email: policycouncil@gov.gg
Web: www.gov.gg

The States of Jersey

Address: States Greffe, Morier House
           2-10 Halkett Place
           St Helier, Jersey JE1 1DD
Tel: 01534 441020
Fax: 01534 441098
Email: statesgreffe@gov.je
Web: www.gov.je

Public Organisations

Air

*Air Transport Users Council

Address: CAA House, 45-59 Kingsway
           London WC2B 6TE
Tel: 020 7240 6061
Fax: 020 7240 7071
Email: n.a.
Web: www.auc.org.uk

*Civil Aviation Authority

Address: CAA House, 45-59 Kingsway
           London WC2 B6TE
Tel: 020 7379 7311
Fax: n.a.
Email: infoservices@caa.co.uk
Web: www.caa.co.uk

Rail

*Office of Rail Regulation

Address: 1 Kemble Street
           London WC2B 4AN
Tel: 020 7282 2000
Fax: 020 7282 2040
Email: contact.cct@orr.gsi.gov.uk
Web: www.rail-reg.gov.uk

Passenger Focus

Address: Whittles House
           14 Pentonville Road
           London N1 9HF
Tel: 0870 336 6000
Fax: 020 7713 2729
Email: contact@passengerfocus.org.uk
Web: www.passengerfocus.org.uk

Road

Driver and Vehicle Licensing Agency

Address: Longview Road
           Swansea SA6 7JL
Tel: 01792 782341
Fax: n.a.
Email: n.a.
Web: www.dvla.gov.uk

Driver & Vehicle Agency (Licensing)

Address: County Hall, Castlerock Road
           Coleraine, Northern Ireland
           BT51 3TA
Tel: 0845 402 4000
Fax: 028 7034 1422
Email: dvlni@doeni.gov.uk
Web: www.dvani.gov.uk

Driver & Vehicle Agency (Testing)
Address: Balmoral Road
           Belfast BT12 6QL
Tel: 028 9068 1831
Fax: 028 9066 5520
Email: dvta@doeni.gov.uk
Web: www.dvani.gov.uk

Driving Standards Agency
Address: Stanley House, 56 Talbot Street
           Nottingham NG1 5GU
Tel: 0870 010 1372
Fax: 0870 010 2372
Email: customer.services@dsa.gsi.gov.uk
Web: www.dsa.gov.uk

Highways Agency
Address: 5 Broadway
           Broad Street
           Birmingham B15 1BL
Tel: 0845 750 4030
Fax: n.a.
Email: ha_info@highways.gsi.gov.uk
Web: www.highways.gov.uk

Vehicle Certification Agency
Address: 1 Eastgate Office Centre
           Eastgate Road
           Bristol BS5 6XX
Tel: 0117 952 4235
Fax: 0117 952 4103
Email: enquiries@vca.gov.uk
Web: www.vca.gov.uk

*Vehicle & Operator Services Agency
Address: Berkeley House, Croydon Street
           Bristol BS5 ODA
Tel: 0117 954 3200
Fax: 0117 954 3212
Email: Enquiries@vosa.gov.uk
Web: www.vosa.gov.uk

Passenger Transport Executive Agencies

*Greater Manchester PTE
Address: 2 Piccadilly Place
           Manchester M1 3BG
Tel: 0161 244 1000
Fax: 0161 244 1011
Email: publicity@gmpte.gov.uk
Web: www.gmpte.com

Merseyside PTE (Merseytravel)
Address: 24 Hatton Garden
           Liverpool L3 2AN
Tel: 0151 227 5181
Fax: 0151 236 2457
Email: n.a.
Web: www.merseytravel.gov.uk

Passenger Transport Executive Group (pteg)
Address: Wellington House
           40-50 Wellington Street
           Leeds, LS1 2DE
Tel: 0113 251 7204
Fax: 0113 251 7333
Email: info@pteg.net
Web: www.pteg.net
Note: Brings together and promotes the
           interests of the six English PTEs;
           SPT and TfL are associate members

South Yorkshire PTE
from late 2007
Address: 11 Broad Street West
           Sheffield S1 2BQ
Tel: 0114 276 7575
Fax: n.a.
Email: comments@sypte.co.uk
Web: www.sypte.co.uk

Strathclyde Partnership for Transport (SPT)
Address: Consort House,
           12 West George Street
           Glasgow G2 1HN
Tel: 0141 332 6811
Fax: 0141 332 3076
Email: webfeedback@spt.co.uk
Web: www.spt.co.uk

Transport for London (TfL)

Address: Central Customer Services
Empress State Building,
Empress Approach
London SW6 1TR
Tel: 020 7222 5600
Fax: 020 7027 6099
Email: enquire@tfl.gov.uk
Web: www.tfl.gov.uk

Tyne and Wear PTE (Nexus)

Address: Nexus House, St James' Boulevard
Newcastle upon Tyne NE1 4AX
Tel: 0191 203 3333
Fax: 0191 203 3180
Email: contactus@nexus.org.uk
Web: www.nexus.org.uk

West Midlands PTE (Centro)

Address: Centro House, 16 Summer Lane
Birmingham, West Midlands
B19 3SD
Tel: 0121 200 2787
Fax: 0121 214 7033
Email: customerrelations@centro.org.uk
Web: www.networkwestmidlands.co.uk

West Yorkshire PTE (Metro)

Address: Wellington House,
40-50 Wellington Street
Leeds LS1 2DE
Tel: 0113 251 7272
Fax: 0113 251 7333
Email: feedback@wypte.gov.uk
Web: www.wymetro.com

Traffic Commissioners

Eastern Traffic Area

Address: City House
126-130 Hills Road
Cambridge CN2 1NP
Tel: 0870 606 0440

North Eastern Traffic Area

Address: Hillcrest House, 386 Harehills Lane
Leeds LS9 6NF
Tel: 0113 254 3291

North Western Traffic Area

Address: Hillcrest House
386 Harehills Lane
Leeds LS9 6NF
Tel: 0113 254 3292

Scottish Traffic Area

Address: J Floor, Argyle House
3 Lady Lawson Street
Edinburgh, EH3 9SE
Tel: 0131 200 4974

South Eastern and Metropolitan Traffic Area

Address: Ivy House, 3 Ivy Terrace
Eastbourne BN21 4QT
Tel: 01323 452473

Welsh Traffic Area

Address: 38 George Road
Edgbaston
Birmingham B15 1PL
Tel: 0121 609 6835

Western Traffic Area

Address: 2 Rivergate, Temple Quay
Bristol BS1 6EH
Tel: 0117 900 8577

West Midland Traffic Area

Address: Cumberland House
200 Broad Street
Birmingham B15 1TD
Tel: 0121 609 6813

Maritime and Inland Waterways

British Waterways

Address: Willow Grange, Church Road
Watford WD17 4QA
Tel: 01923 201120
Fax: 01923 201400
Email: enquiries.hq@britishwaterways.co.uk
Web: www.britishwaterways.co.uk

Corporation of Trinity House

Address: Trinity House, Tower Hill
London EC3N 4DH
Tel: 020 7481 6900
Fax: 020 7480 7662
Email: enquiries@thls.org
Web: www.trinityhouse.co.uk

Maritime and Coastguard Agency

Address: Corporate Secretariat
Bay 3/26, 105 Commercial Road
Southampton SO15 1EG
Tel: 023 8032 9469
Fax: 023 8032 9105
Email: infoline@mcga.gov.uk
Web: www.mcga.gov.uk

Northern Lighthouse Board

Address: 84 George Street
Edinburgh EH2 3DA
Tel: 0131 473 3100
Fax: 0131 220 2093
Email: enquiries@nlb.org.uk
Web: www.nlb.org.uk

United Kingdom Hydrographic Office

Address: Admiralty Way
Taunton TA1 2DN
Tel: 01823 337900
Fax: 01823 284077
Email: helpdesk@ukho.gov.uk
Web: www.ukho.gov.uk

Environmental

Broads Authority

Address: Planning Department, Thomas
Harvey House
18 Colegate
Norwich NR3 1BQ
Tel: 01603 610734
Fax: 01603 765710
Email: webenquiries@
broads-authority.gov.uk
Web: www.broads-authority.gov.uk

Countryside Council for Wales

Address: Maes-y-Ffynnon, Penrhosgarnedd
Bangor LL57 2DW
Tel: 0845 1306229
Fax: 01248 355782
Email: enquiries@ccw.gov.uk
Web: www.ccw.gov.uk

Department of Environment (Northern Ireland)

Address: Clarence House
10-18 Adelaide Street
Belfast BT2 8GB
Northern Ireland
Tel: 028 9054 0540
Fax: 028 9054 1169
Email: doe.internetteam@doeni.gov.uk
Web: www.doeni.gov.uk

Department for Environment, Food & Rural Affairs

Address: Nobel House, 17 Smith Square
London SW1P 3JR
Tel: 020 7238 6000
Fax: 020 7238 2188.
Email: helpline@defra.gsi.gov.uk
Web: www.defra.gov.uk

Department for Environment, Sustainability and Housing (Wales)

Address: Welsh Assembly Government
Cathays Park
Cardiff CF10 3NQ
Tel: 029 2082 5111
Fax: 029 2082 5180
Email: epc.requests@wales.gsi.gov.uk
Web: www.wales.gov.uk

English Heritage

Address: PO Box 569
Swindon SN2 2YP
Tel: 0870 333 1181
Fax: 01793 414926
Email: customers@english-heritage.org.uk
Web: www.english-heritage.org.uk

Environment Agency

Address: Rio House, Waterside Drive
Aztec West, Almondsbury
Bristol BS32 4UD
Tel: 0870 8506 506
Fax: n.a.
Email: enquiries@environment-
agency.gov.uk
Web: www.environment-agency.gov.uk

Environment Agency Wales

Address: Ty Cambria House,
29 Newport Road
Cardiff CF24 0TP
Tel: 0870 850 6506
Fax: n.a.
Email: enquiries@
environment-agency.gov.uk
Web: www.environment-
agency.wales.gov.uk

Environment and Heritage Service (Northern Ireland)

Address: Klondyke Building, Cromac Avenue
Gasworks Business Park,
Lower Ormeau Road
Belfast BT7 2JA
Tel: 0845 302 0008
Fax: n.a.
Email: ehsfeedback@doeni.gov.uk
Web: www.ehsni.gov.uk

Environment and Rural Affairs Department (Scotland)

Address: The Scottish Executive
Room 440, Pentland House
47 Robbs Loan, Edinburgh
EH14 1TY
Tel: 0131 556 8400
Fax: 0131 244 7281
Email: ceu@scotland.gsi.gov.uk
Web: www.scotland.gov.uk/
About/Departments/ERAD

Natural England

Address: 1 East Parade, Sheffield S1 2ET
Tel: 0845 600 3078
Fax: 01733 455103
Email: enquiries@naturalengland.org.uk
Web: www.naturalengland.org.uk

Royal Commission on Environmental Pollution

Address: Third Floor, 5-8 The Sanctuary
London SW1P 3JS
Tel: 020 7799 8970
Fax: 020 7799 8971
Email: enquiries@rcep.org.uk
Web: www.rcep.org.uk

Scottish Environment Protection Agency

Address: Erskine Court
The Castle Business Park
Stirling FK9 4TR
Tel: 01786 457700
Fax: 01786 446885
Web: www.sepa.org.uk

Scottish Natural Heritage

Address: Great Glen House, Leachkin Road
Inverness IV3 8NW
Tel: 01463 725000
Fax: 01463 725067
Email: enquiries@snh.gov.uk
Web: www.snh.gov.uk

Planning and Land Agencies

Land Registry

Address: 32 Lincoln's Inn Fields
London WC2A 3PH
Tel: 0151 473 6137
Fax: n.a
Email: commercial.services@
landregistry.gsi.gov.uk
Web: www.landregistry.gov.uk

Land Registers of Northern Ireland

Address: Lincoln Building
27-45 Great Victoria Street
Belfast BT2 7SL
Tel: 028 9025 1515
Email: Customer.information@lrni.gov.uk
Web: www.lrni.gov.uk

Lands Tribunal (England and Wales)

Address: Procession House
55 Ludgate Hill
London EC4M 7JW
Tel: 020 7029 9780
Fax: 020 7029 9781
Email: lands@dca.gsi.gov.uk
Web: www.landstribunal.gov.uk

Lands Tribunal for Scotland

Address: George House, 126 George Street
Edinburgh EH2 4HH
Tel: 0131 271 4350
Fax: 0131 271 4399
Email: mailbox@lands-tribunal-scotland.org.uk
Web: lands-tribunal-scotland.org.uk

Planning Inspectorate

Address: Temple Quay House
2 The Square, Temple Quay
Bristol BS1 6PN
Tel: 0117 372 6372
Fax: 0117 372 8782
Email: enquiries@planning-inspectorate.gsi.gov.uk
Web: www.planning-inspectorate.gov.uk

Planning Inspectorate (Wales)

Address: Room 1- 004, Cathays Park
Cardiff CF10 3NQ
Tel: 029 2082 3866
Fax: 029 2082 5150
Email: wales@planning-inspectorate.gsi.gov.uk
Web: www.planning-inspectorate.gov.uk

Planning Service (Northern Ireland)

Address: Millenium House,
17-25 Great Victoria Street
Belfast BT2 7BN
Tel: 028 9041 6700
Fax: 028 9041 6802
Email: planning.service.hq@nics.gov.uk
Web: www.planningni.gov.uk

Registers of Scotland

Address: Erskine House, 68 Queen Street
Edinburgh EH2 4NF
Tel: 0845 607 0161
Fax: 0131 200 3932
Email: customer.services@ros.gov.uk
Web: www.ros.gov.uk

Directorate for Planning and Environmental Appeals (Scotland)

Address: 4 The Courtyard
Callendar Business Park
Callendar Road
Falkirk FK1 1XR
Tel: 01324 696400
Fax: 01324 696444
Email: seiru@scotland.gsi.gov.uk
Web: www.scotland.gov.uk/Topics/Planning/Appeals

Regional Development Agencies

Advantage West Midlands

Address: 3 Priestley Wharf, Holt Street
Aston Science Park, Birmingham
B7 4BN
Tel: 0121 380 3500
Fax: 0121 380 3501
Email: n.a.
Web: www.advantagewm.co.uk

East of England Development Agency

Address: The Business Centre, Station Road
Histon, Cambridgeshire CB4 9LQ
Tel: 01223 713900
Fax: 01223 713940
Email: reception@eeda.org.uk
Web: www.eeda.org.uk

East Midlands Development Agency

Address: Apex Court, City Link
Nottingham NG2 4LA
Tel: 0115 988 8300
Fax: 0115 853 3666
Email: info@emd.org.uk
Web: www.emda.org.uk

Invest Northern Ireland

Address: Bedford Square, Bedford Street
            Belfast BT2 7ES
Tel: 028 9023 9090
Fax: 028 9043 6536
Email: website@investni
Web: www.investni.com

London Development Agency

Address: Palestra, 197 Blackfriars Road
            London SE18AA
Tel: 020 7593 8000
Fax: n.a.
Email: info@lda.gov.uk
Web: www.lda.gov.uk

Northwest Development Agency

Address: PO Box 37, Renaissance House
            Centre Park, Warrington WA1 1XB,
            Cheshire
Tel: 01925 400100
Fax: 01925 400400
Email: n.a.
Web: www.nwda.co.uk

One North East

Address: Stella House, Goldcrest Way
            Newburn Riverside,
            Newcastle Upon Tyne, NE15 8NY
Tel: 0191 229 6200
Fax: 0191 229 6201
Email: enquiries@onenortheast.co.uk
Web: www.onenortheast.co.uk

Scottish Enterprise

Address: 5 Atlantic Quay
            150 Broomielaw
            Glasgow
            G2 8LU
Tel: 0141 248 2700
Fax: 0141 221 3217
Email: network.helpline@scotent.co.uk
Web: www.scottish-enterprise.com

South East England Development Agency

Address: Berkeley House, Cross Lanes
            Guildford, Surrey GU1 1YA
Tel: 01483 484200
Fax: 01483 484247
Email: seeda@seeda.co.uk
Web: www.seeda.co.uk

South West of England Development Agency

Address: Sterling House, Dix's Field
            Exeter, Devon EX1 1QA
Tel: 01392 214747
Fax: 01392 214848
Email: enquiries@southwestrda.org.uk
Web: www.southwestrda.org.uk

Yorkshire Forward

Address: Victoria House, Victoria Place
            Leeds LS11 5AE
Tel: 0113 394 9600
Fax: 0113 243 1088
Email: n.a.
Web: www.yorkshire-forward.com

Scottish Regional Transport Partnerships

Highlands & Islands (HITRANS)

Address: Building 25, Inverness Airport
            Inverness IV2 7JB
Tel: 01667 460464
Fax: 01667 460468
Email: info@hitrans.org.uk
Web: www.hitrans.org.uk

North East Scotland (NESTRANS)

Address: Archibald Simpson House
            27-29 King Street, Aberdeen
            AB24 5AA
Tel: 01224 625524
Fax: 01224 626596
Email: info@nestrans.org.uk
Web: www.nestrans.org.uk

South East of Scotland (SEStran)

Address: First Floor, Hopetoun Gate
            8b McDonald Road
            McDonald Road, Edinburgh
            EH7 4LZ
Tel: 0131 524 5150
Fax: 0131 524 5151
Email: enquiries@sestran.gov.uk
Web: www.sestran.gov.uk

South West of Scotland (SWESTRANS)

Address: Kirkbank House, English Street
Dumfries DG1 2HS
Tel: 01387 260141
Fax: 01387 260092
Email: n.a.
Web: www.swestrans.org.uk

Strathclyde Partnership for Transport (SPT)

Address: Consort House,
12 West George Street
Glasgow G2 1HN
Tel: 0141 332 6811
Fax: 0141 332 3076
Email: webfeedback@spt.co.uk
Web: www.spt.co.uk

Tayside & Central Scotland (TACTRAN)

Address: Bordeaux House
31 Kinnoull Street
Perth PH1 5EN
Tel: 01738 475775
Fax: 01738 639705
Email: info@tactran.gov.uk
Web: www.tactran.gov.uk

Zetland (ZetTrans)

Address: Grantfield
Lerwick, Shetland ZE1 0NT
Tel: 01595 744868
Fax: 01595 744503
Email: zettrans@shetland.gov.uk
Web: www.shetland.gov.uk/transport

Other UK organisations

British Safety Council

Address: 70 Chancellor's Road
London W6 9RS
Tel: 020 8741 1231
Fax: 020 8741 4555
Email: ask@britsafe.org
Web: www.britishsafetycouncil.co.uk

BSI Group

Address: 389 Chiswick High Road
London W4 4AL
Tel: 020 8996 9000
Fax: 020 8996 7001
Email: info@bsi-global.com
Web: www.bsigroup.com

Central Office of Information

Address: Hercules House, Hercules Road
London SE1 7DU
Tel: 020 7928 2345
Fax: 020 7928 5037
Email: n.a.
Web: www.coi.gov.uk

Central and Local Government Information Partnership (CLIP)

Address: 5/J5 Eland House, Bressenden Place
London SW1E 5DU
Tel: 020 7944 5514
Fax: 020 7944 5519
Email: CLIP@communities.gsi.gov.uk
Web: www.clip.gov.uk

Commission for Integrated Transport

Address: Ashdown House, 123 Victoria Street
London SW1E 6DE
Tel: 020 7944 8669
Fax: n.a.
Email: cfit@dft.gsi.gov.uk
Web: www.cfit.gov.uk

Communities and Local Government

Address: Eland House, Bressenden Place
London SW1E 5DU
Tel: 020 7944 4400
Email: contactus@communities.gov.uk
Web: www.communities.gov.uk

Companies House

Address: Companies House, Crown Way
Maindy, Cardiff CF14 3UZ
Tel: 0870 333 3636
Fax: n.a.
Email: enquiries@companies-house.gov.uk
Web: www.companieshouse.gov.uk

Competition Commission

Address: Victoria House, Southampton Row
London, WC1B 4AD
Tel: 020 7271 0100
Fax: 020 7271 0367
Email: info@cc.gsi.gov.uk
Web: www.competition-commission.org.uk

Convention of Scottish Local Authorities (COSLA)

Address: Rosebery House
9 Haymarket Terrace
Edinburgh EH12 5XZ
Tel: 0131 474 9200
Fax: 0131 474 9292
Email: enquiries@cosla.gov.uk
Web: www.cosla.gov.uk

The Crown Estate

Address: 16 New Burlington Place
London W1S 2HX
Tel: 020 7851 5070
Fax: 020 7851 5128
Email: enquiries@thecrownestate.co.uk
Web: www.thecrownestate.co.uk

English Partnerships

Address: 110 Buckingham Palace Road
London
SW1W 9SA
Tel: 020 7881 1600
Fax: 020 7730 9162
Email: mail@englishpartnerships.co.uk
Web: www.englishpartnerships.co.uk

Forestry Commission

Address: Silvan House, 231 Corstorphine Road
Edinburgh EH12 7AT
Tel: 0131 334 0303
Fax: 0131 334 6152
Email: enquiries@forestry.gsi.gov.uk
Web: www.forestry.gov.uk

Health and Safety Executive

Address: 2 Southwark Bridge
London SE1 9HS
Tel: 0845 345 0055
Fax: n.a.
Email: hse.infoline@natbrit.com
Web: www.hse.gov.uk

Local Government Association

Address: Local Government House
Smith Square
London SW1P 3HZ
Tel: 020 7664 3131
Fax: 020 7664 3030
Email: info@lga.gov.uk
Web: www.lga.gov.uk

London Councils

Address: 59 Southwark Street
London SE1 0AL
Tel: 020 7934 9999
Fax: 020 7934 9991
Email: info@londoncouncils.gov.uk
Web: www.londoncouncils.gov.uk

*London Travel Watch

Address: 6 Middle Street
London EC1A 7JA
Tel: 020 7505 9000
Fax: 020 7505 9003
Email: info@londontravelwatch.org.uk
Web: www.londontravelwatch.org.uk

Meteorological Office

Address: Fitzroy Road
Exeter EX1 3PB
Tel: 01392 885680
Fax: 01392 885681
Email: enquiries@metoffice.com
Web: www.metoffice.gov.uk

National Consumer Council

Address: 20 Grosvenor Gardens
London SW1W 0DH
Tel: 020 7730 3469
Fax: 020 7730 0191
Email: info@ncc.org.uk
Web: www.ncc.org.uk

National Weights and Measures Laboratory

Address: Stanton Avenue
Teddington TW11 0JZ
Tel: 020 8943 7272
Fax: 020 8943 7270
Email: info@nwml.org.uk
Web: www.nwml.gov.uk

Office for National Statistics

Address: Government Buildings, Cardiff Road
Newport NP10 8XG
Tel: 0845 601 3034
Fax: 01633 652747
Email: info@statistics.gov.uk
Web: www.statistics.gov.uk

Office of Fair Trading

Address: Fleetbank House,
2-6 Salisbury Square
London, EC4Y 8J
Tel: 020 7211 8000 (Switchboard)
0845 722 4499 (Enquiries &
preliminary investigations)
Fax: 020 7211 8800
Email: enquiries@oft.gsi.gov.uk
Web: www.oft.gov.uk

Ordnance Survey

Address: Romsey Road
Southampton SO16 4GU
Tel: 023 8030 5030
Fax: 023 8079 2615
Email: customerservices@
ordnancesurvey.co.uk
Web: www.ordnancesurvey.co.uk

Ordnance Survey of Northern Ireland

Address: Colby House, Stranmillis Court
Malone Lower, Belfast BT9 5BJ
Tel: 028 9025 5755
Fax: 028 9025 5700
Email: osni@osni.gov.uk
Web: www.osni.gov.uk

Transport Tribunal

Address: Procession House
55 Ludgate Hill
London EC4M 7JW
Tel: 020 7029 9790
Fax: 020 7029 9782
Email: transport@tribunals.gsi.gov.uk
Web: www.transporttribunal.gov.uk

UK Intellectual Property Office

Address: Concept House, Cardiff Road
Newport NP10 8QQ
Tel: 01633 814000
Fax: 01633 817777
Email: enquiries@patent.gov.uk
Web: www.ipo.gov.uk

uktradeinfo

Address: Alexander House
21 Victoria Avenue
Southend on sea
SS99 1AA
Tel: 01702 367485
Fax: n.a.
Email: uktradeinfo@hmrc.gsi.gov.uk
Web: www.uktradeinfo.com

*Visit Britain

Address: Department D, Thames Tower
Black's Road, Hammersmith
London W6 9EL
Tel: 020 8846 9000
Fax: 020 8563 0302
Email: industry.relations@visitbritain.org.
Web: www.visitbritain.org

Welsh Local Government Association

Address: Local Government House
Drake Walk, Cardiff CF10 4LG
Tel: 029 2046 8600
Fax: 029 2046 8601
Email: n.a.
Web: www.wlga.gov.

European Union

European Commission: Energy and Transport DG (Directorate General)

Address: rue demot, 24-28
B-1040 Bruxelles/Brussel
Belgium
Tel: +32 22 99 11 11
Web: www.europa.eu.int

European Bank for Reconstruction & Development

Address: One Exchange Square
London EC2A 2JN
Tel: 020 7338 6000
Fax: 020 7338 6100
Email: generalenquiries@ebrd.com
Web: www.ebrd.com

European Commission in the United Kingdom

Address: 8 Storey's Gate
London SW1P 3AT
Tel: 020 7973 1992
Fax: 020 7973 1900/1910
Email: Reijo.Kemppinen@cec.eu.int
Web: www.cec.org.uk

European Investment Bank

Address: 100, Boulevard Konrad Adenauer
Luxembourg 2950
Luxembourg
Tel: +352 43 79 1
Fax: +352 43 77 04
Email: info@eib.org
Web: www.eib.org

UK Office of the European Parliament

Address: 2 Queen Anne's Gate
London SW1H 9AA
Tel: 020 7227 4300
Fax: 020 7227 4302
Email: eplondon@europarl.eu.int
Web: www.europarl.org.uk

*Eurostat

Address: Batiment Jean Monet
rue Alcide de Gasperi
Luxembourg-Kirchberg 2920
Luxembourg
Tel: 01633 813369
Fax: 01633 652699
Email: eustatistics@ons.gsi.gov.uk
Web: epp.eurostat.cec.eu.int

Non-UK Government Organisations

---

*Bundesamt Für Güterverkehr

Address: Werderstraße 34
Postfach 19 01 80
50498 Köln
Germany
Tel: +49 221 5776 2201
Fax: +49 221 5776 1625
Email: presse@bag.bund.de
Web: www.bag.bund.de

*Bureau of Transportation Statistics

Address: 1200 New Jersey Avenue SE
Washington DC 20590
USA
Tel: +1 202 366 1270
Fax: +1 202 366 3759
Email: answers@bts.gov
Web: www.bts.gov

Central Statistical Bureau of Latvia

Address: 1 Lacplesa Street
Riga, LV – 1301
Latvia
Tel: +371 7366803
Fax: +371 7830137
Email: info@csb.gov.lv
Web: www.csb.gov.lv/csp

Commissioners of Irish Lights

Address: 16 Lower Pembroke Street, Dublin 2
Republic of Ireland
Tel: +353 1 632 1900
Fax: +353 1 632 1946
Email: info@cil.ie
Web: www.cil.ie

Czech Statistical Office

Address: Na padesátem 81
100 82 Praha 10
Strašnice
Czech Republic
Tel: +420 274 052 304
Email: infoservis@czso.cz
Web: www.czso.cz

*Direction Generale de L'Aviation Civile

Address: 50 rue Henry-Farman
75 720
Paris Cedex 15
France
Tel: +33 1 58 09 43 21
Fax: +33 1 58 09 35 35
Email: stacweb@aviation-civile.gouv.fr
Web: www.dgac.fr

*European Conference of Ministers of Transport (ECMT)
Address: 2-4 rue André Pascal
Paris Cedex 16
F-75775
France
Tel: +33 1 45 24 97 10
Fax: +33 1 45 24 97 42
Email: ecmt.contact@oecd.org
Web: www.cemt.org

Federal Ministry of Transport, Building and Housing
Address: Invalidenstrasse 44
D10115 Berlin
Germany
Tel: +49 30 18 300 3060
Fax: +49 30 18 300 1942
Email: buergerinfo@BMVBS.bund.de
Web: www.bmvbw.de

*Federal Transit Administration
Address: 1200 New Jersey Avenue SE
4th & 5th Floors – East Building
Washington DC 20590
USA
Fax: +1 202 366 4043
Web: www.fta.dot.gov

*Finnish Maritime Administration
Address: Statistics Division, Porkkalankatu 5
PO Box 171, FIN-00181 Helsinki
Finland
Tel: +358 204 48 4495
Fax: +358 204 48 4355
Email: Henri.Hakkarainen@fma.fi
Web: www.fma.fi

*Finnish National Road Administration
Address: Pasilan virastokeskus
Opastinsilta 12A, PO Box 33
00521 Helsinki
Finland
Tel: +358 204 22 150
Fax: +358 206 90 301
Email: kirajaamo@finnra.fi
Web: www.tiehallinto.fi

*Finnish Rail Administration
Address: PLA 185 Kayntiosoite:
Keskuskatu 8, 7.krs
Helsinki FL 00101
Finland
Tel: +358 207 5111
Email: info@rhk.fi
Web: www.rhk.fi

*INE
Address: Paseo de la Castellana 183
Madrid 28071
Spain
Tel: +34 91 583 9100
Fax: +34 91 579 2713
Email: www.ine.es/infoine
Web: www.ine.es

Institute of Statistics (Albania)
Address: Rr. "Gjergj Fishta",
Nr.3
Tirana, Albania
Tel: +355 4 222411 x 185
Fax: +355 4 228300
Email: marketing@instat.gov.al
Web: www.instat.gov.al

*Institut National de Statistique
Address: Vooruitgangstraat 50
1210 Bruxelles
Belgium
Tel: +32 2 277 55 03
Fax: +32 2 277 55 19
Email: info.stat@s economie.fgov.be
Web: www.statbel.fgov.be

*Instituto Nacional de Estatistica
Address: Avenue de António José de Almeida, 2
1000 Lisbon
Portugal
Tel: +351 218 426 100
Fax: +351 218 426 380
Email: ine@ine.pi
Web: www.ine.pt

*Kraftfahrt-Bundesamt

Address:	Fördestraße 16
	24944
	Flensburg
	Germany
Tel:	+49 461 316 0
Fax:	+49 461 316 14 95
Email:	kba@kba.de
Web:	www.kba.de

*Ministero delle Infrastrutture e dei Trasporti

Address:	Piazzale Porta Pia, 1
	Roma 00161
	Italy
Tel:	+39 6 44125312
Fax:	+39 6 44125312
Email:	biblioteca.Nomentana @ infrastrutturetrasporti.it
Web:	www.infrastrutturetrasporti.it

*National Institute for Statistics and Economic Studies

Address:	195 rue de Bercy
	Tour Gamma A
	75 012 Paris
	France
Tel:	+33 825 800 882
Web:	www.insee.fr

*National Statistical Service of Greece

Address:	46 Pireos & Eponiton Street
	185 10 Pireas
	1st Floor, office no 106
	Greece
Tel:	+30 210 485 313-5
Fax:	+30 210 4852819
Email:	info@statistics.gr
Web:	www.statistics.gr

Polish Statistical Office

Address:	00-925 Warsaw, Al. Niepodległo ci 208
	Poland
Tel:	+48 22 608 30 00
Fax:	+48 22 608 38 69
Email:	dane@stat.gov.pl
Web:	www.stat.gov.pl

Statistical Office of Slovak Republik

Address:	Mileti ova 3
	824 67 Bratislava 26
	Slovak Republic
Tel:	+421 50236 339
Email:	info@statistics.sk
Web:	www.statistics.sk

*Statistics Netherlands

Address:	Postbus 4000
	2270 JM Voorburg
	Netherlands
Tel:	+31 88 570 70 70
Email:	verkoop@cbs.nl
Web:	www.cbs.nl

*Statistik Austria

Address:	Guglasse 13
	1110 Wien
	Austria
Tel:	+43 1 71128 7814
Fax:	+43 1 71128 7738
Email:	Info@statistik.gv.at
Web:	www.statistik.gv.at

*Statistikaamet - Statistical Office of Estonia

Address:	Endla 15,
	15174 Tallinn
	Estonia
Tel:	+372 6259 300
Fax:	372 6259 370
Email:	stat@stat.ee
Web:	www.stat.ee

*Statistisches Bundesamt

Address:	Federal Statistical Office of Germany
	D-65180 Wiesbaden
	Germany
Tel:	+49 611 75 2405
Email:	info@destatis.de
Web:	www.destatis.de

Statistics Lithuania

Address:	29 Gedimino av., LT-01500 Vilnius, Lithuania
Tel:	+370 5 236 48 22
Fax:	+370 5 236 48 45
Email:	statistika@stat.gov.lt
Web:	www.stat.gov.lt

*Swedish Institute for Transport And Communications (SIKA)

Address:	Akademigatan 2
	831 40 Ostersund
	Sweden
Tel:	+46 63 14 00 00
Fax:	+46 63 14 10 00
Email:	info@sika-institute.se
Web:	www.sika-institute.se

*United Nations Statistics Division

Address:	UN Headquarters
	New York NY 10017
	USA
Tel:	+1 212 963 9851
Email:	statistics@org.un
Web:	unstats.un.org

United Nations Information Centre

Address:	1775 K Street, NW
	Suite 400
	Washington, DC 20006
Tel:	+1 202 331 8670
Fax:	+1 202 331 9191
Email:	unicdc@unicwash.org
www:	www.unicwash.org

SECTION 3

Directory of Non-Government Organisations

Privatisation

Government policy after the Second World War saw much of the transport industry taken into public ownership. Only the shipping industry and road haulage remained largely in the private sector.

Following the election of a Conservative Government in 1979, a programme of privatisation was put in hand which saw nearly all of the transport industry back in the hands of the private sector by 1997. Only London Underground, British Waterways, Caledonian McBrayne, Highlands and Islands Airports, the Northern Ireland Transport Holding Company, and a small number of local authority airports, municipal bus companies, PTE rail systems and local authority ports remained in the private sector.

The result of the privatisation process has been the emergence of a small number of large private sector transport companies which have come to dominate sectors of the industry. Competitive pressures and globalisation have also been important drivers for consolidation of the freight transport industry.

In recent years, privatisation of transport activity has been taken up in many countries throughout the world. Some of the privatised British transport companies have been seeking to expand through bidding to acquire overseas companies as they are privatised. And, foreign interests too are bidding for British companies. Therefore, some public organisations (both UK and foreign) are listed in this section. Some local authority owned airport and bus companies also appear in this section, as do certain trust ports and Government-owned transport undertakings.

The (*) icon attached to organisations listed in the directory sections indicates that the organisation provides or publishes transport statistics found in Section 4.

UK Non-Government Organisations

Air

Airclaims Limited
Address: Cardinal Point, Newall Road
         Heathrow Airport, London
         TW6 2AS
Tel: 020 8897 1066
Fax: 020 8897 0300
Email: enquiries.uk@airclaims.com
Web: www.airclaims.co.uk

Aircraft Owners & Pilots Association
Address: 50a Cambridge St
         London SW1V 4QQ
Tel: 020 7834 5631
Fax: 020 7834 8623
Email: info@aopa.co.uk
Web: www.aopa.co.uk

Aircraft Research Association Ltd
Address: Manton Lane
         Bedford MK41 7PF
Tel: 01234 350681
Fax: 01234 328584
Email: ara@ara.co.uk
Web: www.ara.co.uk

*Airport Operators Association
Address: 3 Birdcage Walk
         London SW1H 9JJ
Tel: 020 7222 2249
Fax: 020 7976 7405
Email: info@aoa.org.uk
Web: www.aoa.org.uk

Aviation Insurance Officers Association
Address: London Underwriting Center
         3 Minster Court, Mincing Lane
         London EC3R 7DD
Tel: 020 7617 4444
Fax: 020 7617 4440
Email: info@iua.co.uk
Web: www.iua.co.uk

*BAA plc
Address: Head Office, 130 Wilton Road
         London SW1V 1LQ
Tel: 020 8745 9800
Email: statistics@baa.com
Web: www.baa.com

Baltic Air Charter Association
Address: 38 St Mary Axe
         London EC3R 8BH
Tel: 020 7623 5501
Fax: 020 7369 1623
Email: wvanderpol@balticexchange.com
Web: www.baca.org.uk

British Air Transport Association
Address: Artillery House, 11-19 Artillery Row
         London SW1P 1RT
Tel: 020 7222 9494
Fax: 020 7222 9595
Email: info@bata.uk.com
Web: www.bata.uk.com

British Airport Services & Equipment Association
Address: Homelife House, 26-32 Oxford Road
         Bournemouth BH8 8EZ
Tel: 01202 299088
Fax: 01202 508234
Email: basea@btconnect.com
Web: www.basea.org.uk

British Business and General Aviation Association
Address: 19 Church Street, Brill
         Aylesbury, Bucks HP18 9RT
Tel: 01844 238020
Fax: 01844 238087
Email: info@bbga.aero
Web: www.bbga.aero

*European Regions Airline Association
Address: The Baker Suite, Fairoaks Airport
         Chobham, Woking,
         Surrey GU24 8HX
Tel: 01276 856495
Fax: 01276 857038
Email: info@eraa.org
Web: www.eraa.org

Highlands and Islands Airports Ltd

Address: Head Office, Inverness Airport
Inverness IV2 7JB
Tel: 01667 462445
Fax: 01667 464216
Web: www.hial.co.uk

*International Air Transport Association

Address: Spencer House, 23 Sheen Road
Richmond upon Thames TW9 1BN
Tel: 020 7660 0068
Email: datawarehouse@iata.org
Web: www.iata.org

NATS Ltd

Address: Corporate & Technical Centre
4000 Parkway, Whiteley
Fareham, Hampshire PO15 7FL
Tel: 01489 616001
Web: www.nats.co.uk.

Royal Aeronautical Society

Address: 4 Hamilton Place
London W1J 7BQ
Tel: 020 7670 4300
Fax: 020 7670 4309
Email: raes@raes.org.uk
Web: www.raes.org.uk

*Society of British Aerospace Companies Ltd

Address: Salamanca Square, 9 Albert
Embankment, London SE1 7SP
Tel: 020 7091 4500
Fax: 020 7091 4545
Web: www.sbac.co.uk

UK Airports

Aberdeen Airport

Address: Dyce, Aberdeen
Aberdeenshire AB2 0DU
Tel: 0870 040 006
Fax: 01224 775845
Web: www.aberdeenairport.com

Belfast City Airport

Address: Belfast BT3 9JH
Tel: 028 9093 9093
Fax: 028 9093 9094
Email: info@belfastcityairport.com
Web: www.belfastcityairport.com

Belfast International Airport

Address: Belfast County
Antrim BT29 4AB
Tel: 028 9448 4848
Fax: 028 9448 4849
Email: infodesk@bfs.aero
Web: www.bial.co.uk

*Birmingham International Airport Ltd

Address: Birmingham B26 3QJ
Tel: 08707 335511
Fax: 0121 782 8802
Web: www.bhx.co.uk

Blackpool International Airport Ltd

Address: Squires Gate Lane
Blackpool
FY4 2QY
Tel: 0871 855 6868
Email: info@blackpoolairport.com
Web: www.blackpoolinternational.com

Bournemouth Airport Ltd

Address: Christchurch
Dorset BH23 6SE
Tel: 01202 364 000
Email: enquiries@bournemouthairport.com
Web: www.flybournemouth.com

Bristol International Airport

Address: Bristol BS48 3DY
Tel: 0870 1212747
Email: enquiries@bristolairport.com
Web: www.bristolairport.co.uk

Cardiff International Airport

Address: Vale of Glamorgan
CF62 3BD
Tel: 01446 711111
Email: infodesk@cwl.aero
Web: www.cwlfly.com

Coventry Airport

Address: Coventry Airport South
Siskin Parkway West
Coventry
CV3 4PD
Tel: 024 7630 8600
Email: info@coventryairport.co.uk
Web: www.coventryairport.co.uk

Doncaster Sheffield Robin Hood Airport

Address: Heyford House
First Avenue
Doncaster DN9 3RH
Tel: 08708 33 22 11
Web: www.robinhoodairport.com

Durham Tees Valley Airport

Address: Darlington
Tees Valley DL2 1LU
Tel: 01325 332811
Fax: 01325 332810
Email: information@dtva.co.uk
Web: www.teessideairport.com

Edinburgh Airport

Address: Scotland EH12 9DN
Tel: 0870 040 0007
Fax: 0131 344 3470
Web: www.edinburghairport.com

Exeter International Airport

Address: Exeter, Devon
EX5 2BD
Tel: 01392 367433
Fax: 01392 364593
Email: info@exeter-airport.co.uk
Web: www.exeter-airport.co.uk

Glasgow International Airport

Address: Paisley
Renfrewshire PA3 2SW
Tel: 0870 040 0008
Fax: 0141 848 4769
Web: www.glasgowairport.com

Glasgow Prestwick

Address: Aviation House
Prestwick KA9 2PL
Tel: 0871 223 0700
Fax: 01292 511010
Web: www.gpia.co.uk

Humberside International Airport

Address: Kirmington
North Lincolnshire DN39 6YH
Tel: 01652 688456
Email: enquiries@humbersideairport.com
Web: www.humberside-airport.co.uk

Inverness Airport

Address: Inverness
Scotland IV2 7JB.
Tel: 01667 462445
Fax: 01667 464216
Web: www.hial.co.uk

Isle of Man Airport

Address: Ballasalla
Isle of Man IM9 2AS
Tel: 01624 821600
Fax: 01624 821611
Email: admin@iom-airport.com
Web: www.iom-airport.com

Leeds/Bradford International Airport

Address: Leeds LS19 7TU
Tel: 0113 2509696
Fax: 0113 2505426
Email: general@lbia.co.uk
Web: www.lbia.co.uk

Liverpool John Lennon Airport

Address: South Terminal
Liverpool John Lennon Airport
Liverpool L24 1YD
Tel: 0870 750 8484
Web: www.liverpooljohnlennonairport.com

London City Airport

Address: Royal Docks
London E16 2PX
Tel: 020 7646 0088
Web: www.londoncityairport.com

London Gatwick Airport

Address: Gatwick
West Sussex RH6 ONP
Tel: 0870 000 2468
Web: www.gatwickairport.com

London Heathrow Airport

Address: 234 Bath Road, Hayes
Middlesex UB3 5AP
Tel: 0870 000 0123
Fax: 020 8745 4290
Web: www.heathrowairport.com

London Luton Airport

Address: Navigation House, Airport Way
Luton, Beds LU2 9LY
Tel: 01582 405100
Email: info@ltn.aero
Web: www.london-luton.co.uk

London Stansted Airport

Address: Enterprise House,
Bassingbourne Road
Essex CM24 1QW
Tel: 0870 000 0303
Web: www.stanstedairport.com

Manchester Airport plc

Address: Manchester M90 1QX
Tel: 0161 489 3000
Fax: 0161 489 3813
Web: www.manchesterairport.co.uk

Newcastle International Airport

Address: Woolsington
Newcastle-upon-Tyne NE13 8BZ
Tel: 0191 286 0966
Email: enquiries@
newcastleinternational.co.uk
Web: www.newcastleairport.com

Norwich International Airport

Address: Amsterdam Way
Norwich NR6 6JA
Tel: 01603 411923
Fax: 01603 411923
Email: enquiries@travelnorwichairport.co.uk
Web: www.norwichairport.co.uk

Nottingham East Midlands Airport

Address: Castle Donington
Derby DE74 2SA
Tel: 0871 919 9000
Email: enquiries@eastmidlandsairport.com
Web: www.eastmidlandsairport.com

Southampton Airport

Address: Hampshire SO18 2NL
Tel: 0870 040 0009
Fax: 02380 627193
Web: www.southamptonairport.com

UK and Irish Airlines

Aer Lingus

Address: Dublin Airport, Ireland
Tel: +353 818 365000
Web: www.aerlingus.com

bmi (British Midland Airways Limited)

Address: Donington Hall, Castle Donington
Derby
East Midlands DE74 2SB
Tel: 01332 854000
Web: www.flybmi.com

British Airways plc

Address: Waterside, PO Box 365
Harmondsworth,
Middlesex UB7 0GB
Tel: 0845 7733377
Web: www.britishairways.com

EasyJet Airline Co Ltd

Address: Easyland, London Luton Airport
Bedfordshire LU2 9PF
Web: www.easyjet.com

First Choice Airways Ltd

Address: Diamond House, Peel Cross Road
Salford, Manchester, M5 4DT
Tel: 0161 489 0321
Email: firstchoice@onpack.com
Web: www.firstchoice.co.uk

Flybe

Address: Jack Walker House, Exeter
International Airport EX5 2HL
Tel: 01392 366669
Fax: 01392 366151
Email: CustomerRelationsAdmin@flybe.com
Web: www.flybe.com

Monarch Airlines
Address: London Luton Airport, Luton
Bedfordshire LU2 9NU
Tel: 01582 400000
Web: www.monarch-airlines.com

MyTravel Airways UK
Address: Holiday House, Sandbrook Park
Sandbrook Way, Rochdale
Lancashire OL11 1SA
Tel: 0871 664 7970
Email: mytravelinfo@airtours.co.uk
Web: www.airtours.com

Ryanair
Address: Corporate Head Office,
Dublin Airport
Co. Dublin, Ireland
Tel: +353 1 8121212
Web: www.ryanair.com

Thomas Cook Airlines Ltd
Address: 2nd floor, Commonwealth House
Manchester Airport M90 3FL
Tel: 0161 489 5757
Web: www.thomascookairlines.co.uk

Thomsonfly
Address: Wigmore House, Wigmore Place
Wigmore Lane,
Luton LU2 9TN
Tel: 0870 1900 737
Web: www.thomsonfly.com

Virgin Atlantic Airways Ltd
Address: The Office, Manor Royal
Crawley, West Sussex RH10 9NU
Tel: 01293 562345
Web: www.virgin-atlantic.com

Rail

Associated Society of Locomotive Engineers and Firemen
Address: 9 Arkwright Road
London NW3 6AB
Tel: 020 7317 8600
Fax: 020 7794 6406
Email: info@aslef.org.uk
Web: www.aslef.org.uk

Association of Train Operating Companies
Address: 3rd Floor, 40 Bernard Street
London WC1N 1BY
Tel: 020 7841 8000
Email: enquiry@atoc.org
Web: www.atoc.org

Eurotunnel plc
Address: The Channel Tunnel Group Ltd
UK Terminal, Ashford Road
Folkestone, Kent CT18 8XX
Tel: 01303 282222
Web: www.eurotunnel.co.uk

Heritage Railway Association
Address: 2 Littlestone Road, New Romney
Kent, TN28 8PL
Email: M.Dewell@uel.ac.uk
Web: www.ukhrail.uel.ac.uk

Light Rail Transit Association
Address: c/o Haslams
133 Lichfield Street, Walsall
West Midlands W31 1SL
Tel: 0117 951 7785
Email: office@lrta.org
Web: www.lrta.org

Locomotive & Carriage Institution
Address: 69 Avondale Close, Horley
Surrey RH6 8BN
Tel: 01293 773239
Web: www.lococarriage.org.uk

Network Rail
Address: 40 Melton Street
London NW1 2EE
Tel: 020 7557 8000
Fax: 020 7557 9000
Web: www.networkrail.co.uk

Railway Industry Association
Address: 22 Headfort Place
London SW1X 7RY
Tel: 020 7201 0777
Fax: 020 7235 5777
Email: ria@riagb.org.uk
Web: www.riagb.org.uk

Wagon Building & Repair Association

Address: 48 Clifford Road, Poynton
West Midlands SK12 1HY
Tel: 01625 873012
Fax: 01625 859836

Passenger Rail Operators

Arriva Trains Wales

Address: St Mary's House
47 Penarth Road
Cardiff CF10 5DJ
Tel: 0845 6061 660
Email: customer.relations@
arrivatrainswales.co.uk
Web: www.arrivatrainswales.co.uk

c2c Rail

Address: 10th and 11th Floors
207 Old Street
London, EC1V 9NR
Tel: 0845 601 4873
Email: custrel@c2crail.co.uk
Web: www.c2c-online.co.uk

Central Trains

Address: Stanier House
102 New Street, PO Box 4323
Birmingham B2 4JB
Tel: 0121 634 2040
Fax: 0121 654 1234
Email: customer.responses@
centraltrains.co.uk
Web: www.centraltrains.co.uk

Chiltern Railways

Address: Western House
14 Rickfords Hill, Aylesbury
Buckinghamshire HP20 2RX
Tel: 0845 6005 165
Fax: 01296 332126
Web: www.chilternrailways.co.uk

Eurostar (UK)

Address: Eurostar House
Waterloo Station
London SE1 8SE
Tel: 020 7922 6180
Web: www.eurostar.com

First Capital Connect

Address: 50 Eastbourne Terrace
Paddington
London W2 6LX
Tel: 0845 026 4700
Email: customer.relations.fcc@
firstgroup.com
Web: www.firstcapitalconnect.co.uk

First Great Western

Address: Milford House
1 Milford Street
Swindon SN1 1HL
Tel: 0845 600 5604
Fax: 01793 499516
Email: fgw@custhelp.com
Web: www.firstgreatwestern.co.uk

FirstScotRail

Address: Caledonian Chambers
87 Union Street
Glasgow G1 3TA
Tel: 0845 601 5929
Fax: 0141 335 4592
Email: scotrailcustomer.relations@
firstgroup.com
Web: www.firstscotrail.com

Gatwick Express Railway Co

Address: Terminal House
52 Grosvenor Gardens
London SW1W 0AU
Tel: 0990 301 530
Fax: 020 7973 5038
Email: queries.gex@airexp.co.uk
Web: www.gatwickexpress.co.uk

Great North Eastern Railways

Address: M93 Main Headquarters Building
Station Road
York Y01 6HT
Tel: 0845 722 5333
Fax: 01904 524532
Email: CustomerCare@gner.co.uk
Web: www.gner.co.uk

Heathrow Express

Address: 3rd Floor 30 Eastbourne Terrace,
Paddington, London, W2 6LE
Tel: 020 8750 6600
Fax: 020 8750 6615
Email: queries.hex@airexp.co.uk
Web: www.heathrowexpress.com

Hull Trains

Address: Premier House, Ferensway
Hull HU1 3UF
Tel: 0845 600 1515
Fax: 01904 525208
Email: customer.services@hulltrains.co.uk
Web: www.hulltrains.co.uk

Island Line

Address: St Johns Road Station
St Johns Road, Ryde
Isle of Wight PO33 2BA
Tel: 01983 812591
Fax: 01983 812617
Email: comment@island-line.co.uk
Web: www.island-line.co.uk

Merseyrail

Address: Rail House
Lord Nelson Street
Liverpool L1 1JF
Tel: 0151 702 2534
Fax: 0151 702 3074
Web: www.merseyrail.org

Midland Mainline

Address: Midland House
Nelson St, Derby
East Midlands DE1 2SA
Tel: 0845 712 5678
Fax: 01332 263895
Email: feedback@midlandmainline.com
Web: www.midlandmainline.com

Northern Rail

Address: Prospect House
32 Sovereign Street
Leeds LS1 4JB
Tel: 0113 336 6033
Email: customer.relations@northernrail.org
Web: www.northernrail.org

One Railway (London Eastern Railway Ltd)

Address: Floor 1, Oliver's Yard, 55 City Road
London EC1Y 1HQ
Tel: 020 7549 5900
Fac: 01603 214567
Email: customer.relations@onerailway.com
Web: www.onerailway.com

Silverlink Train Services Limited

Address: 10th and 11th Floors
207 Old Street
London
EC1V 9NR
Tel: 0845 601 4867
Fax: 01603 214517
Email: custrel@silverlink-trains.com
Web: www.silverlink-trains.com

Southern Railway

Address: Go Ahead House
26-28 Addiscombe Road
Croydon
CR9 5GA
Tel: 0845 127 2920
Fax: 0845 727 2930
Web: www.southernrailway.com

South Eastern Trains

Address: Friars Bridge Court
41-45 Blackfriars Road
London
SE1 8PG
Tel: 0845 000 2222
Fax: 0800 783 4548
Web: www.southeasternrailway.co.uk

South West Trains

Address: Overline House
Blechynden Terrace
Southampton
SO15 1GW
Tel: 0845 600 0650
Fax: 020 7620 5177
Web: www.southwesttrains.co.uk

TransPennine Express

Address: Floor 7
Bridgewater House
60 Whitworth Stree
Manchester M1 6LT
Tel: 0845 600 1671
Fax: 0161 228 8120
Email: tpecustomer.relations@
firstgroup.com
Web: www.tpexpress.co.uk

Virgin Trains

Address: West Wing Offices
Euston Station
London NW1 2HS
Tel: 0870 789 1234
Fax: 0121 654 7500
Web: www.virgintrains.co.uk

Freight Rail Companies

Direct Rail Services

Address: Kingmoor Depot, Etterby Road
Carlisle, Cumbria CA3 9NZ
Tel: 01228 406600
Fax: 01228 406601
Email: enquiries@drsl.co.uk
Web: www.directrailservices.com

English, Welsh and Scottish Railway Ltd

Address: Lakeside Business Park
Carolina Way
Doncaster DN4 5PN
Tel: 0870 140 5000
Web: www.ews-railway.co.uk

Freightliner Ltd

Address: The Podium, 1 Eversholt Street
London NW1 2FL
Tel: 020 7200 3974
Fax: 020 7200 3975
Email: pressoffice@freightliner.co.uk
Web: www.freightliner.co.uk

GB Railfreight

Address: 15–25 Artillery Lane, London,
E1 7HA
Tel: 020 7904 3393
Fax: 020 7983 5113
Email: info@gbrailfreight.com
Web: www.gbrailfreight.com

Road

Association for Road Traffic Safety & Management (ARTSM)

Address: Office 8, Epic House
128 Fulwell Road
Teddington TW11 0RQ
Tel: 020 8977 6952
Fax: 020 8977 8339
Email: enquiries@artsm.org.uk
Web: www.artsm.org.uk

Association of British Drivers

Address: P.O. Box 2228, Kenley
Surrey CR8 5ZT
Tel: 07000 781544
Fax: 0870 136 2370
Email: enquiries@abd.org.uk
Web: www.abd.org.uk

Association of British Parking Enforcement Companies

Address: The Imperial Centre, Grange Rd
Darlington DL1 5NQ
Tel: 0114 267 8678
Fax: 0114 267 8009

*Association of Car Fleet Operators

Address: Rivendell House, 2 Winton Road
Petersfield GU32 3LL
Tel: 01730 260162
Fax: 01730 263937
Email: info@acfo.org
Web: www.acfo.org

Automobile Association

Address: Contact Centre
            Lambert House
            Stockport Road
            Cheadle
            SK8 2DY
Tel: 0800 056 8040
Fax: 0161 488 7300
Email: customer.services@theAA.com
Web: www.theAA.com

*Automotive Industry Data Ltd

Address: 31 Cape Road
            Warwick CV34 4JP
Tel: 01926 410040
Fax: 01926 776252
Web: www.eagleaid.com

Automotive Manufacturers Racing Association

Address: The Nook
            27 Top Side
            Grenoside
            Sheffield
            S35 8RD
Tel: 0114 246 4878
Fax: 0114 246 4858
Email: info@amrauk.com
Web: www.amrauk.com

Bicycle Association of Great Britain Ltd

Address: 3 The Quadrant
            Coventry CV1 2DY
Tel: 02476 553838
Fax: 02476 228366
Email: office@ba-gb.org.uk
Web: www.ba-gb.com

British Industrial Truck Association Ltd

Address: 5-7 High Street, Sunninghill
            Ascot, Berkshire SL5 9NQ
Tel: 01344 623 800
Fax: 01344 291 197
Email: info@bita.org.uk
Web: www.bita.org.uk

British Parking Association

Address: Stuart House 41-43 Perrymount Road
            Haywards Heath
            West Sussex RH16 3BN
Tel: 01444 447 300
Fax: 01444 454 105
Email: info@britishparking.co.uk
Web: www.britishparking.co.uk

*British Vehicle Rental And Leasing Association

Address: River Lodge, Badminton Court
            Amersham
            Buckinghamshire HP7 0DD
Tel: 01494 434 747
Fax: 01494 434 499
Email: info@bvrla.co.uk
Web: www.bvrla.co.uk

Bus Users UK

Address: PO Box 320, Portsmouth
            Hampshire PO5 3SD
Tel: 02392 814493
Fax: 02392 863080
Email: enquiries@bususers.org
Web: www.bususers.org

Coach Operators Federation

Address: Oxford, Radway
            Sidmouth, EX10 8TW
Tel: 07768 846138
Email: johnreece@virgin.net
Web: www.cofed.net

Commercial Trailer Association

Address: c/o SMMT Ltd, Forbes House
            Halkin St, London SW1X 7DS
Tel: 020 7235 7000
Fax: 020 7235 7112
Email: taweb@smmt.co.uk
Web: www.smmt.co.uk

Community Transport Association

Address: Highbank, Halton Street
            Hyde, Cheshire SK14 2NY
Tel: 08707 743586
Fax: 08707 743581
Email: info@ctauk.org
Web: www.communitytransport.com

*Confederation of Passenger Transport UK
Address: Drury House, 34-43 Russell Street
London WC2B 5HA
Tel: 020 7240 3131
Fax: 020 7240 6565
Email: admin@cpt-uk.org
Web: www.cpt-uk.org

Fork Truck Association
Address: Manor Farm Buildings, Lasham
Alton, Hampshire GU34 5SL
Tel: 01256 381441
Fax: 01256 381735
Email: mail@fork-truck.org.uk
Web: www.fork-truck.org.uk

*Freight Transport Association
Address: Hermes House, St John's Road
Tunbridge Wells, Kent TN4 9UZ
Tel: 01892 526171
Fax: 01892 534989
Web: www.fta.co.uk

Heavy Transport Association
Address: Century House, High Street
Tattenhall
Chester CH3 9PX
Tel: 01829 771774
Fax: 01829 773109
Email: info@hta.uk.net
Web: www.hta.uk.net

Imported Tyre Manufacturers Association
Address: 5a Pindock Mews
London W9 2PY
Tel: 020 7289 1043
Fax: 020 7286 9859
Email: prt@itma-europe.com
Web: www.itma-europe.com

Institute of Highway Incorporated Engineers
Address: De Morgan House
58 Russell Square
London WC1B 4HS
Tel: 020 7436 7487
Fax: 020 7581 7488
Email: secretary@ihie.org.uk
Web: www.ihie.org.uk

Institute of Road Transport Engineers
Address: 22 Greencoat Place
London SW1P 1PR
Tel: 020 7630 1111
Email: soe@soe.org.uk
Web: www.soe.org.uk

The Institute of the Motor Industry
Address: Fanshaws, Brickendon
Hertford SG13 8PQ
Tel: 01992 511 521
Fax: 01992 511 548
Email: imi@motor.org.uk
Web: www.motor.org.uk

ITIS Holdings plc
Address: Station House
Stamford New Road
Altrincham
Cheshire
WA14 1EP
Tel: 0161 929 5788
Email: info@itisholdings.com
Web: www.itisholdings.com

London Taxi Board
Address: 39-41 Brewery Road
Islington
London N7 9QH
Tel: 020 7700 9881
Email: media@londontaxiboard.org.uk
Web: www.motor.org.uk

*Motor Cycle Industry Association Ltd
Address: 1 Rye Hill Office Park
Birmingham Road
Allesley
Coventry CV5 9AB
Tel: 02476 408 000
Fax: 02476 408 001
Email: n.brown@mcia.co.uk
Web: www.mcia.co.uk

Motor Industry Research Association
Address: Watling Street, Nuneaton
Warwickshire CV10 0TU
Tel: 024 76355000
Fax: 024 76355355
Email: enquiries@mira.co.uk
Web: www.mira.co.uk

Motor Insurance Repair Research Centre

Address: Colthrop Way
T   hatcham RG19 4NR
Tel: 0163 586 8855
Fax: 0163 5871346
Email: enquiries@thatcham.org
Web: www.thatcham.org

Motor Schools Association of Great Britain

Address: 101 Wellington Road North,
           Stockport
           Cheshire SK4 2LP
Tel: 0161 429 9669
Fax: 0161 429 9779
Email: mail@msagb.co.uk
Web: www.msagb.co.uk

Motor Vehicle Dismantlers Association of Great Britain

Address: 33 Market Street
           Lichfield, Staffs WS13 6LA
Tel: 01543 254 254
Fax: 01543 254 274
Email: mail@mvda.org.uk
Web: www.mvda.org.uk

Motor Vehicle Repairers Association

Address: Glenfield Business Park
           Philips Rd
           Blackburn BB1 5QH
Tel: 0870 458 3051
Fax: 0870 458 3052
Email: enquiry@mvra.com
Web: www.mvra.com

National Taxi Association

Address: Infirmary Street, Newtown
           Carlisle, Cumbria CA2 7AA
Tel: 01228 598740
Fax: 01228 598740
Email: secretary@
           national-taxi-association.co.uk
Web: www.national-taxi-association.co.uk

National Trailer & Towing Association Ltd

Address: 1 Alveston Place, Leamington Spa
           Warwickshire CV32 4SN
Tel: 01926 335445
Web: www.ntta.co.uk

National Tyre Distributors Association

Address: 8 Temple Square, Aylesbury
           Bucks HP20 2HQ
Tel: 0870 9000600
Email: info@ntda.co.uk
Web: www.ntda.co.uk

*Natural Gas Vehicle Association

Address: 36 Holly Walk, Leamington Spa
           Warwickshire CV32 4LY
Tel: 01926 462900
Fax: 01926 462919
Email: info@ngva.co.uk
Web: www.ngva.co.uk

Parking Enforcement Association Ltd

Address: 2nd Floor
           145-157 St John Street
           London EC1V 4PY
Tel: 0870 345 9701
Web: www.parkingenforcement
           association.co.uk

*RAC plc

Address: Great Park Road
           Bradley Stock
           Bristol BS32 4QN
Tel: 08705 722 722
Web: www.rac.co.uk

*RAC Foundation for Motoring

Address: 89-91 Pall Mall
           London SW1Y 5HS
Tel: 020 7747 3445
Email: srainer@rac.co.uk
Web: www.racfoundation.org

Retread Manufacturers Association

Address: PO Box 320
           Crewe
           Cheshire CW2 6WY
Tel: 01270 561014
Fax: 01270 668801
Email: rma@greentyres.com
Web: www.retreaders.org.uk

*Road Haulage Association

Address: Roadway House, 35 Monument Hill
Weybridge, Surrey KT13 8RN
Tel: 01932 841 515
Fax: 01932 852 516
Email: weybridge@rha.net
Web: www.rha.net

Road Transport Fleet Data Society

Address: 18 Poplar Close, Biggleswade
Bedfordshire SG18 0EW
Email: info@fleetdata.co.uk
Web: www.fleetdata.co.uk

*Road Users Alliance

Address: Delegate House
30A Hart Street
Henley-on Thames
Oxon RG9 2AL
Email: info@rua.org.uk
Web: www.rua.org.uk

*Society of Motor Manufacturers and Traders

Address: Forbes House, Halkin Street
London SW1X 7DS
Tel: 020 7235 7000
Fax: 020 7235 7112
Email: smmt@smmt.co.uk
Web: www.smmt.co.uk

Trafficmaster

Address: University Way, Cranfield
Bedfordshire MK43 0TR
Tel: 08705 561712
Email: info@trafficmaster.co.uk
Web: www.trafficmaster.net

*Transport Association

Address: Global House
1 Ashley Avenue
Epsom KT18 5AD
Tel: 01372 846482
Fax: 01372 727130
Email: infor@trans-assoc.org.uk
Web: www.trans-assoc.org.uk

TyreSafe

Address: 21-25 St Anne's Court
London W1F 0BJ
Tel: 020 7734 6363
Email: cwakley@Automotivpr.com
Web: www.tyresafety.co.uk

*United Road Transport Union

Address: 76 High Lane, Chorlton-cum-Hardy
Manchester M21 9EF
Tel: 0161 881 6245
Fax: 0161 861 0976
Email: info@urtu.com
Web: www.urtu.com

Vehicle Builders & Repairers Association

Address: Belmont House, Finkle Lane
Gildersome, Leeds
West Yorkshire, LS27 7TW
Tel: 0113 253 8333
Fax: 0113 238 0496
Email: vbra@vbra.co.uk
Web: www.vbra.co.uk

Privately Owned Bus Groups

Arriva plc

Address: 1 Admiral Way, Doxford
International Business Park
Sunderland SR3 3XP
Tel: 0191 520 4000
Fax: 0191 520 4001
Email: enquiries@arriva.co.uk
Web: www.arriva.co.uk

East Yorkshire Motor Services Ltd

Address: 252 Anlaby Road
Hull HU3 2RS
Tel: 01482 327 142
Fax: 01482 217 614
Email: admin@eyms.co.uk
Web: www.eyms.co.uk

FirstGroup plc

Address: 395 King Street
Aberdeen AB24 5RP
Tel: 01224 650 100
Fax: 01224 650 140
Web: www.firstgroup.com

Go-Ahead Group plc

Address: 3rd Floor, 41–51 Grey Street
Newcastle upon Tyne NE1 6EE
Tel: 0191 232 3123
Fax: 0191 221 0315
Web: www.go-ahead.com

National Express Group plc

Address: 75 Davies Street
London W1K 5HT
Tel: 020 7529 2000
Fax: 020 7529 2100
Email: info@natex.co.uk
Web: www.nationalexpressgroup.com

Stagecoach Holdings plc

Address: 10 Dunkeld Road
Perth PH1 5TW
Tel: 01738 442 111
Fax: 01738 443 076
Email: info@stagecoachgroup.com
Web: www.stagecoachplc.com

Transdev plc

Address: Garrick House
Stamford Brook Garage
74 Chiswick High Road
London, W4 1SY
Tel: 020 8400 6052
Fax: 020 8400 6053
Email: information@transdevplc.co.uk
Web: www.transdevplc.com

trent barton

Address: Mansfield Road
Heanor, Derbyshire DE75 7BG
Tel: 01773 712265
Email: enquiries@trentbarton.co.uk
Web: www.trentbuses.co.uk

Local Authority Owned Bus Companies

Blackpool Transport Services Ltd

Address: Rigby Road
Blackpool FY1 5DD
Tel: 01253 473000
Fax: 01253 473101
Web: www.blackpooltransport.com

Cardiff Bus

Address: Sloper Road, Leckwith
Cardiff CF11 8TB
Tel: 029 2066 6444
Fax: 029 2078 7742
Email: enquiries@cardiffbus.com
Web: www.cardiffbus.com

Eastbourne Buses Ltd

Address: Birch Road
Eastbourne BN23 6PD
Tel: 01323 416416
Fax: 01323 643034
Email: mailbox@eastbournebuses.co.uk
Web: www.eastbournebuses.co.uk

Halton Borough Transport Ltd

Address: Moor Lane
Widnes WA8 7AF
Tel: 0151 423 3333
Email: enquiries@haltontransport.co.uk
Web: www.haltontransport.co.uk

Ipswich Buses Ltd

Address: 7 Constantine Road
Ipswich IP1 2DL
Tel: 01473 232 600
Fax: 01473 232 062
Email: info@ipswichbuses.co.uk
Web: www.ipswichbuses.co.uk

Islwyn Borough Transport Ltd

Address: Penmaen Road Depot
Pontllanfraith
Blackwood NP12 2DL
Tel: 01495 226622

Lothian Buses plc

Address: Annadale Street
Edinburgh EH7 4AZ
Tel: 0131 554 4494
Fax: 0131 554 3942
Email: mail@lothianbuses.co.uk
Web: www.lothianbuses.co.uk

Newport Transport Ltd

Address: 160 Corporation Road
           Newport NP19 0WF
Tel: 01633 670563
Fax: 01633 242589
Email: enquiries@newporttransport.co.uk
Web: www.newporttransport.co.uk

Nottingham City Transport Ltd

Address: Lower Parliament Street
           Nottingham NG1 1GG
Tel: 0115 9505 745
Fax: 0115 9504 425
Email: reception@nctx.co.uk
Web: www.nctx.co.uk

Plymouth Citybus Ltd

Address: 1 Milehouse Road
           Milehouse
           Plymouth
           Devon PL3 4AA
Tel: 01752 662271
Fax: 01752 567209
Web: www.plymouthbus.co.uk

Reading Transport Ltd

Address: Great Knollys Street
           Reading RG11 7HH
Tel: 0118 959 4000
Fax: 0118 957 5379
Email: info@reading-buses.co.uk
Web: www.reading-buses.co.uk

Rossendale Transport Ltd

Address: 35 Bacup Road, Rawtenstall
           Rossendale BB4 7NG
Tel: 01706 212337
Fax: 01706 229515
Email: info@rossendalebus.co.uk
Web: www.rossendalebus.co.uk

Thamesdown Transport Ltd

Address: Barnfield Road
           Swindon SN2 2DJ
Tel: 01793 428428
Fax: 01793 428405
Email: j.dosanjh@
           thamesdown-transport.co.uk
Web: www.thamesdown-transport.co.uk

Warrington Borough Transport Ltd

Address: Wilderspool Causeway
           Warrington WA4 6PT
Tel: 01925 634296
Fax: 01925 418382
Email: feedback@
           warringtonboroughtransport.co.uk
Web: www.warringtonborough
           transport.co.uk

Maritime

Association of British Offshore Industries

Address: c/o Society of Maritime Industries
           4th floor, 30 Great Guildford Street
           London SE1 0HS
Tel: 020 7928 9199
Fax: 020 7928 6599
Email: Info@maritimeindustries.org
Web: www.maritimeindustries.org

Association of Marine Scientific Industries

Address: c/o Society of Maritime Industries
           4th floor, 30 Great Guildford Street
           London SE1 0HS
Tel: 020 7928 9199
Fax: 020 7928 6599
Email: Info@maritimeindustries.org
Web: www.maritimeindustries.org

British Marine Equipment Association

Address: c/o Society of Maritime Industries
           4th floor, 30 Great Guildford Street
           London SE1 0HS
Tel: 020 7928 9199
Fax: 020 7928 6599
Email: Info@maritimeindustries.org
Web: www.maritimeindustries.org

*British Marine Industries Federation

Address: Marine House
           Meadlake Place, Thorpe Lea Road
           Egham, Surrey TW20 8HE
Tel: 01784 473 377
Fax: 01784 439 678
Email: info@britishmarine.co.uk
Web: www.britishmarine.co.uk

*British Ports Association

Address: Africa House, 64-78 Kingsway
London WC2B 6AH
Tel: 020 7242 1200
Fax: 020 7430 7474
Email: info@britishports.org.uk
Web: www.britishports.org.uk

British Shippers Council

Address: c/o Freight Transport Association
Hermes House, St Johns Rd
Tunbridge Wells, Kent TN4 9UZ
Tel: 01892 526 171
Fax: 01892 534 989
Email: csnelling@fta.co.uk
Web: www.fta.co.uk

British Tugowners Association

Address: Carthusian Court
12 Carthusian Street
London EC1M 6EZ
Tel: 020 7417 2875
Fax: 020 7600 1534
Web: www.britishtug.org

British Waterways

Address: Willow Grange
Church Road
Watford
Herts
WD17 4QA
Tel: 01923 201120
Fax: 01923 201400
Email: enquiries.hq@fbritishwaterways.co.uk
Web: www.britishtug.org

Cardiff & Bristol Channel Incorporated Shipowners Association

Address: c/o Welsh Industrial & Maritime
Museum
Bute Street
Cardiff CF1 6AN
Tel: 029 2048 1919
Fax: 029 2048 7252

*Chamber of Shipping

Address: Carthusian Court,
12 Carthusian Street
London EC1M 6EZ
Tel: 020 7417 2800
Fax: 020 7726 2080
Email: postmaster@british-shipping.org
Web: www.british-shipping.org

Electric Boat Association

Address: 150 Wayside Green, Woodcote
Reading, Berks RG8 0QJ
Tel: 01491 681 449
Fax: 01491 681 945
Email: mail@electric-boat-association.org.uk
Web: www.electric –boat-association.org.uk

Hovercraft Society

Address: Argus Gate, Chark Lane
Lee-on-Solent PO13 9NY
Tel: 023 92552090
Fax: 023 92552090
Web: www.hovercraft-museum.org/
society.htm

Immarsat Global Ltd

Address: 99 City Road
London EC1Y 1AX
Tel: 020 7728 1000
Fax: 020 7728 1044
Email: customercare@inmarsat.com
Web: www.inmarsat.com

Inland Waterways Association

Address: PO Box 114, Rickmansworth
Hertfordshire WD3 1ZY
Tel: 01923 711 114
Fax: 01923 897 000
Email: iwa@waterways.org.uk
Web: www.waterways.org.uk

Institute of Chartered Shipbrokers

Address: 85 Gracechurch Street
London EC3V 0AA
Tel: 020 7623 1111
Fax: 020 7623 8118
Email: info@ics.org.uk
Web: www.ics.org.uk

Institute of Marine Engineering, Science and Technology

Address: 80 Coleman Street
             London EC2R 5BJ
Tel: 020 7382 2600
Fax: 020 7382 2670
Email: info@imarest.org
Web: www.imarest.org

International Cargo Handling Association

Address: Suite 2, 85 Western Road
             Romford, Essex RM1 3LS
Tel: 01708 735 295
Fax: 01708 735 225
Email: info@ichcainternational.co.uk
Web: www.ichcainternational.co.uk

International Council of Marine Industry Associations

Address: Marine House, Thorpe Lea Road
             Egham, Surrey TW20 8BF
Tel: 01784 223 700
Fax: 01784 223 705
Email: info@icomia.com
Web: www.icomia.com

International Marine Contractors Association

Address: 5 Lower Belgrave Street
             London SW1W 0NR
Tel: 020 7824 5520
Fax: 020 7824 5521
Email: imca@imca-int.com
Web: www.imca-int.co

International Maritime Organisation

Address: 4 Albert Embankment
             London SE1 7SR
Tel: 020 7735 7611
Fax: 020 7587 3210
Email: publications-sales@imo.org
Web: www.imo.org

International Ship Suppliers Association

Address: The Baltic Exchange, St Mary Axe
             London EC3A 8BH
Tel: 020 7626 6236
Fax: 020 7626 6234
Email: issa@dial.pipex.com
Web: www.shipsupply.org

Liverpool Shipowners and Port Users Association

Address: c/o Liverpool Chamber of Commerce
             & Industry, One Old Hall Street
             Liverpool L3 9HG
Tel: 0151 227 1234
Fax: 0151 236 0121
Email: chamber@liverpoolchamber.org.uk
Web: www.liverpoolchamber.org.uk

*Lloyd's Register of Shipping/Fairplay

Address: 71 Fenchurch Street
             London EC3M 4BS
Tel: 020 7709 9166
Fax: 020 7488 4796
Email: emea@lr.org
Web: www.lr.org

NAUTILUS UK

Address: Oceanair House, 750-760 High Road
             Leytonstone, London E11 3BB
Tel: 020 8989 6677
Fax: 020 8530 1015
Email: telegraph@nautilus.org
Web: www.nautilus.org

Oil and Gas UK

Address: 2nd Floor
             232-242 Vauxhall Bridge Road
             London SW1V 1AU
Tel: 020 7802 2400
Fax: 020 7802 2401
Email: info@oilandgasuk.co.uk
Web: www.oilandgas.co.uk

Passenger Shipping Association

Address: 1st Floor
             41/42 Eastcastle Street
             London W1W 8DU
Tel: 020 7436 2449
Email: hayley@psa-psara.org
Web: www.the-psa.co.uk

*Royal Institution of Naval Architects

Address: 10 Upper Belgrave Street
             London SW1X 8BQ
Tel: 020 7235 4622
Fax: 020 7259 5912
Email: hq@rina.org.uk
Web: www.rina.org.uk

*Society of Maritime Industries

Address: 4th floor, 30 Great Guildford Street
London SE1 0HS
Tel: 020 7928 9199
Fax: 020 7928 6599
Email: Info@maritimeindustries.org
Web: www.maritimeindustries.org

UK Major Ports Group Ltd

Address: 2nd Floor
Africa House
64-78 Kingsway
London WC2B 6AH
Tel: 020 7430 7460
Fax: 020 7405 7461
Email: Richardbird@ukmajorports.org.uk
Web: www.ukmajorports.org.uk

Major UK Ports

Associated British Ports (ABP)

Address: 150 Holborn
London EC1N 2LR
Tel: 020 7430 1177
Fax: 020 7430 1384
Email: pr@abports.co.uk
Web: www.abports.co.uk

Port of Belfast

Address: Harbour Office, Corporation Square
Belfast BT1 3AL
Tel: 028 9055 4422
Fax: 028 9055 4411
Email: corporate@belfast-harbour.co.uk
Web: www.belfast-harbour.co.uk

The Bristol Port Company

Address: St Andrews House, St Andrews Road
Avonmouth, Bristol BS11 9DQ
Tel: 0117 982 0000
Fax: 0117 982 0698
Email: enquiries@bristolport.co.uk
Web: www.bristolport.co.uk

Clydeport Ltd

Address: 16 Robertson Street
Glasgow G2 8DS
Tel: 0141 221 8733
Fax: 0141 248 3167
Email: info@clydeport.co.uk
Web: www.clydeport.co.uk

*Dover Harbour Board

Address: Harbour House, Marine Parade
Dover, Kent CT17 9BU
Tel: 01304 240400
Fax: 01304 240465
Email: marketing@doverport.co.uk
Web: www.doverport.co.uk

Port of Felixstowe

Address: Tomline House
The Dock
Suffolk IP11 3SY
Tel: 01394 604500
Fax: 01394 604949
Email: enquiries@fdrc.co.uk
Web: www.portoffelixstowe.co.uk

Forth Ports plc

Address: 1 Prince of Wales Dock, Leith
Edinburgh EH6 7DX
Tel: 0131 555 8700
Fax: 0131 553 7462
Web: www.forthports.co.uk

Harwich International Port

Address: Parkeston, Harwich
Essex CO12 4SR
Tel: 01255 242000
Fax: 01255 241400
Web: www.harwich.co.uk

Hutchison Ports (UK) Ltd

Address: Tomlin House
The Dock
Felixstowe
Suffolk 1P11 8SY
Tel: 01394 604500
Fax: 01394 604949
Web: www.portoffelixstowe.co.uk

Isle of Man Harbours

Address: Sea Terminal Building
Douglas IM1 2RF
Tel: 01624 686626
Fax: 01624 626403
Email: enquiries@harbours.dot.gov.im
Web: www.gov.im/harbours

Port of London Authority

Address: London River House
Royal Pier Road
Gravesend
Kent DA12 2BG
Tel: 01474 562200
Fax: 01474 562281
Web: www.portoflondon.co.uk

Mersey Docks & Harbour Company

Address: Maritime Centre, Port of Liverpool
Liverpool L21 1LA
Tel: 0151 949 6000
Fax: 0151 949 6300
Web: www.merseydocks.co.uk

Milford Haven Port Authority

Address: PO Box 14
Gorsewood Drive, Milford Haven
Pembrokeshire SA73 3ER
Tel: 01646 696100
Fax: 01646 696125
Email: enquiries@mhpa.co.uk
Web: www.mhpa.co.uk

PD Teesport

Address: Tees Dock, Grangetown
Middlesbrough TS6 6UD
Tel: 01642 277 564
Fax: 01642 277 565
Email: commercial@pdports.co.uk
Web: www.thpal.co.uk

Peel Ports

Address: Maritime Centre
Port of Liverpool
Liverpool L21 1LA
Tel: 0151 949 6000
Fax: 0151 949 6300
Web: www.peeladmin.co.uk

Sullom Voe Harbour Authority

Address: Port Administration Building,
Sella Ness, Sullom Voe
Shetland ZE2 9QR
Tel: 01806 244200
Fax: 01806 242237
Email: port.reception@shetland.gov.uk.
Web: www.shetland.gov.uk/
ports/sullomvoe

Thamesport

Address: Grain Road
Isle of Grain
Rochester
Kent, ME3 0EP
Tel: 01634 271511
Fax: 01634 270384
Web: www.hph.com

Port of Tyne Authority

Address: Maritime House, Tyne Dock
South Shields,
Tyne and Wear NE34 9PT
Tel: 0191 455 2671
Fax: 0191 455 4687
Email: enquiries@portoftyne.co.uk
Web: www.portoftyne.com

Major Passenger Ferry Operators

Brittany Ferries

Address: Millbay
Plymouth
Devon
England PL1 3EW
Tel: 0870 9 076 103
Web: www.brittany-ferries.co.uk

Caledonian MacBrayne Ltd

Address: The Ferry Terminal
Gourock PA19 1QP
Tel: 01475 650 100
Fax: 01475 650268
Web: www.calmac.co.uk

Condor Ferries
Address: The Quay
          Weymouth
          Dorset DT4 8DX
Tel: 01202 207216
Email: info@condorferries.fr
Web: www.condorferries.co.uk

DFDS Seaways
Address: Scandinavia House
          Parkeston
          Harwich
          Essex CO12 4QG
Tel: 0871 522 9955
Web: www.dfdsseaways.co.uk

Hovertravel
Address: Quary Road
          Ryde
          Isle of Wight PO33 2HB
Tel: 01983 811 000
Fax: 01983 562 216
Email: info@hovertravel.co.uk
Web: www.hovertravel.co.uk

Irish Ferries
Address: Breakwater Road Off Alexandra Road
          Ferryport
          Dublin 1, Ireland
Tel: 08705 17 17 17
Email: info@irishferries.co.uk
Web: www.irishferries.com

Isle of Man Steam Packet
Address: PO Box 5
          Imperial Buildings, Douglas
          Isle of Man, IM1 2BY
Tel: 01624 645 645
Email: info@steampacket.com
Web: www.steampacket.com

Isles of Scilly Steamship Company Ltd
Address: Steamship House
          Quay Street
          Penzance
          Cornwall, TR18 4BZ
Tel: 01624 645 645
Email: Sales@islesofscilly-travel.co.uk
Web: www.islesofscilly-travel.co.uk

LD Transmanche Ferries
Address: Terminal de la Citadelle
          BP 907 46
          76060
          Le Havre, cedex
Tel: 0033 235 197878
Email: nadin.corbel@ldlines.fr
Web: www.transmancheferries.com

Norfolk Line
Address: Export Freight Plaza
          Eastern Docks Dover
          CT16 1JA Kent
Tel: 01304 218400
Fax: 01304 218420
Email: doverpax@norfolkline.com
Web: www.norfolkline.com

Northlink Ferries
Address: Kiln Corner, Ayre Road,
          Kirkwall, Orkney
          Scotland KW15 1QX
Tel: 01856 885500
Fax: 01856 879588
Email: info@northlinkferries.co.uk
Web: www.northlinkferries.co.uk

Orkney Ferries
Address: Shore Street
          Kirkwall
          Orkney KW15 1LG
Tel: 01856 872044
Fax: 01856 872921
Email: info@orkneyferries.co.uk
Web: www.orkneyferries.co.uk

P&O Ferries
Address: Channel House
          Channel View Road
          Dover CT17 9TJ
Tel: 08705 980333
Email: help@poferries.co.uk
Web: www.poferries.com

Red Funnel
Address: 12 Bugle Street
          Southampton SO14 2JY
Tel: 0870 444 8898
Fax: 0870 444 8897
Email: post@redfunnel.co.uk
Web: www.redfunnel.co.uk

Sea France

Address: Whitefield Court
            Honeywood Close
            Kent CT16 3PX
Tel: 01304 828 300
Web: www.seafrance.com

Shetland Island Ferries

Address: Shetland Islands Council
            Town Hall
            Upper Hillhead, Lerwick
            Shetland ZE1 0HB
Tel: 01595 693535
Fax: 01595 744509
Email: info@shetland.gov.co.uk
Web: www.shetland.gov.uk/ferries

Speed Ferries

Address: Western Docks, Dover
            Kent CT17 9TG
Tel: 0870 220 0 570
Fax: 01304 20 8000
Email: mail@speedferries.com
Web: www.speedferries.com

Stena Line

Address: 1 Suffolk Way
            Sevenoaks
            Kent TN13 1YL
Tel: 0870 5707070
Web: www.stenaline.com

Wightlink Ltd

Address: PO Box 59
            Portsmouth PO1 2XB
Tel: 0239 2812 011
Email: info@wightlink.co.uk
Web: www.wightlink.co.uk

Travel and Tourism

*Association of British Travel Agents Ltd (ABTA)

Address: 68-71 Newman Street
            London W1T 3AH
Tel: 020 7637 2444
Fax: 020 7637 0713
Email: information@abta.co.uk
Web: www.abta.co.uk

Association of Independent Tour Operators

Address: 133a St Margaret's Road,
            Twickenham
            Middlesex TW1 1RG
Tel: 020 8744 9280
Fax: 020 8744 3187
Email: info@aito.co.uk
Web: www.aito.co.uk

Association of Leading Visitor Attractions

Address: 4 Westminster Palace
            Gardens Artillery Row
            London SW1P 1RL
Tel: 020 7222 1728
Fax: 020 7222 1729
Email: email@alva.org.uk
Web: www.alva.org.uk

Association of National Tourist office Representatives

Address: PO Box 5017
            Hove
            East Sussex BN23 3ZD
Tel: 0870 241 9084
Email: secretary@antor.com
Web: www.tourist-offices.org.uk

Association of Scottish Visitor Attractions

Address: Argyll's Lodging, Castle Wynd
            Stirling FK8 1EG
Tel: 01786 475 152
Fax: 01786 474 288
Email: info@asva.co.uk
Web: www.asva.co.uk

British Holiday & Home Parks Association

Address: 6 Pullman Court, Great Western Rd
            Gloucester GL1 3ND
Tel: 01452 526 911
Fax: 01452 508 508
Email: enquiries@bhhpa.org.uk
Web: www.bhhpa.org.uk

Coach Tourism Council

Address: 10 Bermondsey Exchange
179-181 Bermondsey Street
London SE1 3UW
Tel: 0870 850 2839
Fax: 020 7407 6880
Email: admin@coachtourismcouncil.co.uk
Web: www.coachtourismcouncil.co.uk

Federation of Tour Operators

Address: 1st Floor, Graphic House
14-16 Sussex Road
Haywards Heath
West Sussex RG16 4EA
Tel: 01444 457900
Fax: 01444 457901
Email: info@fto.co.uk
Web: www.fto.co.uk

*National Caravan Council Ltd

Address: Catherine House, Victoria Rd
Aldershot,
Hampshire GU11 1SS
Tel: 01252 318 251
Fax: 01252 322 596
Email: info@nationalcaravan.co.uk
Web: www.nationalcaravan.co.uk

Outdoors Industries Association

Address: Morritt House, 58 Station Approach
South Ruislip, Middlesex HA4 6SA
Tel: 020 8842 1111
Fax: 020 8842 0090
Email: info@go-outdoors.org.uk
Web: www.go-outdoors.org.uk

Sustrans

Address: National Cycle Network Centre
2 Cathedral Square
College Green
Bristol BS1 5DD
Tel: 0117 926 8893
Fax: 0117 929 4173
Email: info@sustrans.org.uk
Web: www.sustrans.org.uk

UKinbound

Address: 3rd Floor
388 The Strand
London WC2R 0LT
Tel: 020 7395 7500
Fax: 020 7240 6618
Email: info@ukinbound.org
Web: www.ukinbound.org

Other UK Organisations

*Association of British Insurers

Address: 51 Gresham Street,
London, EC2V 7HQ
Tel: 020 7600 3333
Fax: 020 7696 8999
Email: info@abi.org.uk
Web: www.abi.org.uk

British International Freight Association

Address: Redfern House, Browells Lane
Feltham
Middlesex TW13 7EP
Tel: 020 8844 2266
Fax: 020 8890 5546
Email: bifa@bifa.org
Web: www.bifa.org

*Business and Trade Statistics Ltd

Address: 45 More Lane
Esher, Surrey KT10 8AP
Tel: 01372 463121
Fax: 01372 469847
Email: sales@worldtradestats.com

Campaign to Protect Rural England

Address: 128 Southwark Street
London SE1 0SW
Tel: 020 7981 2800
Fax: 020 7981 2899
Email: Info@cpre.org.uk
Web: www.cpre.org.uk

Chartered Institue of Logistics and Transport

Address:	Logistics and Transport Centre
	Elstrees Court
	Elstrees Road
	Corby, Northants NN17 4AX
Tel:	01536 740 100
Fax:	01536 740 101
Email:	enquiry@cilt.org.uk
Web:	www.ciltuk.org.uk

*Chartered Institute of Public Finance and Accountancy (CIPFA)

Address:	3 Robert Street
	London WC2N 6RL
Tel:	020 7543 5600
Fax:	020 7543 5700
Email:	technical.enquiry@cipfa.org
Web:	www.cipfa.org.uk

Chartered Insurance Institute

Address:	42- 48 High Road, South Woodford
	London E18 2JP
Tel:	020 8989 8464
Fax:	020 8530 3052
Email:	customer.serv@cii.co.uk
Web:	www.cii.co.uk

Environmental Transport Association

Address:	68 High Street, Weybridge
	Surrey KT13 8RS
Tel:	0845 389 1010
Fax:	0845 389 1015
Email:	eta@eta.co.uk
Web:	www.eta.co.uk

*Energy Institute

Address:	61 New Cavendish Street
	London W1G 7AR
Tel:	020 7467 7100
Email:	info@energyinst.org.uk
Web:	www.energyinst.org.uk

Freight Forward International

Address:	PO Box 4076
	Bracknell, Berkshire
	England, RG42 9EG
Tel:	+44 (0)1344 862964
Fax:	+44 (0)1344 744352
Email:	carol@ffi-admin.com
Web:	www.freightforwardinternational.net

Institute of Materials, Minerals and Mining

Address:	1 Carlton House Terrace
	London SW1Y 5DB
Tel:	020 7451 7300
Fax:	020 7839 1702
Web:	www.iom3.org

*Institute of Public Finance (IPF)

Address:	No 1 Croydon
	12-16 Addiscombe Road
	Croydon
	Surrey CR0 0XT
Tel:	020 8667 1144
Fax:	020 8681 8058
Email:	info@ipf.co.uk
Web:	www.ipf.com

Institute of Transport Administration

Address:	The Old Studio
	25 Greenfield Road, Westoning
	Bedfordshire MK45 5JD
Tel:	01525 634940
Fax:	01525 750016
Email:	director@iota.org.uk
Web:	www.iota.org.uk

Institution of Civil Engineers

Address:	One Great George Street,
	Westminster
	London SW1P 3AA
Tel:	020 7222 7722
Fax:	020 7222 7500
Email:	library@ice.org.uk
Web:	www.ice.org.uk

*Institution of Highways and Transportation

Address:	6 Endsleigh Street
	London WC1H 0DZ
Tel:	020 7387 2525
Fax:	020 7387 2808
Email:	info@iht.org
Web:	www.iht.org

Institution of Mechanical Engineers

Address: 1 Birdcage Walk
         London SW1H 9JJ
Tel: 020 7222 7899
Fax: 020 7222 0557
Email: journals@pepublishing.com
Web: www.imeche.org.uk

Institution of Structural Engineers

Address: 11 Upper Belgrave Street
         London SW1X 8BH
Tel: 020 7235 4535
Fax: 020 7235 4294
Web: www.istructe.org.uk

Rail, Maritime & Transport Union

Address: Unity House, 39 Chalton Street
         London NW1 1JD
Tel: 020 7387 4771
Fax: 020 7387 4123
Email: info@rmt.org.uk
Web: www.rmt.org.uk

Royal Institution of Chartered Surveyors

Address: 12 Great George Street
         Parliament Square
         London SW1P 3AD
Tel: 0870 333 1600
Fax: 020 7334 3811
Email: contactrics@rics.org
Web: www.rics.org

Royal Town Planning Institute

Address: 41 Botolph Lane
         London EC3R 8DL
Tel: 020 7929 9494
Fax: 020 7929 9490
Email: online@rtpi.org.uk
Web: www.rtpi.org.uk

*Scottish Association for Public Transport

Address: 11 Queens Crescent, Glasgow
         Scotland G4 9BL
Tel: 07760 381729
Email: mail@sapt.org.uk
Web: www.sapt.org.uk

*Scottish Transport Studies Group

Address: 26 Palmerston Place
         Edinburgh EH12 5AL
Tel: 0870 350 4202
Fax: 0131 455 5141
Email: enquiries@stsg.org
Web: www.stsg.org

Transport and Health Study Group

Address: Stockport Primary Care Trust
         Regent House
         Stockport SK4 1BS
Tel: 0161 426 2014
Fax: 0161 477 8272
Email: mary.brooks@stockport-pct.gov.uk
Web: www.stockport.nhs.uk/thsg

Transport & General Workers Union

Address: Transport House
         128 Theobald's Road
         Holborn, London WC1X 8TN
Tel: 020 7611 2500
Fax: 020 7611 2555
Email: tgwu@tgwu.org.uk
Web: www.tgwu.org.uk

*Transport 2000

Address: The Impact Centre
         12-18 Hoxton Street
         London N1 6NG
Tel: 020 7613 0743
Fax: 020 7613 5280
Email: sales@transport2000.org.uk
Web: www.transport2000.org.uk

Transport Planning Society

Address: 1 Great George Street
         London SW1P 3AA
Tel: 020 7665 2231
Email: tps@ice.org.uk
Web: www.tps.org.uk

Transport Research Laboratory

Address: Crowthorne House,
         Nine Mile Ride Wokingham
         Berkshire RG40 6GA
Tel: 01344 773131
Fax: 01344 770356
Email: enquiries@trl.co.uk
Web: www.trl.co.uk

Transport Salaried Staffs Association
Address: Walkden House, 10 Melton Street
London NW1 2EJ
Tel: 020 7387 2101
Fax: 020 7383 0656
Email: enquiries@tssa.org.uk
Web: www.tssa.org.uk

Traveline
Address: Confederation of Passenger
Transport
Drury House
34-43 Russell Street
London WC2B 5HA
Tel: 0871 200 22 33
Web: www.traveline.info

*United Kingdom Petroleum Industry Association
Address: 9 Kingsway
London WC2B 6XF
Tel: 020 7240 0289
Email: info@ukjpia.com
Web: www.ukpia.com

International Non-Government Organisations

*Airbus Industries
Address: 1 Rond Point Maurice Bellonte
31700 Blagnac Cedex
France
Tel: +33 5 61 93 33 33
Web: www.airbus.com

*Airports Council International
Address: PO Box 16, 1215 Geneva 15 – Airport
Switzerland
Tel: +41 22 717 8585
Fax: +41 22 717 8888
Email: aci@airports.org
Web: www.airports.org

*Air Transport Action Group
Address: 33 route de l'aéroport, P.O. Box 49,
1215 Geneva 15 Airport, Switzerland
Tel: +41 22 770 2672
Fax: +41 22 770 2686
Email: information@atag.org
Web: www.atag.org

*American Public Transport Association (APTA)
Address: 1666 K Street, NW, Suite 1100
Washington DC 20006
USA
Tel: +1 202 496 4800
Fax: +1 202 496 4321
Email: info@apta.com
Web: www.apta.com

*Armateurs de France
Address: 47 rue Monceau
75008 Paris
France
Tel: +33 1 53 89 52 52
Fax: +33 1 53 89 52 53
Email: info@armateursdefrance.org
Web: www.armateursdefrance.org

*Association of European Airlines
Address: Avenue Louise 350
B-1150 Brussels
Belgium
Tel: +32 (0)26 39 89 89
Fax: +32 (0)26 39 89 99
Email: aea.secretariat@aea.be
Web: www.aea.be

Association of European Travel Agents
Address: Rue Dautzenberg
36 (Box 6)
B- 1050 Brussels
Belgium
Tel: +32 2 644 34 50
Web: www.ectaa.org

*Boeing Commercial Airplanes
Address: P. O. Box 3707
Seattle, Washington 98124
Tel: +1 206-655-2121
Web: www.boeing.com

*European Car and Truck Rental Association
Address: Avenue de Tervuren
402 - 1150
Brussels
Belgium
Tel: +32 2 761 6614
Fax: +32 2 777 0505
Email: ecatra@ecatra.org

European Community Association of Ship Brokers and Agents
Address: Ground Floor North
85 Gracechurch Street
London EC3V OAA
Tel: +44 207 7623 3113
Email: generalmanager@fonasba.com
Web: www.ecasba.com

European Express Organisation
Address: Avenue Cortenbergh 118
Box 8
B-1000 Brussels
Belgium
Tel: +32 2 737 95 76
Fax: +32 2 737 95 01
Email: ghodgson@hillandknowlton.com
Web: www.euroexpress.org

*European Union Road Federation
Address: Avenue Louise 113
B-1050 Brussels
Belgium
Tel: +32 2 644 58 77
Fax: +32 2 647 59 34
Email: info@erf.be
Web: www.erf.be

Federation of National Associations of Ship Brokers and Agents
Address: Ground Floor North
85 Gracechurch Street
London EC3V OAA
Tel: +44 207 7623 3113
Email: generalmanager@fonasba.com
Web: sslrelay.com/fonasba.com

*Forecast International
Address: 22 Commerce Road
Newtown CT 06470
USA
Tel: +1 203 426 0800
Fax: +1 203 426 0223
Email: info@forecast1.com
Web: www.forecastinternational.com

*Institute of Shipping Economics and Logistics (ISL)
Address: Universitatsallee GW1, Block A
D-28359, Bremen
Germany
Tel: +49 421 22096 0
Fax: +49 421 22096 55
Email: info@isl.org
Web: www.isl.org

The International Air Cargo Association (TIACA)
Address: P.O. Box 661510
Miami, FL 33266-1510
Tel: +1 786 265 7011
Fax: +1 786 265 7012
Email: secgen@tiaca.org
Web: www.tiaca.org

International Association of Ports and Harbors (IAPH)
Address: 7th Floor, South Tower New Pier
Takeshiba
1-16-1 Kaigan, Minato-ku,
Tokyo 105-0022
Japan
Tel: +81-3-5403-2770
Fax: +81-3-5403-7651
Email: info@iaphworldports.org
Web: www.iaphworldports.org

*International Association of Public Transport
Address: 6, rue Sainte Marie
B-1080 Brussels
Belgium
Tel: +32 2 673 6100
Fax: +32 2 660 1072
Email: hans.rat@uitp.com
Web: www.uitp.com

*International Civil Aviation Organisation

Address: 999 University Street, Montreal
Quebec H3C 5H7
Canada
Tel: + 1 514 954 8219
Fax: + 1 514 954 6077
Email: icaohq@icao.int
Web: www.icao.int

International Federation of Freight Forwarders Associations

Address: Schaffhauserstr. 104
P.O. Box 364
CH-8152 Glattbrugg
Switzerland
Tel: +41 (0)43 211 65 00
Fax: +41 (0)43 211 65 65
Web: www.fiata.com

*International Organisation of Motor Vehicle Manufacturers

Address: 4 rue de Berri
75008 Paris
France
Tel: +331 43 59 00 13
Fax: +331 45 63 84 41
Email: webmaster@oica.net
Web: www.oica.net

*International Road Federation

Address: 2 Chemin de Blandonnet
CH-1214 Vernier, Geneva
Switzerland
Tel: +41 22 306 0260
Fax: +41 22 306 0270
Email: info@irfnet.org
Web: www.irfnet.org

*International Road Transport Union (IRU)

Address: Centre International,
3 rue de Varembe
PO Box 44, CH-1211 Geneva 20
Switzerland
Tel: +41 22 918 27 00
Fax: +41 22 918 27 41
Email: iru@iru.org
Web: www.iru.org

*International Union of Combined Road-Rail Transport Companies (UIRR)

Address: 31 rue Montoyer bte 11
B - 1000 Brussels
Tel: +32 2 548 78 90
Fax: +32 2 512 63 93
Email: headoffice.brussels@uirr.com
Web: www.uirr.com

*International Union of Railways

Address: Sales Department, 16 rue Jean Rey
F-75015 Paris
France
Tel: +33 1 44 49 20 20
Fax: +33 1 44 49 20 29
Web: www.uic.asso.fr

Irish International Freight Association

Address: Strand House, Strand Street
Malahide, Co. Dublin
Republic of Ireland
Tel: +353 1845 5411
Fax: +353 0184 5531
Email: iifa@eircom.net
Web: www.iifa.ie

Irish Road Haulage Association

Address: C.G.I. Building, Unit 12
Blanchardstown
Corporate Park, Blanchardstown,
Dublin 15
Republic of Ireland
Tel: +353 (0)1 8224888
Fax: +353 (0)1 8224898
Email: info@irha.ie
Web: www.irha.ie

Irish Ship Agents Association

Address: Ormonde Housey, 26 Harbour Row
Cobh, County Cork
Republic of Ireland
Tel: +353 21813180
Fax: +353 21811849
Email: info@irishshipagents.com
Web: www.irishshipagents.com/

Irish Tourist Industry Confederation

Address: 17 Longford Terrace, Monkstown
Co Dublin
Republic of Ireland
Tel: +353 (0)1 2844222
Fax: +353 (0)1 2804218
Email: itic@eircom.net
Web: www.itic.ie

*Motor & Equipment Manufacturers Association

Address: PO Box 13966, 10 Laboratory Drive
Research Triangle Park, NC 27709-3966 U.S.A.
Tel: +1 919 549 4800
Fax: + 919 549 4824
Email: info@mema.org
Web: www.mema.org

*Travel Industry Association of America

Address: 1100 New York Avenue, NW
Suite 450
Washington, DC 20005-3934
USA
Tel: +1 202 408 8422
Fax: +1 202 408 1255
Email: feedback@tia.org
Web: www.tia.org

*Verband der Automobilindustrie

Address: Westendstraße 61
D-60325 Frankfurt/M.
Germany
Tel.: +49 69 9 75 07 – 0
Fax: +49 69 9 75 07 – 261
Web: www.vda.de

SECTION 4

Sources of Transport Statistics

UK and International

This directory of sources of transport statistics is compiled from amendments to entries in the last edition and the addition of new entries. Entries in the last edition have been checked with the relevant organisation for amendments and updates.

All organisations listed in Sections 2 and 3 were investigated to ascertain if they produced relevant publications for inclusion. However, certain statutory publications such local authority transport plans and annual reports and accounts have not been listed although they are often sources of transport statistics.

Air

ACI CUSS Survey Report
Org: Airports Council International
Freq: Ad hoc
Type: Common Use Self Service Kiosk
Desc: Snapshot of the current CUSS deployments. PDF and print versions available.
Price: €300, members €150.
Contact: Order from website
Tel: +41 22 717 8585
Web: www.airports.org

ACI World Economics Survey
Org: Airports Council International
Freq: Annual
Type: Airport finances
Desc: Employment trends, financial results, capital expenditure, financial benchmarking, and regional breakdown of non-aeronautical revenue by source. PDF and print versions available.
Price: €500, members €400.
Contact: Order from website
Tel: +41 22 717 8585
Web: www.airports.org

Air Cargo Annual

Org: International Air Transport
           Association
Freq: Annual
Type: Freight
Price: IATA Member Airline US$250.00;
           Strategic Partners US$292.50; others
           US$390
Contact: Order via website
Tel: +41 22 770 2751
Web: www.iata.org

Air Traffic Analysis - Birmingham

Org: Birmingham International
           Airport Ltd
Freq: Annual
Type: Passenger and freight
Desc: Passenger and aircraft movements
Price: On application
Contact: Mark Scourse
Tel: 0121 767 8346
Web: www.bhx.co.uk

Air Traffic Management International

Org: Euromoney Publications plc
Freq: Annual
Price: £349
Contact: Order online
Tel: +44 020 7779 8673
Web: www.euromoney.com

Air Transport Between The EU And The USA

Org: Eurostat
Freq: Annual
Type: Passengers and Freight
Desc: Covers the number of passengers at
           country, airport and route level as well
           as number of flight plus data on air
           freight transport.
Price: Free
Contact: Download via website
Tel: 01633 813369
Web: epp.eurostat.ec.europa.eu

Air Transport in Europe in 2005

Org: Eurostat
Freq: Annual
Type: Passengers and Freight
Desc: Air passenger and freight transport in
           the EU Member States, Candidate
           Countries and EFTA countries. The
           figures are presented at country,
           airport and route level.
Price: Free
Contact: Download via website
Tel: 01633 813369
Web: epp.eurostat.ec.europa.eu

Airline Economic Results and Prospects

Org: International Air Transport
           Association
Freq: Annual
Type: Passengers and Freight
Desc: Detailed information on airline
           revenues, costs, traffic, capacity,
           labour efficiency etc.
Price: IATA Member Airline US$384.25;
           Strategic Partners US$399.20; others
           US$499
Contact: Order via website
Tel: +41 22 770 2751
Web: www.iata.org

Airline Economic Task Force Quarterly Report: 2006 Quarter One

Org: International Air Transport
           Association
Freq: Annual
Type: Passengers and Freight
Desc: Quarterly update about airlines' three
           key performance indicators for each
           route area
Price: IATA Member Airline US$149.25;
           others US$199
Contact: Download via website
Tel: +41 22 770 2751
Web: www.iata.org

Airline Financial Performance Benchmarks, 2004

Org:	International Air Transport Association
Freq:	Annual
Type:	Airline finances
Desc:	Summarized data on airline traffic, capacity, revenues, costs, profitability and return on investment.
Price:	IATA Member Airline US$292.50; others US$390
Contact:	Download via website
Tel:	+41 22 770 2751
Web:	www.iata.org

Airports - Annual and Monthly Traffic Data

Org:	Airports Council International
Freq:	Monthly and annual
Price:	Free on web
Web:	www.airports.org

Airline Statistics - Monthly

Org:	European Regions Airline Association
Freq:	Monthly
Type:	Passenger and freight
Desc:	Monthly reports contain traffic, departure punctuality and fleet data.
Price:	Free
Contact:	Download from website
Tel:	01276 856495
Web:	www.eraa.org

Airline Statistics - Quarterly

Org:	European Regions Airline Association
Freq:	Quarterly
Type:	Passenger and freight
Desc:	Analyis of the traffic including passenger numbers, load factors along with departure punctuality, regularity and fleet data.
Price:	Free
Contact:	Download from website
Tel:	01276 856495
Web:	www.eraa.org

Airport Capacity/Demand Profile, 2003

Org:	International Air Transport Association
Freq:	Every two years
Type:	Airport capacity database
Desc:	a joint ACI/ATAG/IATA publication, compiled by IATA, which provides airport capacity, development, operations and infrastructure information for nearly 200 international airports.
Price:	US$165
Contact:	Order via website
Tel:	+41 22 770 2751
Web:	www.iata.org

Airport Statistics

Org:	European Regions Airline Association
Freq:	Monthly
Type:	Passenger and freight
Desc:	A monthly traffic analysis which includes passenger, movement and freight data.
Price:	Free
Contact:	Download from website
Tel:	01276 856495
Web:	www.eraa.org

Annual Worldwide Airport Traffic Reports

Org:	Airports Council International
Freq:	Annual
Type:	Common Use Self Service Kiosk
Desc:	Airport traffic statistics covering passenger, cargo (freight and mail) and aircraft movements. PDF and Excel versions available.
Price:	PDF €450, members €225. Excel €1,500, members €600
Contact:	Order from website
Tel:	+41 22 717 8585
Web:	www.airports.org

Association of European Airlines Yearbook

Org:	Association of European Airlines
Freq:	Annual
Type:	Passenger and freight
Desc:	General overview of European airline industry
Price:	Free on website
Web:	www.aea.be

ATOL Business

Org:	Civil Aviation Authority (CAA)
Freq:	Monthly
Type:	Passengers
Desc:	The travel industry's recent performance under their Air Travel Organisers' Licences as well as their projected business.
Price:	Free
Contact:	Download from website
Tel:	020 7379 7311
Web:	www.caa.co.uk

Aviation Facts

Org:	Airport Operators Association
Freq:	Annual
Type:	Passenger and freight
Desc:	Overview of UK airline industry
Price:	Free on website
Web:	www.aoa.org.uk

BAA Airport Traffic Statistics

Org:	BAA plc
Freq:	monthly
Type:	Passenger and freight
Desc:	Comparative airport information
Price:	Free on the website
Contact:	Research Department
Tel:	020 7932 6600
Web:	www.baa.co.uk

Birmingham International Airport - Facts & Statistics

Org:	Birmingham International Airport Ltd
Freq:	Annual
Type:	Passenger and freight
Price:	Free
Contact:	Mark Scourse
Tel:	0121 767 8346
Web:	www.bhx.co.uk

Carrier Tracker

Org:	International Air Transport Association
Freq:	Monthly
Type:	Passenger and freight
Desc:	A monthly analysis by airline of top-line year on year traffic and capacity trends.
Price:	US$675 per year. Bundle deal with Route Tracker costs US$1012.50
Contact:	Download via website
Tel:	+41 22 770 2751
Web:	www.iata.org

Charter Airline Delay League Table

Org:	Air Transport Users Council
Freq:	Annual
Type:	Passenger
Desc:	Charter flight delay statistics.
Price:	Free
Contact:	James Fremantle
Tel:	020 7240 6061
Web:	www.auc.org.uk

Corporate Air Travel Survey - Full Report All Regions

Org:	International Air Transport Association
Freq:	Annual
Type:	Passengers and freight
Desc:	A Survey of long haul business. Contains key information on the behaviour of business travellers and identifies key issues in business air travel.
Price:	Available on request
Contact:	Order via website
Tel:	+41 22 770 2751
Web:	www.iata.org

Custom Statistical Report 1 – Regional Outlook

Org: International Air Transport Association
Freq: Ad hoc
Type: Passenger and freight
Desc: Provides with highlights on the air transport activity in one specific region for one specific year.
Price: US$290 Ad hoc
Contact: Order via website
Tel: +41 22 770 2751
Web: www.iata.org

Custom Statistical Report 2 - Industry Outlook

Org: International Air Transport Association
Freq: Ad hoc
Type: Passenger and freight
Desc: Custom Statistical Reports on specific markets - passenger or freight -, on specific locations - airports or regions - and for specific periods
Price: US$390 Ad hoc; US$3120 12-month Subscription
Contact: Order via website
Tel: +41 22 770 2751
Web: www.iata.org

Custom Statistical Report 3 – Airport Outlook

Org: International Air Transport Association
Freq: Ad hoc
Type: Passenger and freight
Desc: International traffic information for one specific airport for one month or one year
Price: US$490 Ad hoc; US$3920 12-month Subscription
Contact: Order via website
Tel: +41 22 770 2751
Web: www.iata.org

Departing Passenger Survey Reports

Org: Civil Aviation Authority (CAA)
Freq: Annual
Type: Passengers
Desc: Questions on journey purpose, final and intermediate surface origins/destinations, means of transport to and from airports, route flown, country of residence and income
Price: Free if downloaded, £50 on CD
Contact: Download from website or for CD contact Linda Alfred
Tel: 020 7453 6245
Web: www.caa.co.uk

Departure Punctuality

Org: European Regions Airline Association
Freq: Annual
Type: Punctuality figures
Desc: Historical aggrgate punctuality data of ERAA members and reasons for delays
Price: Free
Contact: Download from website
Tel: 01276 856495
Web: www.eraa.org

The Economic & Social Benefits of Air Transport, 2005

Org: Air Transport Action Group
Freq: Ad hoc
Desc: Data, including statistics, on the economic and social benefits of air transport
Price: Free on website
Contact: website
Tel: +41 22 770 2672
Web: www.atag.org

The Economic Impact of Air Service Liberalisation, 2006

Org: Air Transport Action Group
Freq: Ad hoc
Desc: Data, including statistics, on the impact of liberalisation: a study, carried out by InterVISTAS-ga
Price: Free on website
Contact: website
Tel: +41 22 770 2672
Web: www.atag.org

Economic Impact Report, September 2006

Org: Airport Operators Association
Freq: Ad hoc
Desc: The economic and social impact of airports, including some statistics
Price: Free on website
Contact: website
Tel: 020 7222 2249
Web: www.aoa.org.uk

European Leisure Air Travel Survey 2007 (CD-ROM)

Org: International Air Transport Association
Freq: Annual
Type: Passengers
Desc: The needs, attitudes and general preferences of leisure travellers
Price: IATA Member Airline US$1,750; others US$2,250
Contact: Order via website
Tel: +41 22 770 2751
Web: www.iata.org

European Regional Airlines Association Yearbook

Org: European Regions Airline Association
Freq: Annual
Desc: Reference guide to the industry, includes some statistics
Price: £85
Contact: Order form online
Tel: 01276 857038
Web: www.eraa.org

Fast Facts, English

Org: Air Transport Action Group
Freq: Ad hoc
Desc: Flyer detailing the aviation industry's key facts and figures
Price: Free on website
Contact: website
Tel: +41 22 770 2672
Web: www.atag.org

Fleet Information

Org: European Regions Airline Association
Freq: Annual
Type: Aircraft fleet
Desc: Series of seven publications showing fleet of ERAA members by type.
Price: Free
Contact: Download from website
Tel: 01276 856495
Web: www.eraa.org

Freight Forecast 2006-2010 (CD-ROM)

Org: International Air Transport Association
Freq: Annual
Type: Freight
Desc: IATA's outlook for the next 5 years
Price: IATA Member Airline US$849.15; Strategic Partners US$899.10; others US$999
Contact: Order via website
Tel: +41 22 770 2751
Web: www.iata.org

Freight Forecast 2006-2010 (Website Download)

Org: International Air Transport Association
Freq: Annual
Type: Passengers
Desc: IATA's outlook for the next 5 years
Price: IATA Member Airline US$1,610.75; Strategic Partners US$1,705.50; others US$1,895.00
Contact: Download via website
Tel: +41 22 770 2751
Web: www.iata.org

Global Aviation Business Intelligence (GABI)

Org: International Air Transport Association

Freq: Various

Type: Passengers, freight, mail and others

Desc: Subscription based online service that provides key statistical information found in key IATA pubications like Airline Economic Results & Prospects, Airport Capacity and Demand Profiles, Aviation Financial Performance, Freight Forecast, Monthly International Statistics, Passenger Forecast and World Air Transport Statistics

Price: On request

Contact: Customer Service Department

Tel: +1 514 390 6726

Web: www.iata.org

IATA Custom Analysis & Statistical Services

Org: International Air Transport Association

Freq: Annual

Type: Passengers and freight

Desc: Customised analysis an individually tailored reports to meet a specific statistical requirements for monitoring global and regional trends, identifying market opportunities or benchmarking.

Price: Available on request

Contact: bis@iata.org

Tel: +41 22 770 2751

Web: www.iata.org

ICAO Data Website

Org: International Civil Aviation Organisation

Freq: Annual

Desc: Online

Price: £1,050 +

Web: www.icaodata.com

Jane's Air Traffic Control

Org: Jane's Information Group

Freq: Weekly online

Type: Passenger and freight

Desc: Weekly online intelligence review of air traffic control systems, including an annual ATS survey.

Price: Online £980, CD £900, Printed Yearbook £375

Contact: Jenny Beechener

Tel: 020 8700 3700

Web: http://jatc.janes.com

Jane's World Airlines

Org: Jane's Information Group

Freq: Weekly

Type: Passenger and freight

Desc: The structure, business operations and performance of more than 500 of the world's most significant commercial airlines.

Price: Online £1280, CD £1185, Printed Yearbook £920

Contact: Danny Pratt

Tel: 020 8700 3700

Web: jwa.janes.com

Market Characteristics

Org: European Regions Airline Association

Freq: Annual

Type: Passengers

Desc: Historical passeger data for ERAA members.

Price: Free

Contact: Download from website

Tel: 01276 856495

Web: www.eraa.org

Monthly International Statistics

Org: International Air Transport Association

Freq: Monthly

Type: Passenger and freight

Desc: Timely monthly information on carrier traffic and capacity for 115 airlines.

Price: US$1950 per year

Contact: Order via website

Tel: +41 22 770 2751

Web: www.iata.org

Monthly International Passengers & Freight Report

Org: Airports Council International
Freq: Monthly
Type: Passenger and freight
Price: PDF: 1 issue - €75 (members €25), 12 issues €750 (members €250). Excel: 1 issue €300 (members €150), 12 issues: €3,000 (members €1,500)
Contact: Order from website, delivered by email
Tel: +41 22 717 8585
Web: www.airports.org

Monthly Worldwide Airport Traffic Report

Org: Airports Council International
Freq: Monthly
Type: Passenger, freight and aircraft movements
Price: PDF: 1 issue - €75 (members €25), 12 issues €750 (members €250). Excel: 1 issue €300 (members €150), 12 issues: €3,000 (members €1,500)
Contact: Order from website, delivered by email
Tel: +41 22 717 8585
Web: www.airports.org

Monthly Stats Package WATR and IPFR

Org: Airports Council International
Freq: Monthly
Type: Passenger and freight
Desc: Combined International Passengers & Freight Report and Worldwide Airport Traffic Report
Price: PDF: 12 issues €900 (members €400). Excel: 12 issues: €5,500 (members €2,500)
Contact: Order from website, delivered by email
Tel: +41 22 717 8585
Web: www.airports.org

Origin Destination Statistics 2005

Org: International Air Transport Association
Freq: Monthly
Type: Passengers and freight
Desc: Collection of scheduled international passenger, freight and mail statistics. Only available to participating airlines
Price: Available on request
Contact: Order via website
Tel: +41 22 770 2751
Web: www.iata.org

Origin Destination Freight Statistics

Org: International Air Transport Association
Freq: Monthly
Type: Freight
Desc: Collection of international freight Statistics. Only available to participating airlines
Price: Available on request
Contact: Order via website
Tel: +41 22 770 2751
Web: www.iata.org

Origin Destination Statistics Ad-hoc data request

Org: International Air Transport Association
Freq: Ad hoc
Type: Passengers and freight
Desc: Collection of scheduled international passenger, freight and mail statistics. Only available to participating airlines
Price: US$1,500
Contact: Order via website
Tel: +41 22 770 2751
Web: www.iata.org

Passenger Growth

Org: European Regions Airline Association
Freq: Annual
Type: Passengers
Desc: Historical passenger growth data for ERAA members.
Price: Free
Contact: Download from website
Tel: 01276 856495
Web: www.eraa.org

Passenger Forecasts 2006-2010 (CD-ROM)

Org: International Air Transport Association
Freq: Annual
Type: Passengers
Desc: IATA's outlook for the next 5 years
Price: IATA Member Airline US$849.15; Strategic Partners US$899.10; others US$999
Contact: Order via website
Tel: +41 22 770 2751
Web: www.iata.org

Passenger Forecasts 2006-2010 (Website Download)

Org: International Air Transport Association
Freq: Annual
Type: Passengers
Desc: IATA's outlook for the next 5 years
Price: IATA Member Airline US$1,610.75; Strategic Partners US$1,705.50; others US$1,895.0
Contact: Download via website
Tel: +41 22 770 2751
Web: www.iata.org

Passenger Load Factors

Org: European Regions Airline Association
Freq: Annual
Type: Passengers
Desc: Historical passenger load data for ERAA members.
Price: Free
Contact: Download from website
Tel: 01276 856495
Web: www.eraa.org

Regional International

Org: European Regions Airline Association
Freq: Monthly
Desc: ERA's monthly journal, which contains a Business Databank section showing quarterly data on traffic passenger numbers, load factors, along with departure punctuality, regularity and fleet data
Price: Free
Contact: Barry Dunstall, Managing Editor. Latest issue downloadable from website.
Tel: 01276 488039
Web: www.eraa.org

Route Tracker

Org: International Air Transport Association
Freq: Monthly
Type: Passenger and freight
Desc: A monthly analysis of passenger and freight trends for five of the world's major route areas
Price: US$675 per year. Bundled deal with Carrier Tracer costs US$1012.50
Contact: Download via website
Tel: +41 22 770 2751
Web: www.iata.org

SBAC Annual Review

Org: Society of British Aerospace Companies Ltd
Freq: Annual
Type: Passenger and freight
Desc: Includes a summary of the facts and figures of the UK aerospace industry and a review of the various market sectors.
Price: Free
Contact: Download from website
Tel: 020 7091 4500
Web: www.sbac.co.uk

Survey on Apron Incidents/Accidents, 2004

Org: Airports Council International
Freq: Ad hoc
Type: safety incidents/accidents
Price: €40 (members €20)
Contact: Order from website
Tel: +41 22 717 8585
Web: www.airports.org

UK Aerospace Industry Survey - Facts and Figures

Org: Society of British Aerospace
           Companies Ltd
Freq: Annual
Type: Turnover, sales by segment and
           product
Desc: Data taken from SBAC's annual
           survey of the UK aerospace industry.
Price: Free
Contact: Download from website
Tel: 020 7091 4500
Web: www.sbac.co.uk

UK Airline Financial Tables

Org: Civil Aviation Authority (CAA)
Freq: Annual
Type: Airline finances
Desc: Annual Profit and Loss, Airline
           Appropriation & Balance Sheet
           statistics
Price: Free if downloaded. CD £25.
Contact: Download from website or for CD
           contact Linda Alfred
Tel: 020 7453 6245
Web: www.caa.co.uk

UK Airline Statistics - Annual

Org: Civil Aviation Authority (CAA)
Freq: Annual
Type: Passengers, freight, operating and
           Traffic Statistics
Desc: Annual aggregate information on
           each route served together with
           returns of fleet and personnel data
           and, for the major carriers, annual
           standardised profit and loss accounts
           and balance sheets.
Price: Free if downloaded. CD: Annual
           Airlines (excl Financial Suite) £25;
           Airline Financial Statistics £25.
Contact: Download from website or for CD
           contact Linda Alfred
Tel: 020 7453 6245
Web: www.caa.co.uk

UK Airline Statistics - Monthly

Org: Civil Aviation Authority (CAA)
Freq: Monthly
Type: Passengers, freight, operating and
           Traffic Statistics
Desc: Monthly aggregate information on
           each route served together with
           quarterly returns of fleet and
           personnel data and, for major carriers,
           annual standardised P & L accounts
           and balance sheets.
Price: Free
Contact: Download from website
Tel: 020 7379 7311
Web: www.caa.co.uk

UK Airport Statistics - Annual

Org: Civil Aviation Authority (CAA)
Freq: Annual
Type: Passengers, freight and mail
Desc: Statistics from more than 60 UK
           Airports. Information is supplied on
           each individual air transport flight
           with other movements.
Price: Free if downloaded, £25 on CD
Contact: Download from website or for CD
           contact Linda Alfred
Tel: 020 7453 6245
Web: www.caa.co.uk

UK Airport Statistics - Monthly

Org: Civil Aviation Authority (CAA)
Freq: Monthly
Type: Passengers, freight and mail
Desc: Statistics from more than 60 UK
            Airports. Information is supplied on
            each individual air transport flight
            with other movements.
Price: Free
Contact: Download from website
Tel: 020 7379 7311
Web: www.caa.co.uk

UK Punctuality Statistics - Monthly

Org: Civil Aviation Authority (CAA)
Freq: Monthly
Type: Operations
Desc: Detailed and summary punctuality
            statistics for 10 UK Airports
Price: Free
Contact: Download from website
Tel: 020 7379 7311
Web: www.caa.co.uk

UK Punctuality Statistics - Annual

Org: Civil Aviation Authority (CAA)
Freq: Annual
Type: Operations
Desc: Detailed and summary punctuality
            statistics for 10 UK Airports
Price: Free if downloaded. CD detailed £50,
            summary £25
Contact: Download from website or for CD
            contact Linda Alfred
Tel: 020 7453 6245
Web: www.caa.co.uk

World Air Transport Statistics – website download

Org: International Air Transport
            Association
Freq: Annual
Type: Passenger and freight
Desc: Contains detailed information for
            over 200 of IATA's member airlines as
            well as summary top line analysis of
            industry trends. (Book in PDF
            format, WATS data in MS Excel)
Price: IATA Member Airline US$809.1;
            Strategic Partners US$845.06; others
            US$899
Contact: Download via website
Tel: +41 22 770 2751
Web: www.iata.org

World Air Transport Statistics – Book and CD ROM

Org: International Air Transport
            Association
Freq: Annual
Type: Passenger and freight
Desc: Contains detailed information for
            over 200 of IATA's member airlines as
            well as summary top line analysis of
            industry trends
Price: IATA Member Airline US$629.10;
            Strategic Partners US$664.05; others
            US$699
Contact: Purchase via website
Tel: +41 22 770 2751
Web: www.iata.org

World Air Transport Statistics – Book and CD ROM, plus monthly updates

Org: International Air Transport Association

Freq: Annual

Type: Passenger and freight

Desc: Contains detailed information for over 200 of IATA's member airlines as well as summary top line analysis of industry trends. (Book + CD ROM. Monthly data updates are delivered to your email).

Price: IATA Member Airline US$898.20; Strategic Partners US$948.10; others US$998

Contact: Purchase via website

Tel: +41 22 770 2751

Web: www.iata.org

World Air Transport Statistics - 10 year traffic results

Org: International Air Transport Association

Freq: Annual

Type: Passenger and freight

Desc: Contains detailed information for 10 years on over 200 of IATA's member airlines as well as summary top line analysis of industry trends

Price: IATA Member Airline US$1,601; Strategic Partners US$1,691; others US$1,799

Contact: Download from website

Tel: +41 22 770 2751

Web: www.iata.org

Worldwide and Regional Forecasts, Airport Traffic 2005-2020

Org: Airports Council International

Freq: Annual

Type: Passengers and freight

Desc: Overview of the current and future trends of the air transport industry. PDF and print version available

Price: €300, members €150

Contact: Order from website

Tel: +41 22 717 8585

Web: www.airports.org

The Railway Consultancy Ltd
Specialists in Planning Economics and Management

The Railway Consultancy is a specialist consultancy with a keen understanding of the railway industry and its data. Train Operators, freight shippers, Central and local government have all found us useful through our practical and creative approach to solving problems associated with railway planning, economics and management.

Our key areas of expertise include:

- **Management Consultancy & Business Planning**
- **Operational Planning & Simulation**
- **Demand & Revenue Forecasting**
- **Data Collection & Analysis**
- **Project Appraisal**

1st Floor South Tower
Crystal Palace Station
London SE19 2AZ

T +44 20 8676 0395
F +44 20 8778 7439
E info@railcons.com
www.railcons.com

Registered Office: 43a Palace Square, Crystal Palace, London SE19 2LT Registered in England & Wales no. 3270536

Rail

International Railway Statistics
Org: International Union of Railways
Freq: Annual
Type: Passenger and freight
Desc: Composition and resources of railway systems, operating results and financial results
Price: € 245
Country: France
Tel: +33 1 44 49 20 20
Web: www.uic.asso.fr

Jane's Locomotives and Rolling Stock Forecasts
Org: Jane's Information Group
Freq: Annual
Type: Passenger and freight
Desc: Country-by-country strategic analysis of the current and future trends in the global locomotive and rolling-stock markets.
Price: Online £1090, Printed £760
Contact: David Burns
Tel: 020 8700 3700
Web: jhmt.janes.com

Jane's World Railways

Org: Jane's Information Group
Freq: Ad hoc
Type: Passenger and freight
Desc: The structure, business operations and performance of railways in 120 countries
Price: Online £1200, CD £1115, Printed Yearbook £515
Contact: Ken Harris
Tel: 020 8700 3700
Web: jwa.janes.com

Metro Report

Org: Railway Gazette International
Freq: Annual
Type: Passenger
Desc: Worldwide urban rail features/surveys statistics and city reports.
Price: £30 or free with annual subscription to Railway Gazette. Order online.
Contact: Chris Jackson
Tel: 0208 652 8608
Web: www.railwaygazette.com

National Rail Perfromance Reports

Org: London Watch
Freq: Quarterly
Type: Passenger
Desc: Quarterly operating performance of South East train companies.
Price: Free
Tel: 020 7505 9000
Web: www.londontravelwatch.org.uk

National Rail Trends

Org: Office of Rail Regulation
Freq: Quarterly
Desc: Usage and performance of trains
Price: Free
Tel: 020 7282 2000
Web: www.rail-reg.gov.uk

Passenger Transport By Rail In 2004-2005

Org: Eurostat
Freq: Annual
Type: Passengers
Desc: Focuses on developments in different Member States in national and international rail passenger transport.
Price: Free
Contact: Download via website
Tel: 01633 813369
Web: epp.eurostat.ec.europa.eu

Quarterly Statistics - UIC

Org: International Union of Railways
Freq: Quarterly
Type: Passenger and freight
Desc: Recent global trends for passenger and freight traffic in Europe, covering operator's traffic and infrastructure managers performance, access via website
Price: Free
Contact: Olivier Georger
Country: France
Tel: +33 1 44 49 20 20
Web: www.uic.asso.fr

Rail Freight Transport 2005

Org: Eurostat
Freq: Annual
Type: Freight
Desc: Based on the annual and quarterly freight transport statistics reported according to the Regulation 91/2003.
Price: Free
Contact: Download via website
Tel: 01633 813369
Web: epp.eurostat.ec.europa.eu

Railisa Database

Org: International Union of Railways
Freq: Daily
Type: Passenger, freight, infrastructure, staff and rolling stock
Desc: Contains statistics data of the UIC Railways. Access via website
Price: Free
Contact: Olivier Georger
Country: France
Tel: +33 1 44 49 20 20
Web: www.uic.asso.fr

Rail Industry Monitor (5 volumes)

Org: The TAS Partnership Ltd
Freq: Annual
Type: Passenger and freight
Desc: General statistics, covering the market for rail services, public spending and support, vehicles and investment, the passenger railway and the freight railway.
Price: £235 PDF, £240 CDROM, £260 Printed version.
Contact: Philip Higgs
Tel: 01772 204988
Web: www.tas-part.co.uk

Railway time-series Data

Org: International Union of Railways
Type: Passenger and freight
Desc: Trends in key railway statistical data
Price: € 230
Contact: Olivier Georger
Country: France
Tel: +33 1 44 49 20 20
Web: www.uic.asso.fr

Rail transport accidents in the European Union in 2004-2005

Org: Eurostat
Freq: Annual
Type: Passengers
Desc: The types of accidents and categories of victims.
Price: Free
Contact: Download via website
Tel: 01633 813369
Web: epp.eurostat.ec.europa.eu

Station Usage

Org: Office of Rail Regulation
Freq: Annual
Desc: Estimates of the total numbers of people entering, exiting and interchanging at stations.
Price: Free
Tel: 020 7282 2000
Web: www.rail-reg.gov.uk

Road

AID Passenger Car Parc Study

Org: Automotive Industry Data Ltd
Freq: Annual
Desc: Analysis of vehicles in use throughout Western Europe
Price: £1375 / €1990
Tel:: 01926 410040
Web: www.eagleaid.com

Annual Casualty Figures Summary

Org: West Sussex County Council
Freq: Annual
Type: Passenger
Desc: Annual traffic accident data
Price: Free on website
Tel: 01243 777100
Web: www.westsussex.gov.uk

Automotive Data Services

Org: Society of Motor Manufacturers and Traders
Freq: Regular
Desc: Source for UK data on production, exports, parc and used vehicle transactions. Also collates world data on new registrations, production, exports and parc. Produces standard and tailored reports.
Price: Price depends on the nature of the information required
Tel: 020 7235 7000

Automotive Focus

Org: Society of Motor Manufacturers and Traders
Freq: Quarterly
Desc: Free quarterly snapshot of new vehicle registrations, production and trade.
Price: Free on website
Tel: 020 7235 8278
Web: www.smmt.co.uk

Breakdown Britain 2006

Org: RAC plc
Freq: Annual
Type: Passenger
Desc: Report focuses on why vehicles breakdown as well as considering how the modern motoring experience has altered.
Price: Free on web
Contact: Media Centre
Web: www.racnews.co.uk

Bus and Coach Statistics

Org: Scottish Executive
Freq: Annual
Type: Passenger
Desc: Trends in bus and coach services in Scotland
Price: Free on the website
Tel: 0131 556 8400
Web: www.scotland.gov.uk

Bus Industry Monitor

Org: The TAS Partnership Ltd
Freq: Annual
Type: Passenger
Desc: The market for bus services; industry structure and ownership; public spending & support; investment & fleet analysis; industry performance; and company reports
Price: £299 PDF, £299 CDROM, £325 Printed version. PDFs of volumes: Vol 1,2 and 5 £35 each, Vol 3 £39, Vol 4 £53, Vol 6 £167
Contact: Philip Higgs
Tel: 01772 204988
Web: www.tas-part.co.uk

Bus Quality Indicators

Org: Department for Transport
Freq: Quarterly
Type: Passenger
Desc: Quarterly bulletin. Download from website
Price: Free
Contact: Iain Ritchie
Tel: 020 7944 4139.
Web: www.dft.gov.uk

Car Aftermarket in Europe, 2007

Org: Datamonitor
Freq: Annual
Desc: Key developments in the European Aftermarket, highlighting changes in market size and structure. Download from website
Price: US$2295
Tel: 020 7675 7000
Web: www.datamonitor.com

Castrol Business Services Car Servicing Trend Tracker - January 2006

Freq: Bi-annual
Org: Trend Tracker Ltd
Type: Passenger
Desc: Contains both primary consumer research data and secondary data on the aftermarket.
Price: £345 or £625 both Castrol reports
Contact: Robert MacNab
Tel: 870 421 4350
Web: www.trendtracker.co.uk

Castrol Business Services Car Repair Trend Tracker 2006

Freq: Bi-annual
Org: Trend Tracker Ltd
Type: Passenger
Desc: Focuses on the repair and MoT test Markets.
Price: £345 or £625 both Castrol reports
Contact: Robert MacNab
Tel: 870 421 4350
Web: www.trendtracker.co.uk

Casualty Report 2005 and Road Safety Plan (2006/07)
Org: Oxfordshire County Council
Freq: Annual
Type: Passenger and freight
Desc: Summary of accident data in county.
Price: Free
Contact: Environmental Services
Tel: 01865 792422
Web: www.oxfordshire.gov.uk

CAT Distribution Trend Index
Freq: Bi-annual
Org: Trend Tracker Ltd
Type: Passenger
Desc: B2B research into motor factors, accessory shops, franchised dealer parts departments and independent garages.
Price: £425 per year, £245 per report
Contact: Robert MacNab
Tel: 870 421 4350
Web: www.trendtracker.co.uk

Concessionary Fares UK
Org: The TAS Partnership Ltd
Freq: Annual
Type: Passenger
Desc: Totals for spending on concessions in different parts of the country, with trend and unit cost data. Data on the qualifying population and an understanding of the influences on demand.
Price: £69.50 PDF, £79
Contact: Philip Higgs
Tel: 01772 204988
Web: www.tas-part.co.uk

Compendium of Motorcycling Statistics
Org: Department for Transport
Freq: Annual
Type: Passenger
Desc: Statistics on motorcycle use from a range of sources, including ownership, purchases stocks, traffic, crime and accidents.
Price: Free
Tel: 020 7944 3095
Web: www.dft.gov.uk

Casualty Figures And Crash Data
Org: Kent County Council
Freq: Annual
Type: Passenger
Desc: Personal injury statistics
Price: Summary data free on website. Detailed statistics on application
Contact: Kent Highway Services
Tel: 08458 247 800
Web: www.kent.gov.uk

Cycling – Personal Travel Factsheet
Org: Department for Transport
Freq: Ad hoc
Type: Passenger
Desc: Statistical report
Price: Free on the website
Contact: National Travel Survey
Tel: 020 7944 3097
Web: www.dft.gov.uk

Datamonitor Aftermarket - Fleet Market Overview
Org: Datamonitor
Freq: Annual
Desc: An overview of the fleet sector and the operational leasing market in key European markets.
Price: On application
Tel: 020 7675 7000
Web: www.datamonitor.com

EU Road Safety 2004: Regional Differences
Org: Eurostat
Freq: Annual
Type: Passengers
Desc: The number of fatalities per million passenger cars registered both in EU & CC countries and with division to NUTS 2.
Price: Free
Contact: Download via website
Tel: 01633 813369
Web: epp.eurostat.ec.europa.eu

European Aftermarket Database 2007 (15 Markets)

Org:	Datamonitor
Freq:	Annual
Desc:	Quantifies the value and volume of key aftermarket product groups and distribution channels in 15 countries.
Price:	On application
Tel:	020 7675 7000
Web:	www.datamonitor.com

European Aftermarket Database 2007 (5 Markets)

Org:	Datamonitor
Freq:	Annual
Desc:	Quantifies the value and volume of key aftermarket product groups and distribution channels in 5 countries.
Price:	On application
Tel:	020 7675 7000
Web:	www.datamonitor.com

European Aftermarket Database 2006 (25 Markets)

Org:	Datamonitor
Freq:	Annual
Desc:	Quantifies the value and volume of key aftermarket product groups and distribution channels in 25 countries
Price:	On application
Tel:	020 7675 7000
Web:	www.datamonitor.com

European Fleet Market Database 2006 (25 Markets)

Org:	Datamonitor
Freq:	Annual
Desc:	Insight into the market dynamics of 25 key European fleet markets
Price:	Price on application
Tel:	020 7675 7000
Web:	www.datamonitor.com

European Fleet Market Database - Top 7 Markets

Org:	Datamonitor
Freq:	Annual
Desc:	Insight into the market dynamics of the leading 7 European fleet markets.
Price:	US$18,995
Tel:	020 7675 7000
Web:	www.datamonitor.com

European Fleet Lessor Database 2006

Org:	Datamonitor
Freq:	Annual
Desc:	This database gives a detailed overview of leading players in the fleet market, providing market positioning by country.
Price:	On application
Tel:	020 7675 7000
Web:	www.datamonitor.com

European Road Statistics

Org:	European Union Road Federation
Freq:	Annual
Desc:	Comprehensive collection of data on road networks
Price:	Free on website
Tel:	+41 22 306 0260
Web:	www.erf.be

Facts and Figures – Transport 2000

Org:	Transport 2000 Trust
Freq:	Regular
Type:	Passenger
Desc:	Various statistics on road transport from the National Travel Survey and others
Price:	Free on web
Web:	www.transport2000.org.uk

Fleet Statistics

Org:	Fleet Audits Ltd
Freq:	Ad hoc
Type:	Passenger and freight
Desc:	Various
Price:	On special request
Contact:	Stewart Whyte
Tel:	01730 266666
Web:	www.fleet–audits.com

Focus on Freight 2006

Org: Department for Transport
Freq: Tri-annual
Type: Freight
Desc: Statistical focus report
Price: £33 from The Stationary Office or
free on the website
Tel: 020 7944 3095
Web: www.dft.gov.uk

The Future of the Car Body Repair Market 2006

Org: Trend Tracker Ltd
Type: Passenger
Desc: The structure and future
development of the car body repair
market in the UK.
Price: £795
Contact: Robert MacNab
Tel: 870 421 4350
Web: www.trendtracker.co.uk

The Future of the Used Car Market 2006

Org: Trend Tracker Ltd
Type: Passenger
Desc: The structure and future
development of the used car market
in the UK.
Price: £795
Contact: Robert MacNab
Tel: 870 421 4350
Web: www.trendtracker.co.uk

Goods Vehicle Operating Costs

Org: Road Haulage Association
Freq: Annual
Type: Freight
Desc: Survey of real costs from a large
range and sample of road transport
companies
Price: Free for members on website
Contact: Brian Fish
Tel: 0117 938 0400
Web: www.rha.net

Hampshire Local Transport Plan 2006-2011

Org: Hampshire County Council
Freq: Ad hoc
Type: Passenger
Desc: Includes indicators and targets for
road transport in Hampshire
Price: Free on website
Tel: 01962 870 500
Web: www.hants.gov.uk

Hampshire Road Safety Statistics

Org: Hampshire County Council
Freq: Annual
Type: Passenger
Desc: Data from surveys in Hampshire
Price: Free on website
Tel: 01962 870 500
Web: www.hants.gov.uk

Hertfordshire Traffic and Transport Data Report

Org: Hertfordshire County Council
Freq: Annual
Type: Passenger and freight
Desc: Report covers changes in road based
traffic movements in the country and
compares it with national changes.
Price: Free on website
Contact: Sue Jackson
Tel: 01992 558615
Web   http://www.hertsdirect.org/
yrccouncil/hcc/env/plan/transplan/

Jane's Urban Transport System

Org: Jane's Information Group
Freq: Monthly online
Type: Passenger and freight
Desc: Review of the transoprt systems of
over 155 cities around the world
Price: Online £1,140, CD £1060, Printed
£495
Contact: Mary Webb
Tel: 020 8700 3700
Web: juts.janes.com/public/
juts/index.shtml

Key Road Accident Statistics

Org: Scottish Executive
Freq: Annual
Type: Passenger
Desc: Key statistics on injury road accidents in Scotland
Price: Free on website
Tel: 0131 244 7256
Web: www.scotland.gov.uk

Latest Figues on the Urban Bus Fleet in the European Union

Org: International Association of Public Transport
Freq: 2007
Desc: CD
Price: €80.00
Web: www.uitp.org

Local Transport Plan 2006 - 2011

Org: Northamptonshire County Council
Freq: Annual
Type: Passenger
Desc: Includes statistics covering details of traffic flows, accident data, street lighting, air quality, public transport within the county of Northamptonshire
Price: Free
Contact: Chris Wragg
Tel: 01604 654411
Web: www.northamptonshire.gov.uk

Manager's Fuel Price Information Service

Org: Freight Transport Association
Freq: Quarterly
Type: Freight
Price: Subscription/Membership
Tel: 08717 11 22 22
Web: www.fta.co.uk

Manager Guide to Distribution Costs

Org: Freight Transport Association
Freq: Quarterly
Type: Freight
Price: Subscription/Membership
Tel: 08717 11 22 22
Web: www.fta.co.uk

Millennium Cities Database for Sustainable Transport

Org: International Union for Public Transport
Freq: 2000
Desc: Statistics on 100 cities on CD
Price: €800.00
Web: www.uitp.org

Milton Keynes Intelligence Observatory

Org: Milton Keynes Council
Freq: Annual
Type: Passenger
Desc: A one-stop-shop for information about Milton Keynes and the surrounding area, including transport information
Price: Free on website
Tel: 01908 691691
Web: www.mkiobservatory.org.uk

Monthly Statistics - SMMT

Org: Society of Motor Manufacturers and Traders
Freq: Monthly
Type: Passenger and freight
Desc: free monthly data on vehicle registrations and production and used vehicle sales.
Web: www.smmt.co.uk

Monthly Statistical Review

Org: Society of Motor Manufacturers and Traders
Freq: Monthly
Type: Passenger and freight
Desc: Monthly statistics and commentary covering UK and international production and new registrations; quarterly updates of used vehicle transactions and an annual update of PARC and UK overseas trade.
Contact: msrweb@smmt.co.uk
Price: PDF (email) annual sub: Members (£150), Non-members (£220). Hard copy annual sub: Members (£155), Non-members (£225). PDF single copy Members (£40), Non-members (£50).Hard copy single copy: Members (£40), Non-mmbers (£50).
Web: www.smmt.co.uk

Motor Cycle Industry - Pocket Guide

Org: Motor Cycle Industry Association Ltd
Freq: Annual
Type: Passenger
Desc: The association also offers a range of statistical services including standardised and bespoke reports on all aspects of the motorcycle industry.
Price: Free
Web: www.mcia.co.uk

Motor Industry Facts 2007

Org: Society of Motor Manufacturers and Traders
Freq: Annual
Type: Passenger and freight
Desc: pocket-sized guide to facts and figures for the UK automotive sector.
Price: Download Free on website
Web: www.smmt.co.uk

Motor Industry of Great Britain – World Automotive Statistics

Org: Society of Motor Manufacturers and Traders
Freq: Annual
Desc: A guide to trends in the UK and world automotive sector. Available in paper hardcopy or fully indexed CD-ROM
Price: Members £125. Non-members £175. application
Web: www.smmt.co.uk

Motoring towards 2050 – Shopping and Transport Policy

Org: RAC Foundation
Freq: One
Type: Passenger
Desc: Independent enquiry published 2006
Price: Free on web
Web: www.racfoundation.org.uk

Motorstat Express

Org: Society of Motor Manufacturers and Traders
Freq: Fortnightly
Type: Passenger
Desc: Subscription for members
Price: £125
Web: www.smmt.gov.uk

Motor Vehicle Registration Information System (MVRIS)

Org: Society of Motor Manufacturers and Traders
Freq: Regular
Desc: Comprehensive source of new registration details in the UK. Produces standard and tailored reports for members (at discounted rates), and for the general public
Price: Price depends on the nature of the information required
Tel: 020 7235 7000

National Road Maintenance Condition Survey: Bulletin

Org: Department for Transport
Freq: Annual
Desc: Report on the condition of public roads, footways, kerbs and verges in England and Wales.
Price: Free on the website
Contact: roadmaintenance.stats@dft.gov.uk
Tel: 020 7944 3095
Web: www.dft.gov.uk

New Vehicle Regstrations (UK)

Org: Society of Motor Manufacturers and Traders
Freq: Regular
Desc: Covers cars, buses and coaches, LGVs, HCVs with data broken down by body type, and model range. Data can be supplied in standard format or be tailored to your exact requirements.
Price: Depends on vehicle type and nature of information. Non-member prices range from £428 to £6890
Tel: 020 7235 8278
Web: www.smmt.co.uk

Northern Ireland Road and Rail Transport Statistics Quarterly Bulletin

Org: Northern Ireland: Department for Regional Development
Freq: Quarterly
Type: Passenger and freight
Desc: Northern Ireland Road and Rail Transport quarterly statistics.
Price: Free
Tel: 028 9054 0801
Web: www.drdni.gov.uk/index/statistics.htm

Park and Ride Great Britain 2007

Org: The TAS Partnership Ltd
Freq: Annual
Type: Passenger
Desc: An analysis of schemes and expenditure, looking at both the extent and type of provision.
Price: £49 PDF, £579
Contact: Philip Higgs
Tel: 01772 204988
Web: www.tas-part.co.uk

Motoring Report 2006

Org: RAC plc
Freq: Annual
Type: Passenger
Desc: Research into the views of UK motorists.
Price: Free on web
Contact: Media Centre
Web: www.racnews.co.uk

Road File

Org: Road Users Alliance
Freq: Annual
Type: Passenger
Price: Free on web
Web: www.rua.org.uk

Selected Statistics on bus and coach transport in Europe

Org: International Road Transport Union (IRU)
Type: Passenger
Desc: Hard copy
Price: CHF 50
Web: www.iru.org

Selected Statistics on bus and coach transport in Europe

Org: International Road Transport Union (IRU)
Type: Freight
Desc: Hard copy
Price: CHF 50
Web: www.iru.org

The Regional Dimension of Road Freight Transport Statistics

Org: Eurostat
Freq: Annual
Type: Freight
Desc: Series of maps that present the NUTS 2 regions in relation to goods transport journeys which started or ended at their territory.
Price: Free
Contact: Download via website
Tel: 01633 813369
Web: epp.eurostat.ec.europa.eu

Road Casualties in Great Britain, 2005

Org: Department for Transport
Freq: Annual
Type: Passenger
Desc: Contains final figures giving detailed information on the number of people killed and injured on the roads in Great Britain in 2005
Price: Free download on website. £25 print version from The Stationery Office.
Contact: roadacc.stats@dft.gsi.gov.uk
Tel: 020 7944 6595
Web: www.dft.gov.uk

Road Casualties in West Sussex

Org: West Sussex County Council
Freq: Annual
Type: Passenger and freight
Desc: Road casualty report
Price: Free and free summry on website
Tel: 01243 777100
Web: www.westsussex.gov.uk

Road Freight Statistics, 2005

Org: Department for Transport
Freq: Annual
Type: Passenger and freight
Desc: Data on the activities of UK-registered heavy goods vehicles, both domestically and internationally, non-UK registered heavy goods vehicles in Great Britain, and GB-registered vans.
Contact: Download via website
Price: Free
Tel: (0)20 7944 4261
Web: www.dft.gov.uk

Road Freight Transport By Type Of Goods 1999-2004

Org: Eurostat
Freq: Annual
Type: Freight
Desc: Main trends in road freight transport for national, international, cross-trade and cabotage transport.
Price: Free
Contact: Download via website
Tel: 01633 813369
Web: epp.eurostat.ec.europa.eu

Road freight transport 1999-2004: cabotage and transport with non-EU countries

Org: Eurostat
Freq: Annual
Type: Freight
Desc: Main trends in road freight transport for cabotage transport.
Price: Free
Contact: Download via website
Tel: 01633 813369
Web: epp.eurostat.ec.europa.eu

Road Freight Transport 2000-2004: Average Vehicle Load And Regional Aspects

Org: Eurostat
Freq: Annual
Type: Freight
Desc: Average vehicle load is analysed by national and international transport and also broken down by load capacity of the vehicle and by distance class. Regional data goes down to NUTS level 1 and 3.
Price: Free
Contact: Download via website
Tel: 01633 813369
Web: epp.eurostat.ec.europa.eu

Road Goods Vehicles Travelling to Mainland Europe 2007

Org: Department for Transport
Freq: Quarterly
Type: Freight
Desc: Number of road goods vehicles travelling to mainland Europe from Great Britain
Price: Free on website
Contact: roadfreight.stats@dft.gsi.gov.uk
Tel: 020 7944 3093.
Web: www.dft.gov.uk

Road Traffic Statistics

Org: Department for Transport
Freq: Annual
Type: Passenger and freight
Desc: Traffic data, information of road lengths and vehicles. Download from website
Price: Free
Tel: 020 7944 3095
Web: www.dft.gov.uk

Schmidt's 2006 Auto Aid

Org: Automotive Industry Data Ltd
Freq: Annual
Desc: Forecasts of the European truck market and truck markets in other key countries
Price: Price: Book £385/€560. CD-ROM £410/€610
Tel::   01926 410040
Web: www.eagleaid.com

Schmidt's Diesel Car Prospects to 2011

Org: Automotive Industry Data Ltd
Freq: Annual
Desc: Market sales and forecasts of the Western European diesel car market.
Price: £1828/€2710/US$3475
Tel::   01926 410040
Web: www.eagleaid.com

Schmidt's 2006 Truck Aid

Org: Automotive Industry Data Ltd
Freq: Annual
Desc: Forecasts of the Western European truck market
Price: Price: Book £435 / €645. CD-ROM £470/€695. Book + CD-ROM: £610/€905
Tel::   01926 410040
Web: www.eagleaid.com

Surrey Road Casualty Report

Org: Surrey County Council
Freq: Annual
Desc: A Summary showing an analysis of casualties in the latest year and long term trends in casualties and accidents. Available in hardcopy and electronic copy (via email or Web)
Price: Free
Contact: SCC Contact Centre
Tel: 08456 009 009
Web: www.surreycc.gov.uk

Traffic and Collisions in Cornwall 2006

Org: Local Intelligence Network Cornwall (LINC) - Cornwall County Council
Freq: Annual
Type: Passenger and freight
Desc: Summary of traffic and accident in Cornwall
Price: Free on website
Contact: Ben Bolton
Tel: 01872 323556
Web: www.cornwallstatistics.org.uk

Traffic and Transport Statistics Including Accident Data - Leeds

Org: Leeds City Council
Freq: Constantly updated
Type: Passenger
Desc: Various reports covering transport in West Yorkshire
Price: On application
Contact: Ray Heywood. Transport Policy Monitoring
Tel: 01132 2476342
Web: www.leeds.gov.uk

Traffic in Great Britain

Org: Department for Transport
Freq: Annual
Type: Passenger and freight
Desc: Data on traffic levels
Price: Free
Tel: 020 7944 3095
Web: www.dft.gov.uk

Traffic Speeds In English Urban Area, 2004

Org: Department for Transport
Freq: Bi-annual
Type: Passenger and freight
Desc: Bulletin
Price: Free
Contact: vehicles.stats@dft.gov.uk
Tel: 020 7944 3046
Web: www.dft.gov.uk

Transport Monitoring – Data Summaries

Org: Oxfordshire County Council
Freq: Annual
Type: Passenger and freight
Desc: Summary of traffic counts in county
Price: Free on website
Contact: Transport Monitoring Team
Tel: 01865 815574
Web: www.oxfordshire.gov.uk

Transport In The Urban Enviroment

Org: The Institution of Highways and Transportation
Desc: Reference work for practitioners in the fields of highway and traffic engineering, transportation and town planning
Price: £49
Contact: IHT Office Manager
Tel: 020 7391 9970
Web: www.iht.org.uk

Transport of Goods by Road in Great Britain, 2004

Org: Department for Transport
Freq: Annual
Type: Freight
Desc: Bulletin of annual report of the continuing survey of road goods transport. Now Superceded by 'Road Freight Statistics'
Price: Free
Tel: 020 7944 4261
Web: www.dft.gov.uk

Travel by Scottish Residents: some National Travel Survey results

Org: Scottish Executive
Freq: Ad hoc
Type: Passenger
Desc: Travel within Great Britain by Scottish residents
Price: Free on website
Tel: 01397 795 001
Web: www.scotland.gov.uk

Trends In Road Freight Transport 1999 - 2005

Org: Eurostat
Freq: Annual
Type: Freight
Desc: Main trends in road freight transport for national, international, cross-trade and cabotage transport.
Price: Free
Contact: Download via website
Tel: 01633 813369
Web: epp.eurostat.ec.europa.eu

Urban Public Transport - Statistics

Org: International Association of Public Transport
Freq: Annual
Desc: Statistics on 310 public urban networks
Price: €100.00
Web: www.uitp.org

Used Vehicle Sales

Org: Society of Motor Manufacturers and Traders
Freq: Regular
Desc: Data can be used to create customised reports, from simple reports detailing volumes of sales within a local area, or complex reports mapping sales across the whole of Great Britain.
Price: Varies by data required
Tel: 020 7235 8278
Web: www.smmt.co.uk

Used Vehicle Sales – Vehicles in Use

Org: Society of Motor Manufacturers and Traders
Freq: Regular
Desc: Series of reports produced by SMMT's Motorparc service: a set of standard reports is produced annually which can be either purchased in whole or as an extract. Alternatively, individually tailored Report can be provided.
Price: Varies by data required
Tel: 020 7235 8278
Web: www.smmt.co.uk

Vehicle & Fuel Statistics – Natural Gas Vehicles Duty

Org: Natural Gas Vehicle Association
Freq: Annual
Desc: Web
Price: Free
Web: www.ngva.org.uk

Vehicle Data Sales - Vehicle Data Sales-Production & Exports

Org: Society of Motor Manufacturers and Traders
Freq: Regular
Desc: Monthly UK production and quarterly exports of vehicles by manufacturer and model.
Price: On application.
Tel: 020 7235 8278
Web: www.smmt.co.uk

Vehicle Licensing Statistics

Org: Department for Transport
Freq: Annual
Type: Passengers and freight
Desc: Bulletin. Downloadable from website
Price: Free on website
Tel: 020 7944 3095
Web: www.dft.gov.uk

Vehicle Operator and Services Agency Corporate Reports: 2007-2008 Report Suite

Org: Vehicle & Operator Services Agency
Freq: Annual
Type: Passenger and freight
Desc: These include the yearly Business Plan, and successive Annual Report and Accounts, and Effectiveness Report for 2007-2008. Effectiveness report is a detailed breakdown of the Vehicle Inspectorate activities with commentary on the state of the various vehicle fleets
Price: Free
Tel: 0870 6060440
Web: www.vosa.gov.uk

Vehicle Recall Database

Org: Vehicle & Operator Services Agency
Freq: Annual
Type: Passenger and freight
Desc: Records all UK recalls from manufacturers, broken down by month manufacturer and model.
Price: Free
Tel: 0870 6060440
Web: www.vosa.gov.uk

Vehicle Speeds in Great Britain: Bulletin

Org: Department for Transport
Freq: Annual
Desc: Bulletin. Downloadable from website
Price: Free on website
Tel: 020 7944 3095
Web: www.dft.gov.uk

Welsh Local Government Finance Statistics, 2006

Org: National Assembly for Wales
           (Transport Statistics)
Freq: Annual
Type: Passenger and freight
Desc: Annual report on local authorities
           including expenditure on roads and
           transport
Price: Free on website
Contact: stats.transport@wales.gsi.gov.uk
Tel: 029 2082 5085
Web: www.wales.gov.uk

Welsh Transport Statistics

Org: National Assembly for Wales
           (Transport Statistics)
Freq: Annual
Type: Passenger and freight
Desc: Transport Statistics covering a variety
           of topics.
Price: Free on website
Contact: stats.transport@wales.gsi.gov.uk
Tel: 029 2082 5085
Web: www.wales.gov.uk

West Sussex Transport Plan

Org: West Sussex County Council
Freq: Annual
Type: Passenger and freight
Desc: Data in traffic flows, accidents etc.
Price: Free on website
Tel: 01243 777100
Web: www.westsussex.gov.uk

World Automotive Market Report

Org: Educational & Research Foundation
           of MEMA Inc and Overseas
           Automotive Council (OAC)
Freq: Annual
Type: Passenger and freight
Desc: Production/assembly, vehicle census
           summary, U.S. automotive parts trade,
           world trade in new vehicles and world
           motor vehicle markets.
Price: $75 for OAC members and members
           of MEMA market segment, $200 for
           non-members
Contact: Download from Website
Web: www.mema.org
Tel: +1 919 549 4800

The World's Automotive Industry

Org: International Organisation of Motor
           Vehicle Manufacturers
Freq: Annual
Desc: Statistics on production and exports
Price: Free on website
Tel: +331 43 59 00 13
Web: www.oica.net

World Road Statistics

Org: International Road Federation
Freq: Annual
Desc: Comprehensive collection of data on
           road networks
Price: Book CHF 300 Pdf CHF 200
Tel: +41 22 306 0260
Web: www.irfnet.org

World Transport Statistics

Org: International Road Transport Union
           (IRU)
Type: Passenger and Freight
Desc: Hard copy
Price: CHF 75
Web: www.iru.org

The World's Automotive Industry

Org: International Organisation of Motor
Vehicle Manufacturers
Freq: Annual
Type: Passenger and freight
Desc: Statistics on production and key
figures on the global motor industry
Price: Free on website
Tel: +331 43 59 00 13
Web: www.oica.net

Maritime

AMOR - The APEX Monthly Oil Review

Org: Lloyd's Maritime Intelligence Unit
Freq: Monthly
Type: Freight
Desc: Overview of the latest trends in
tanker supply and seaborne oil trades.
Price: £1500
Contact: Sales
Tel: 020 7017 5788
Web: www.lloydsmiu.com

Annual Cruise Holiday Market Digest UK And Europe, 2006

Org: IRN Research
Freq: Annual
Type: Passenger
Desc: Detailed statistical analysis of the UK
cruise market
Price: £300 + VAT
Contact: Fred Hitchins
Tel: 0121 635 5210
Web: www.irn-research.com

Annual Reefer Shipping Market Review and Forecast 2006/07

Org: Drewry Shipping Consultants Ltd
Freq: Annual
Type: Freight
Desc: Data on the demand for cargo, supply
of tonnage, reefer vehicles and reefer
economics.
Price: PDF £1195. PDF and printed £1290
Tel: 020 7538 0191
Web: www.drewry.co.uk

Annual Review of the Global Container Terminal Operators, 2006

Org: Drewry Shipping Consultants Ltd
Freq: Annual
Type: Freight
Desc: Includes regional and operator
capacity projections, throughput data
etc.
Price: PDF £1195. PDF and printed £1290
Tel: 020 7538 0191
Web: www.drewry.co.uk

APEX (Analysis of Petroleum Exports) Database

Org: Lloyd's Maritime Intelligence Unit
Freq: Twice Weekly
Desc: Contains port specific accounts of all
crude laden voyages in tankers over
10,000 dwt and all product laden
voyages in tankers over 60,000 dwt.
Price: On application
Contact: Sales
Tel: 020 7017 5788
Web: www.lloydsmiu.com

APEX Trade Reports: Yearly Tanker Review

Org: Lloyd's Maritime Intelligence Unit
Freq: Annual
Desc: A report utilising data from the
APEX Database. Historical
breakdown of a given year's tanker
trade and broken down by vessel size,
vessel age and trade route
Price: £1500
Contact: Sales
Tel: 020 7017 5788
Web: www.lloydsmiu.com

APEX Trade Reports: APEX Oil Exports Roundup

Org: Lloyd's Maritime Intelligence Unit
Freq: Monthly
Desc: A monthly synopsis of crude oil trade, showing seaborne crude import and export volumes to and from the most significant regions.
Price: £2500
Contact: Sales
Tel: 020 7017 5788
Web: www.lloydsmiu.com

APEX Trade Reports: Middle East Oil Exports Report

Org: Lloyd's Maritime Intelligence Unit
Freq: Weekly
Desc: Report showing oil leaving the Middle East with all the latest Middle East sailings and Crude Oil on the Water broken down by export direction (East or West) and route (via Suez, via Sumed, via Cape).
Price: £1800
Contact: Sales
Tel: 020 7017 5788
Web: www.lloydsmiu.com

Autumn 2006 IndustryTrends Survey

Org: British Marine Industries Federation
Freq: Spring and Autumn
Type: Passengers
Desc: Detailed the state of the UK marine industry.
Price: Free on website
Tel: 01784 473377
Web: www.britishmarine.co.uk

British Shipping - Annual Review

Org: Chamber of Shipping
Freq: Annual
Price: Free on web
Web: www.british-shipping.org

British Ports Association Review

Org: British Ports Association
Freq: Annual
Type: Passenger and freight
Price: Free on web
Web: www.britishports.org.uk

BRL Marine Database

Org: BRL Shipping Consultants
Freq: Various
Type: Vessels
Desc: Online database holding the following information: newbuild data (worldwide newbuild orderbook), contracts under negotiation, commercially trading fleet, scrapped vessels, vessel events, comprehensive contact details
Price: Contact for quotation
Tel: 020 8316 2005
Web: www.brldata.com

BRL Market Analysis

Org: BRL Shipping Consultants
Freq: Various
Type: Vessels
Desc: Bespoke data services on shipbuilding and sales market. Includes: specialist data reports; statistics/graphical analysis; complex data analysis and consulting services.
Price: Contact for quotation
Tel: 020 8316 2005
Web: www.brldata.com

Car Carriers: The Fast Lane of International Shipping

Org: Drewry Shipping Consultants Ltd
Freq: Annual
Type: Freight
Desc: Includes world vehicle trade to 2015, port and terminal operations etc.
Price: PDF £1195. PDF and printed £1290
Tel: 020 7538 0191
Web: www.drewry.co.uk

Chemical Forecaster

Org: Drewry Shipping Consultants Ltd
Freq: Quarterly
Type: Freight
Desc: Analysis and forecast of all key market variables.
Price: PDF £1995, PDF and hardcopy £2250 per year
Tel: 020 7538 0191
Web: www.drewry.co.uk

Container Capacity Forecast

Org:	MDS Transmodal
Freq:	Quarterly
Type:	Freight
Desc:	Three year forecast of containership supply by route and operator.
Price:	On application
Tel:	01244 348301
Web:	www.mdst.co.uk

Container Forecaster

Org:	Drewry Shipping Consultants Ltd
Freq:	Quarterly
Type:	Freight
Desc:	Analysis and forecast of all key market variables.
Price:	£2500 per year
Tel:	020 7538 0191
Web:	www.drewry.co.uk

Container Freight Rate Insight

Org:	Drewry Shipping Consultants Ltd
Freq:	Bi-monthly
Type:	Freight
Desc:	Freight rates, including access to Containerbenchmark.com and interative online database.
Price:	£750 per year
Tel:	020 7538 0191
Web:	www.drewry.co.uk

Container Shipper Insight

Org:	Drewry Shipping Consultants Ltd
Freq:	Quarterly
Type:	Freight
Desc:	Freight rates benchmarks, supply/demand forecasts by route, and schedule reliability indicators.
Price:	£860 per year
Tel:	020 7538 0191
Web:	www.drewry.co.uk

Containership Databank

Org:	MDS Transmodal
Freq:	Quarterly
Type:	Freight
Desc:	The world standard containership deployment database supplied on CD
Price:	£2,200
Tel:	01244 348301
Web:	www.mdst.co.uk

Cruise Industry Statistical Review 2005

Org:	GP Wild International Ltd
Freq:	Annual
Type:	Passenger
Desc:	Industry Statistical Report
Price:	£425
Contact:	G P Wild
Tel:	01444 413931
Web:	www.gpwild.com

Dover Harbour – Annual and Monthly Traffic Statistics

Org:	Dover Harbour Board
Freq:	Annual/monthly
Type:	Passenger
Price:	Free on web
Web:	www.doverport.co.uk

Dry Bulk Insight

Org:	Drewry Shipping Consultants Ltd
Freq:	Monthly
Type:	Freight
Desc:	Analysis of the dry bulk market.
Price:	£500 per year
Tel:	020 7538 0191
Web:	www.drewry.co.uk

Dry Bulk Forecaster

Org:	Drewry Shipping Consultants Ltd
Freq:	Quarterly
Type:	Freight
Desc:	Analysis and forecast of all key market variables.
Price:	PDF £1725, PDF and hardcopy £1895 per year
Tel:	020 7538 0191
Web:	www.drewry.co.uk

Drewry Annual Container Market Review and Forecast, 2006/07

Org: Drewry Shipping Consultants Ltd
Freq: Annual
Type: Freight
Desc: Data on container trade growth, structure of the container fleet, global demand/supply balance to 2011 and freight and charter rates.
Price: PDF £1195. PDF and printed £1290
Tel: 020 7538 0191
Web: www.drewry.co.uk

Economic Benefits of UK Leisure Boating Industry

Org: British Marine Industries Federation
Freq: Annual
Price: Free on web
Tel: 01784 223615
Web: www.britishmarine.co.uk

The European Ferry Industry – A Business in Transition

Org: Drewry Shipping Consultants Ltd
Freq: Ad hoc
Type: Freight
Desc: Data and analysis of the ferry market.
Price: PDF £495. PDF and printed £690
Tel: 020 7538 0191
Web: www.drewry.co.uk

Ferrystat: PSA Monthly Digest of Ferry Statistics

Org: IRN Research
Freq: Monthly
Type: Passenger
Desc: Passenger, car and coach traffic, based on the monthly returns of all leading UK ferry operators
Price: £650 + VAT per annum
Contact: Fred Hitchins
Tel: 0121 635 5210
Web: www.irn-research.com

Focus on Ports 2006

Org: Department for Transport
Freq: Ad hoc
Type: Freight
Desc: Statistical information about commercially active UK ports, including trends in traffic since the 1960s for unitised cargo types such as containers, road goods vehicles and trailers, and by broad commodity groups Statistical focus report
Price: £40 or free on website
Contact: Steve Wellington
Tel: 020 7944 4131
Web: www.dft.gov.uk

Global Energy and the Prospects for the LNG Trades to 2020

Org: GP Wild International Ltd
Freq: Ad hoc
Type: Freight
Desc: Covers the international energy market, the current market for LNG, receiving and export LNG terminals, analysis of the current LNG tanker fleet, new vessels under construction and shipyards involved.
Price: £850
Contact: Peter Wild
Tel: 01444 413931
Web: www.gpwild.com

Global Ports - Major Coal & Ore Ports

Org: SSY Consultancy And Research Ltd
Freq: Continuous
Type: Passenger and Freight
Desc: Details on over 500 ports and berths including over 110 new port entries including details of the latest expansion plans.
Price: £395
Tel: 020 7977 7404
Web: www.ssyonline.com

HSC Incident Statistics – High Speed Craft

Org: Royal Institution of Naval Architects
Freq: 2004
Type: Passenger
Price: £10
Tel: 020 7235 4622
Web: www.rina.org.uk

Implications of Fleet Changes for Cruise Market Prospects to 2014

Org: GP Wild International Ltd
Freq: Ad hoc
Type: Passenger
Desc: Future study of cruise passenger ships.
Price: £750
Contact: Peter Wild
Tel: 01444 413931
Web: www.gpwild.com

Inland Waterways Freight Transport in Europe in 2005

Org: Eurostat
Freq: Annual
Type: Freight
Desc: Data on inland waterways freight transport in Europe for 2005, covering the Member States and the Candidate Countries.
Price: Free
Contact: Download via website
Tel: 01633 813369
Web: epp.eurostat.ec.europa.eu

International Cruise Market Monitor 2005

Org: GP Wild International Ltd
Freq: Quarterly
Type: Passenger
Desc: Industry Statistical Report
Price: £415 harcopy or pdf. £425 hardcopy and pdf
Contact: G P Wild
Tel: 01444 413931
Web: www.gpwild.com

Jane's High Speed Marine Transportation

Org: Jane's Information Group
Freq: Monthly online
Type: Passenger and freight
Desc: Coverage of the world's high-speed vessels and their operators.
Price: £1,110 online, £1025 CD. Yearbook £425
Contact: Stephen J Phillips
Tel: 020 8700 3700
Web: www.janes.com

Lloyd's Casualty Reporting Service

Org: Lloyd's Maritime Intelligence Unit
Freq: Continuous
Desc: Database from which tailor made reports on causalities can be generated.
Price: On application
Contact: Sales
Tel: 020 7017 5788
Web: www.lloydsmiu.com

Lloyd's MIU Data Services

Org: Lloyd's Maritime Intelligence Unit
Freq: Continuous
Desc: Service to answer bespoke requests for data and information on the following areas: Vessel Movements, Vessel Characteristics, Ownership, Casualty. Port State Control, Ports, AIS Data
Price: On application
Contact: Data sales
Tel: 020 7017 4625
Web: www.lloydsmiu.com

Lloyd's Shipping Index

Org: Lloyd's Maritime Intelligence Unit
Freq: Weekly
Desc: Publication providing important up to date data on shipping movements from all over the globe.
Price: £1700
Contact: Sales
Tel: 020 7017 5788
Web: www.lloydsmiu.com

Lloyd's Shipping Information Database
Org: Lloyd's Maritime Intelligence Unit
Freq: Quarterly
Desc: CDROM holding information on vessels, owners, characteristics, and casualty statistics.
Price: £999
Contact: Sales
Tel: 020 7017 5788
Web: www.lloydsmiu.com

Lloyd's List Ports of the World 2007
Org: Lloyd's Maritime Intelligence Unit
Freq: Quarterly
Desc: Port directory plus information on vessel and port statistics.
Price: £269
Contact: Sales
Tel: 020 7017 5788
Web: www.lloydsmiu.com

Lloyd's Maritime Directory 2007
Org: Lloyd's Maritime Intelligence Unit
Freq: Quarterly
Desc: Directory of IMO numbers, owners, vessels, fleets, towage & salvage and off- shore services, plus global maritime statistics
Price: £345
Contact: Sales
Tel: 020 7017 5788
Web: www.lloydsmiu.com

Lloyd's Register Fairplay Ships Data Service
Org: Lloyd's Register Fairplay
Freq: Continuous
Type: Passenger and Freight
Desc: Data service allowing customised data to be extracted from 20 databases, covering ships, companies and ports information
Price: On application
Tel: 01737 379000
Web: www.lrfairplay.com

LPG Insight
Org: Drewry Shipping Consultants Ltd
Freq: Monthly
Type: Freight
Desc: Analysis of the LPG market.
Price: £500 per year
Tel: 020 7538 0191
Web: www.drewry.co.uk

LPG Forecaster
Org: Drewry Shipping Consultants Ltd
Freq: Quarterly
Type: Freight
Desc: Analysis and forecast of all key market variables.
Price: PDF £1725, PDF and hardcopy £1895 per year
Tel: 020 7538 0191
Web: www.drewry.co.uk

Maritime Statistics
Org: Department for Transport
Freq: Annual
Type: Passenger and freight
Desc: Report contains figures giving detailed information on port traffic, and UK and world fleet statistics.
Price: £36 hardcopy (from TSO), of free via website.
Contact: maritime.stats@dft.gov.uk
Tel: 020 7944 4131
Web: www.dft.gov.uk

Maritime transport of goods and passengers 1997-2004
Org: Eurostat
Freq: Annual
Type: Passengers and Freight
Desc: Gross weight of goods handled in European ports is presented by country and for the main ports. Passengers embarked and disembarked in European ports are presented by country and for the main ports
Price: Free
Contact: Download via website
Tel: 01633 813369
Web: epp.eurostat.ec.europa.eu

Market Information: Dry Cargo

Org: SSY Consultancy And Research Ltd
Freq: Continuous
Type: Freight
Desc: Series of dry cargo charts (some of which are free on the website) and dry cargo report (for SSY members only).
Price: £395
Tel: 020 7977 7404
Web: www.ssyonline.com

Market Information: Tankers

Org: SSY Consultancy And Research Ltd
Freq: Continuous
Type: Freight
Desc: Series of tanker data charts (some of which are free on the website) and reports - Dirty Fixture Report, Clean Fixture Report and Tanker Report - for SSY members only.
Price: On application
Tel: 020 7977 7404
Web: www.ssyonline.com

Market Information: Sales and Purchase

Org: SSY Consultancy And Research Ltd
Freq: Continuous
Type: Freight
Desc: Series of data charts (some of which are free on the website) and the Sales and Purchase report (for SSY members only).
Price: On application
Tel: 020 7977 7404
Web: www.ssyonline.com

Monthly Container Port Monitor

Org: Institute of Shipping Economics and Logistics (ISL)
Freq: Annual
Type: Freight
Desc: Shipping markets, world shipbuilding, world port traffic, sea canals
Price: Hard Copy/online €365
Tel: +49 421 220 960
Web: www.isl.org

Monthly Shipping Review

Org: SSY Consultancy And Research Ltd
Freq: Monthly
Type: Freight
Desc: Trade movements publication.
Price: £395
Tel: 020 7977 7404
Web: www.ssyonline.com

Monthly World Newbuilding Enquiry

Org: BRL Shipping Consultants
Freq: Quarterly
Type: Vessels
Desc: Detailing all vessels on order worldwide plus business under negotiation or planned. Includes newbuild statistics.
Price: £200 per year
Tel: 020 8316 2005
Web: www.brldata.com

Oil Tanker Intelligence Service (OTIS)

Org: Lloyd's Maritime Intelligence Unit
Freq: Weekly
Desc: First alert service shows changes in volumes from major producing regions, allowing clients to anticipate crude inventory changes in key consuming regions.
Price: On application
Contact: Sales
Tel: 020 7017 5788
Web: www.lloydsmiu.com

Port of Dover, Ferry Traffic Statistics

Org: Dover Harbour Board
Freq: Monthly and annual
Type: Passenger and freight
Desc: Summary of monthly traffic statistics
Price: Free on website
Contact: marketing@doverport.co.uk
Tel: 01304 240 400
Web: www.doverport.co.uk

Provisional Port Statistics, 2006

Org: Department for Transport
Freq: Annual
Type: Passenger and freight
Desc: National Statistics on freight traffic handled at UK ports in 2006.
Price: Free via website.
Contact: steve.wellington@dft.gsi.gov.uk
Tel: 020 7944 4131
Web: www.dft.gov.uk

Quarterly World Newbuilding Enquiry

Org: BRL Shipping Consultants
Freq: Quarterly
Type: Vessels
Desc: Detailing all vessels on order world-wide plus business under negotiation or planned. Includes cumulative Shipyard deliveries and newbuild statistics.
Price: £100 per year
Tel: 020 8316 2005
Web: www.brldata.com

Sea Web: Lloyd's Register of Ships Online

Org: Lloyd's Register Fairplay
Freq: Continuous
Type: Passenger and Freight
Desc: An online maritime reference tool, combining ships, companies, shipbuilders, fixtures, casualties, port state control, ISM, real-time positions and historic vessel movements data into a single application
Price: Singe user £1420. Company User (up to 5 users) £2475.
Tel: 01737 379000
Web: www.sea-web.com

Shipbuilding Market Forecast

Org: Lloyd's Register - Fairplay Ltd
Freq: Monthly
Type: Passenger and Freight
Desc: Detailed analysis of the current order book, world fleet summary and newbuilding forecast, for ships over 100 GT, over the next five years.
Price: £730 per year
Tel: 01737 379000
Web: www.lrfairplay.com

Shipping Insight (UK/Europe)

Org: Drewry Shipping Consultants Ltd
Freq: Monthly
Type: Freight
Desc: Data on fixture and sale listing o dry cargo and freight market related data.
Price: PDF £725, PDF and hardcopy £815 per year
Tel: 020 7538 0191
Web: www.drewry.co.uk

Shipping-markets.com

Org: Lloyd's Register - Fairplay Ltd and Maritime Research Inc
Freq: Continuous
Type: Freight
Desc: Online integrated markets information system with data on tanker and dry bulk markets, including the latest fixtures, ship sales, newbuildings and market background information.
Price: Single user £1470. Company User (up to five users) £2415.
Tel: 01737 379000
Web: www.shipping-markets.com/

Shipping Markets Forecast

Org: Lloyd's Register - Fairplay Ltd
Freq: Twice yearly
Type: Passenger and Freight
Desc: Series of three reports covering: the passenger, liquid and dry cargo markets
Price: £415 each or £578 all three
Tel: 01737 379000
Web: www.lrfairplay.com

Shipping Statistics and Market Review

Org: Institute of Shipping Economics and Logistics (ISL)
Freq: Annual
Type: Freight
Desc: Shipping markets, world shipbuilding, world port traffic, sea canals
Price: Hard Copy/online €395
Country: World
Tel: +49 421 220 960
Web: www.isl.org

Shipping Statistics Yearbook

Org: Institute of Shipping Economics and Logistics (ISL)
Freq: Annual
Type: Freight
Desc: Shipping markets, world shipbuilding, world port traffic, sea canals
Price: Hard Copy/online €270
Country: World
Tel: +49 421 220 960
Web: www.isl.org

Short Sea Shipping of goods 2000-2004

Org: Eurostat
Freq: Annual
Type: Freight
Desc: Transport of goods between ports in the EU 25, Bulgaria, Romania and Norway, on the one hand, and ports situated in geographical Europe, the Mediterranean and the Black Sea on the other hand.
Price: Free
Contact: Download via website
Tel: 01633 813369
Web: epp.eurostat.ec.europa.eu

Society of Maritime Industries Information System (SMIIS)

Org: Society of Maritime Industries
Type: Passenger and Freight
Desc: Subscription and product search service
Price: £495 full service for members
Tel: 020 7928 9199
Web: www.maritimeindustries.org

SSY's Bulk Trade Monitor

Org: SSY Consultancy And Research Ltd
Freq: Quarterly
Type: Freight
Desc: Quarterly forecasts of shipping demand for all major dry bulk commodities plus fleet analysis, new buildings for the year ahead.
Price: £775
Tel: 020 7977 7404
Web: www.ssyonline.com

SSY's Coal Trade Monitor

Org: SSY Consultancy And Research Ltd
Freq: Quarterly
Type: Freight
Desc: Global and regional forecast of steam and coking coal trades for four-year forecast period on route-by-route basis
Price: £1900
Tel: 020 7977 7404
Web: www.ssyonline.com

The Survey of UK Short Sea Freight RoRo and LoLo Capacity 2007

Org: PRB Associates Limited
Freq: Annual
Type: Freight
Desc: Short Sea freight RoRo and LoLo market survey, analysis and report with detailed service, port and vessel information in appendices.
Price: £500 for first time, £150 for existing subscribers
Tel: 01472 353532
Web: www.prbassociates.co.uk

Tanker Insight

Org: Drewry Shipping Consultants Ltd
Freq: Monthly
Type: Freight
Desc: Analysis of the tanker market.
Price: £500 per year
Tel: 020 7538 0191
Web: www.drewry.co.uk

Tanker Forecaster

Org: Drewry Shipping Consultants Ltd
Freq: Quarterly
Type: Freight
Desc: Analysis and forecast of all key market variables.
Price: PDF £1725, PDF and hardcopy £1895 per year
Tel: 020 7538 0191
Web: www.drewry.co.uk

UK Leisure Marine Industry Bulletin

Org: British Marine Industries Federation
Freq: Annual
Price: Free on web
Tel: 01784 223615
Web: www.britishmarine.co.uk

UK Leisure and Small Commercial Marine Industry Key Performance Indicators

Org: British Marine Industries Federation
Freq: Annual
Type: Passengers
Desc: Detailed information on the marine industry of leisure and small commercial craft for a range of economic indicators, from turnover and value added to exports and employment.
Price: Free on website
Tel: 01784 473377
Web: www.britishmarine.co.uk

UK Seafarer Statistics: 2006

Org: Department for Transport
Freq: Annual
Type: Passenger and freight
Desc: National Statistics on seafarers
Price: Free via website.
Contact: maritime.stats@dft.gov.uk
Tel: 020 7944 4131
Web: www.dft.gov.uk

VLCC and Suezmax Weekly Monitor

Org: Lloyd's Maritime Intelligence Unit
Freq: Twice Weekly
Type: Freight
Desc: Details current vessel status, load and discharge ports and ETAs, including laden tanker movements by port of load/discharge
Price: On application
Contact: Sales
Tel: 020 7017 5788
Web: www.lloydsmiu.com

Waterborne Freight Benchmark Report

Org: Department for Transport
Freq: Ad hoc
Type: Passenger and freight
Desc: Inventory of waterway track, wharves and craft in GB
Price: Free via website.
Contact: Maritime Statistics Branch of Department for Transport (DfT),
Tel: 020 7944 4131
Web: www.dft.gov.uk

Waterborne freight in the United Kingdom: 2005

Org: Department for Transport
Freq: Annual
Type: Passenger and freight
Desc: National Statistics on freight traffic carried on UK inland waters, around the UK coast, to and from UK offshore installations and sea dredging.
Price: Free via website.
Contact: Maritime Statistics Branch of Department for Transport (DfT),
Tel: 020 7944 4131
Web: www.dft.gov.uk

Watersports and Leisure Participation Survey, 2006

Org: British Marine Industries Federation
Freq: Annual
Type: Passengers
Desc: Details participation amongst adults in a range of 21 different activities
Price: Free on website
Tel: 01784 473377
Web: www.britishmarine.co.uk

Weekly Newbuilding Contracts Report

Org: BRL Shipping Consultants
Freq: Weekly
Type: Vessels
Desc: A seven day overview of newbuilding contracts placed and newbuilding contracts planned or under negotiation
Price: £500 per year
Tel: 020 8316 2005
Web: www.brldata.com

World Casualty Statistics

Org: Lloyd's Fairplay
Freq: Annual
Type: Freight and passenger
Desc: Produced annually, this publication lists all vessels removed from the propelled sea-going merchant fleet, as Losses or Disposals.
Price: £260
Tel: 01737 379180
Web: www.irfairplay.com

World Fleet Statistics

Org: Lloyd's Fairplay
Freq: Annual
Type: Freight and passenger
Desc: This annual publication shows the composition of the current self-propelled, sea-going merchant fleet of 100 GT or above.
Price: £260
Tel: 01737 379180
Web: www.irfairplay.com

World Oil Tanker Trends

Org: SSY Consultancy And Research Ltd
Freq: Semi-annual
Type: Freight
Desc: A statistical review/outlook of tanker market.
Price: £350 annual subscription
Tel: 020 7977 7404
Web: www.ssyonline.com

World Shipbuilding Statistics

Org: Lloyd's Fairplay
Freq: Quarterly
Type: Freight
Desc: Quarterly summary of the shipbuilding activity for all self-propelled, sea-going merchant ships of 100 GT or above.
Price: £360 annual subscription
Tel: 01737 379180
Web: www.irfairplay.com

All Modes

Annual Review of London Travel Watch

Org: London Travel Watch
Freq: Annual
Type: Passenger
Desc: Narrative review of committee's work
Price: Free
Tel: 020 7505 9000
Web: www.londontravelwatch.org.uk

Annual Bulletin of Transport Statistics for Europe and North America

Org: United Nations
Freq: Annual
Type: Passenger and freight
Desc: General statistical data
Price: $48
Web: www.un.org

Britain Inbound 2007

Org: Visit Britain
Freq: Annual
Type: Passenger
Desc: Overview of overseas visitors to the UK
Price: Free on website
Contact: david.edwards@visitbritain.org
Tel: 020 8846 9000
Web: www.visitbritain.com

Key Tourism Facts

Org: Visit Britain
Freq: Ongoing
Price: Free on web
Tel: 020 8846 9000
Web: www.visitbritain.com

Energy, transport and environment indicators pocketbook

Org: Eurostat
Freq: Annual
Type: Passenger and freight
Desc: An overview of the most relevant indicators on energy, transport and environment, with particular focus on sustainable development.
Price: Free on website. €13 in hardcopy.
Country: Luxembourg
Tel: +352 4301 34580
Web: europa.eu.int/comm/eurostat

European Travel Monitor - World Travel Monitor

Org: IPK International
Freq: Annual
Type: Passenger
Desc: Continuous survey measuring the outbound travel demand and travel behavior of the Europeans in all Western and Eastern European countries.
Price: On application. The costs for a complete standard outbound / set of tables report vary from 6,000 EUR to 20,000 EUR. Costs for single data: Minimum 300 EUR
Contact: Barbara Partel
Country: Germany
Tel: +49 8982 92370
Web: www.ipkinternational.com

Eurostat Transport Database

Org: Eurostat
Freq: Annual
Type: Passenger and freight
Desc: Online database to Eurostat's transport information covering all modes
Price: Free
Contact: Download data from website –
Tel: 01633 652699
Web: epp.eurostat.ec.europa.eu

External Trade Statistics

Org: Business And Trade Statistics Ltd
Freq: Monthly
Price: Depends on the amount and type of data required
Tel: 01372 463121

Focus on Personal Travel, 2005

Org: Department for Transport
Freq: Every four years
Type: Passenger
Desc: Statistical focus report. This is designed to bring together information about personal travel in Great Britain.
Price: Free on website
Tel: 020 7944 2164
Web: www.dft.gov.uk

Foresight

Org: Visit Britain
Freq: Monthly
Type: Passenger
Desc: Monthly commentary on significant issues within the tourism sector, including figures on inbound tourism.
Price: Free on website
Contact: david.edwards@visitbritain.org
Tel: 020 8846 9000
Web: www.visitbritain.com

Generation Project" A forecast study about travel behavior in 2010 and 2020

Org: IPK International
Freq: Annual
Type: Passenger
Desc: The outbound travel behavior of the Germans, British, French, Dutch, Italians, Belgians, Spanish, Swedish, Canadians, US-Americans and Russians forecasted on the basis of the comprehensive World Travel Monitor data pool.
Price: Any other single market € 20,000. Price deductions for two and more markets: all Eleven markets € 95,000
Contact: Barbara Partel
Country: Germany
Tel: +49 8982 92370
Web: www.ipkinternational.com

Highways and Transportation – Statistics based on Actuals 2004/05

Org: Chartered Institute of Public Finance and Accountancy (CIPFA)
Freq: Annual
Price: £85
Tel: 020 8667 1144
Web: www.cipfastats.net

Highways and Transportation – Statistics based on Estimates 2006/07

Org: Chartered Institute of Public Finance and Accountancy (CIPFA)
Freq: Annual
Price: £85
Tel: 020 8667 1144
Web: www.cipfastats.net

Inbound Tourism Statistics & Research

Org: Visit Britain
Freq: Monthly
Type: Passenger
Desc: Data on overseas visitors to the UK based on the International Passenger Survey.
Price: Free on website
Contact: david.edwards@visitbritain.org
Tel: 020 8846 9000
Web: www.visitbritain.com

International Passenger Survey

Org: MDS Transmodal
Freq: Quarterly
Type: Passenger
Desc: Passenger movements
Price: Bespoke
Contact: Mrs Meda Frost
Tel: 01244 348301
Web: www.mdst.co.uk

International Passenger Survey (IPS)

Org: IRN Research
Freq: Ad hoc
Type: Passenger
Desc: Statistical analysis of in/outbound passengers to/from UK
Price: On application
Contact: Fred Hitchins
Tel: 0121 635 5210
Web: www.irn-research.com

Jane's Urban Transport

Pub: Jane's Information Group
Freq: Monthly
Desc: Surveys the systems, manufacturers and consultants within the global market, including traffic statistics
Price: Online £1140, CD £1060, Yearbook £495
Tel: 020 8700 3700
Email: customerservices.uk@janes.com
Web: http://juts.janes.com

London Travel Report

Org: Transport for London
Freq: Annual
Type: Passenger and freight
Desc: London travel patterns and employment/demographic background
Price: Free
Web: www.tfl.gov.uk

Manager's Fuel Price Information Service

Org: Freight Transport Association
Freq: Monthly
Desc: Bulk prices used for gas oil. Only available to FTA members.
Price: On application
Contact: FTA Members services
Tel: 08717 11 22 22.
Web: www.fta.co.uk

Marine, Aviation and Transport (MAT) Insurance & Non-MAT Reinsurance Statistics

Org: Association of British Insurers
Freq: Annual
Type: Passengers and freight
Desc: Statistics on premiums split by Direct & Facultative Premiums and Reinsurance Treaties Accepted, claims, underwriting results, commission and expenses, change in provisions, and equalisation reserves for annual and funded business
Price: Summary statistics free on web. Annual subscription to detailed data £110
Tel: 0207 600 3333
Web: www.abi.org.uk

Monthly Bulletin of Statistics Online

Org: United Nations
Freq: Various
Type: Passenger and freight
Desc: Generic statistical database which includes transportation data (International maritime freight transport, registrations of new motor vehicles, civil aviation traffic)
Price: $635 for profit organisations, £370 for non-profit
Web: www.un.org

Motor Insurance Statistics

Org: Association of British Insurers
Freq: Annual
Type: Passengers and freight
Desc: Statistics on premiums and claims, commission and expenses, change in provisions, equalisation reserves, underwriting result, operating ratios, and overseas data, for the UK and worldwide
Price: Summary statistics free on web. Annual subscription to detailed data £150
Tel: 0207 600 3333
Web: www.abi.org.uk

National Travel Survey

Org: Department for Transport
Freq: Annual
Type: Passenger
Desc: A household survey designed to provide a databank of personal travel information for Great Britain.
Price: Free
Contact: national.travelsurvey@dft.gov.uk
Tel: 020 7944 3097
Web: www.dft.gov.uk

Northern Ireland Transport Statistics Annual

Org: Northern Ireland: Department for Regional Development
Freq: Annual
Type: Passenger and freight
Desc: Transport statistics for Northern Ireland
Price: Free on website
Contact: Miss Stephanie Diffin
Tel: 028 9054 0801
Web: www.doeni.gov.uk/statistics/doestats.htm

Northern Ireland Road and Rail Transport Statistics

Org: Northern Ireland: Department for Regional Development
Freq: Quarterly
Type: Passenger and freight
Desc: Road and rail statistics for Northern Ireland
Price: Free on website
Contact: Miss Stephanie Diffin
Tel: 028 9054 0801
Web: www.doeni.gov.uk/statistics/doestats.htm

Northern Ireland Travel Survey

Org: Northern Ireland: Department for Regional Development
Freq: Annual
Type: Passengers
Desc: The source of information on how, over the region as a whole, people as individuals or family groups use different forms of transport to meet their travel needs.
Price: Free on website
Contact: Department for Regional Development (Northern Ireland) Roads Service.
Tel: 028 9054 0022
Web: www.doeni.gov.uk/statistics/doestats.htm

On The Move 2006 – FACTS 2006

Org: Confederation of Passenger Transport UK
Freq: Annual
Type: Passenger
Desc: Summary of key data
Price: Free
Web: www.cpt-uk.org

Operational Performance Report

Org: Transport for London
Freq: Quarterly
Type: Passenger and freight
Desc: Data on service provision and reliability.
Price: Free
Web: www.tfl.gov.uk

Outbound Travel Information & Booking Behavior of the Europeans, 2006

Org: IPK International
Freq: Ad hoc
Type: Passenger
Desc: Data based on the IPK European Travel Monitor, it shows data on booking behaviour exhibited by the Europeans relative their outbound holiday trips.
Price: 2,850 EUR
Contact: Barbara Partel
Country: Germany
Tel: +49 8982 92370
Web: www.ipkinternational.com

Passenger Transport in the European Union, 2006

Org: Eurostat
Freq: Annual
Type: Passenger
Desc: Data on passenger transport in the EU Member States, and EFTA countries. The figures are presented at country level and includes all inland transport modes.
Price: Free on website
Tel: 01633 652699
Web: epp.eurostat.ec.europa.eu

Petroleum Review: Retail Marketing Survey

Org: Energy Institute
Freq: Annual
Type: Passenger and freight
Desc: A comprehensive review of forecourt retailing in the UK, including the number of vehicles registered in the UK
Price: Free as part of subscription to Petroleum Review. However, individual copies may be purchased for £50.
Contact: Chris Baker
Tel: 020 7467 7114
Web: www.energyinst.org.uk

Petroleum Statistics Service

Org: Energy Institute
Freq: Regular
Price: £80 annual to non-members
Tel: 0207 467 7100
Web: www.energyinst.org.uk

Rapid Transit Monitor 2006

Org: The TAS Partnership Ltd
Freq: Ad hoc
Type: Passenger and freight
Desc: Has data on light rail systems, underground systems, bus rapid transit and rapid transit planning and finance.
Price: £215 hardcopy; £195 CD-Rim, £190 PDF.
Tel: 01729 840756
Web: www.tas-part.co.uk

Regional Transport Statistics

Org: Department for Transport
Freq: Annual
Type: Passenger and freight
Desc: Brings together a wide range of transport statistics for Great Britain and Northern Ireland at Government Office Region and former Metropolitan County level.
Price: Free on website
Contact: publicationgeneral.enq@dft.gsi.gov.uk
Tel: 020 7944 3098
Web: www.dft.gov.uk

Scottish Household Survey

Org: Scottish Executive
Freq: Annual
Type: Passenger
Desc: Information about bus and car availability, frequency of driving, walking, cycling, travel; to work and school
Price: Free on website
Tel: 0131 556 8400
Web: www.scotland.gov.uk

Scottish Transport Statistics

Org: Scottish Executive
Freq: Annual
Type: Passenger and freight
Desc: Has figures on road vehicles, traffic, accidents, toll bridges, bus and rail passengers, road and rail freight, air and water transport ,finance, personal travel and international comparisons.
Price: Free on website
Tel: 0131 244 7256
Web: www.scotland.gov.uk

Scottish Transport Review

Org: Scottish Transport Studies Group
Freq: Quarterly
Type: Both
Desc: Updated statistics for Scotland and general articles, news.
Price: Free on web
Web: www.stsg.org

SPT – Statistics & trends

Org: Strathclyde Partnership for Transport
Freq: Annual
Type: Passenger
Desc: Statistics relating to travel in west central Scotland, which cover all major public transport modes.
Price: Free
Web: www.spt.co.uk

Public Transport Statistical Report

Org: International Union (Association) of Public Transport
Freq: Frequent but irregular
Type: Passenger
Desc: Each issue provides in–depth data on a specific topic of strategic importance for the sector.
Price: Summary data free on website, more detailed statistics on a CDROM, € 80
Contact: Jerome Pourbaix (statistics@uitp.org)
Tel: +32 2 673 6100
Web: www.uitp.com

Short-term Trends in Transport

Org: European Conference of Ministers of Transport (ECMT)
Freq: Quarterly
Type: Passenger and freight
Desc: Monthly and quarterly general statistical data on road, rail and inland waterways. Covers all European countries.
Price: Free on website
Contact: Mario Barreto
Tel: +33 1 4524 9722
Web: www.cemt.org

Tourism Trends & Forecasts

Org: Visit Britain
Freq: Annual wth mid year update
Type: Passenger
Desc: Forecasts of both the volume and value of inbound tourism
Price: Free on website
Contact: david.edwards@visitbritain.org
Tel: 020 8846 9000
Web: www.visitbritain.com

Transport by air and sea - National and international intra- and extra-EU - Data 2004/2005 - CD-ROM 2007 edition

Org: Eurostat
Freq: Annual
Type: Passenger and freight
Desc: Detailed statistics on passenger and freight transport by air and sea for the EU Member States, Canada, Candidate and EEA countries 2004/2005
Price: 20 EUR
Tel: 01633 652699
Web: epp.eurostat.ec.europa.eu

Transport - Kent

Org: Kent County Council
Freq: Annual
Type: Passenger
Desc: Reports on public and private transport movement in Kent
Price: On application
Tel: 01622 671 411
Web: www.kent.gov.uk

Travel Statistics and Trends

Org: Association of British Travel Agents
Freq: Annual
Type: Passenger
Desc: Annual statistical report
Price: Free on website
Web: www.abta.co.uk

Trends and Statistics GMPTE

Org: Greater Manchester PTE
Freq: Ad hoc
Type: Passenger
Price: On application
Tel: 0161 242 6000
Web: www.gmpte.gov.uk

Trends in the Transport Sector

Org: European Conference of Ministers of Transport (ECMT)
Freq: Annual
Type: Passenger and freight
Desc: Internationally comparable figures on key transport trends. Analyses of the transport situation in the western and eastern European countries, as well as the Baltic States and the CIS. Excludes air transport.
Price: € 24
Contact: OECD Bookshop
Web: www.oecdbookshop.org
Country: France
Tel: +33 1 4524 9722
Web: www.cemt.org

Transport Statistics Great Britain

Org: Department for Transport
Freq: Annual
Type: Passenger and freight
Desc: Statistical compendium report. Download from website
Price: Free on website
Contact: Colin Brailsford
Tel: 020 7944 3098
Web: www.dft.gov.uk

Transport Trends

Org: Department for Transport
Freq: Annual
Type: Passenger and freight
Desc: Statistical focus report. Download from website
Price: Free on website
Contact: Lyndsey Avery
Tel: 020 7944 3098
Web: www.dft.gov.uk

Travelstat

Org:	IRN Research
Freq:	Quarterly
Type:	Passenger
Desc:	Bespoke analysis of the International Passenger Survey
Price:	Varies according to the nature and range of data required
Contact:	Fred Hitchins
Tel:	0121 635 5210
Web:	www.irn-research.com

UK - Continent Passenger Profiles

Org:	IRN Research
Freq:	Quarterly + an annual report
Type:	Passenger
Desc:	UK - Continent Passenger Profile
Price:	£950 + VAT
Contact:	Fred Hitchins
Tel:	0121 635 5210
Web:	www.irn-research.com

UK Travel Demand: Trends and Insights, 2004 Edition

Org:	Travel Industry Association of America
Freq:	Ad hoc
Desc:	2003 market data and 2004 forecast.
Price:	Public price: $90 – Member price: $50
Web:	www.tia.org

UKPIA Statistical Review

Org:	United Kingdom Petroleum Industry Association
Freq:	Annual
Desc:	A source of facts and figures on the UK Downstream Oil Industry
Price:	Free on web
Web:	www.ukpia.com

United Nations Common Database

Org:	United Nations
Freq:	Various
Type:	Passenger and freight
Desc:	Generic statistical database which includes transportation data
Price:	Free access via website

Vital Statistics

Org:	National Caravan Council Ltd
Freq:	Monthly
Type:	Passenger
Desc:	Production and sales figures for touring, caravans, motor caravans, caravan holiday homes and residential park homes.
Price:	Free on email application
Web:	www.nationalcaravan.co.uk

World Cargo Database

Org:	MDS Transmodal
Freq:	Quarterly
Type:	Freight
Desc:	Detailed estimates of the volume of traded and empty containers by TEU on a country - country basis associated with each 5 digit SITC commodity classification.
Price:	On application
Tel:	01244 348301
Web:	www.mdst.co.uk

World Trade Statistics

Org:	Business And Trade Statistics Ltd
Freq:	Monthly
Type:	Freight
Desc:	Electronic database covering 25 reporting countries
Price:	Varies by type and amount of data taken
Tel:	01372 469847

Non-UK

Air

The Airbus Market Outlook for 2006-2025

Org:	Airbus Industries
Freq:	Annual
Type:	Passenger, freight and aircraft
Price:	Free on website
Tel:	+ 33 5 61 93 33 33
Web:	www.airbus.com

Air Transport

Org: Statistisches Bundesamt
Freq: Monthly/Annual
Type: Passenger and freight
Desc: Federal results on air transport.
            Detailed data (e.g. individual airport)
            available via GENESIS Online
            system, tables via the www.destatis.de
            website and summary data on
            www.statistik-portal.de site.
Price: Free online
Country: Germany
Tel: +49-611 75-2405
Web: www.destatis.de

Air Transport

Org: INE
Freq: Annual
Type: Passengers and freight
Price: Free on website via INEBase
Country: Spain
Tel: +34 91 583 9100
Web: www.ine.es

Annual report in French and English - 2006

Org: Direction Generale de L'Aviation
            Civile
Freq: Annual
Type: Passenger and freight
Desc: Commentary, analysis and statistics
            on the activities of DGAC
Price: Free on website
Country: France
Tel: +33 1 58 09 43 21
Web: www.dgac.fr

Annuario statistico trasporto aereo

Org: Ministero delle Infrastrutture e dei
            Trasporti
Freq: Annual
Type: Passenger and freight
Desc: Data on air traffic in Italy, including
            the destination of the flights, accounts
            of airports etc.
Price: On application
Contact: Paolo Staderini
Country: Italy
Tel: +39 6 590 83290
Web: www.infrastrutturetrasporti.it

Aviation Statistics

Org: Statistik Austria
Freq: Varies
Type: Passenger and Freight
Desc: Series of online tables on the civil
            aviation industry
Price: Free from website
Country: Austria
Tel: +43 1 71128 7070
Web: www.statistik.at

Aviation Statistics

Org: Bureau of Transportation Statistics
Freq: Ad hoc
Type: All
Desc: Wide range of reports and statistics
            on US and international airlines and
            commodity flows in the US.
Price: On application
Country: USA
Tel: +1 800 853 1351
Web: www.bts.gov

The Boeing World Air Cargo Forecast, 2006-2007

Org: Boeing Commercial Airplanes
Freq: Annual
Type: Freight
Price: Free on website
Contact: Tom Crabtree
Tel: +1 206-766-1030
Web: www.boeing.com

Current Market Outlook, 2006

Org: Boeing Commercial Airplanes
Freq: Annual
Type: Passengers, freight and fleet
Price: Free on website
Tel: +1 206-766-1030
Web: www.boeing.com

Civil Aircraft Forecast

Org: Forecast International
Freq: Updated daily
Type: Passenger and freight
Desc: Reports on worldwide civil aircraft
            market with 10 year forecasts
Price: $1,935 real time
Country: USA
Tel: +1 203 426 0800
Web: www.forecastinternational.com

Civil Aviation

Org: Swedish Institute for Transport And
          Communications (SIKA)

Freq: Annual

Desc: Development of the air transport
          sector with regard to infrastructure,
          aircraft, traffic and transport,
          accidents and environmental effects.

Price: Free on web

Contact: Anette Myhr

Country: Sweden

Tel: +46 631 40009

Web: www.sika-institute.se

Military Aircraft Forecast

Org: Forecast International

Freq: Updated daily

Type: Passenger and freight

Desc: Reports on worldwide military
          aircraft market with 10 year forecasts

Price: $1,935 real time

Country: USA

Tel: +1 203 426 0800

Web: www.forecastinternational.com

Observatory of Civil Aviation

Org: Direction Generale de L'Aviation
          Civile

Freq: Monthly

Type: Passenger and freight

Desc: The current situation of air transport
          in France and in the world

Price: Free on website

Country: France

Tel: +33 1 58 09 43 21

Web: www.dgac.fr

Observatory of Civil Aviation, 2005-06

Org: Direction Generale de L'Aviation
          Civile

Freq: Annual

Type: Passenger and freight

Desc: Commentary, analysis and statistics
          on the current situation of air
          transport in France and in the world

Price: Free on website

Country: France

Tel: +33 1 58 09 43 21

Web: www.dgac.fr

Management report of Air Traffic Control (Rapport d'activité de la Direction des services de la Navigation Aérienne)

Org: Direction Generale de L'Aviation
          Civile

Freq: Annual

Type: Passenger and freight

Desc: Commentary, analysis and statistics
          on air traffic control in France

Price: Free on website

Country: France

Tel: +33 1 58 09 43 21

Web: www.dgac.fr

Monthly Figures on Aviation

Org: Statistics Netherlands

Freq: Monthly

Type: Passengers and Freight

Desc: Data on flight movements,
          passengers, cargo and mail

Price: Free - only on website and
          downloadable from
          http//:statline.cbs.nl

Country: Netherlands

Tel: +31 0900 0227

Web: www.cbs.nl

U.S. Domestic Business and Convention Travel, 2006

Org: Travel Industry Association of America
Type: Passenger
Desc: Profiles business and convention trips and travelers in the United States in 2005.
Price: Members $165, Non-members $275
Contact: Download from website
Tel: +1 202 408 8422
Web: www.tia.org

U.S. Domestic Leisure Travel, 2006

Org: Travel Industry Association of America
Type: Passenger
Desc: Information on leisure travelers and trips, including spending, transportation, lodging, and activities,
Price: Members $165, Non-members $275
Contact: Download from website
Tel: +1 202 408 8422
Web: www.tia.org

World Commercial Aircraft/Engine Order Forecast

Org: Forecast International
Freq: Updated daily
Type: Passenger and freight
Desc: Binder
Price: $1,355
Country: USA
Tel: +1 203 426 0800
Web: www.forecastinternational.com

Statistics of Civil Aviation

Org: Statistik Austria
Freq: Annual
Type: Passenger and Freight
Desc: Includes data referring to commercial air traffic and scheduled traffic
Price: ATS 40 including CDROM or free if downloaded from website
Contact: Order on website
Country: Austria
Tel: +43 1 71128 7070
Web: www.statistik.at

Rail

Finnish Railway Statistics

Org: Finnish Rail Administration
Freq: Annual
Type: Rail
Desc: Information on Finnish railway traffic and rail network (in Finnish with English and French summaries)
Price: Free on website
Contact: Harri Lahelma
Country: Finland
Tel: +358 9 5840 5111
Web: www.rhk.fi/defeng.htm

Rail Statistics

Org: Statistik Austria
Freq: Varies
Type: Passenger and Freight
Desc: Series of online tables on the rail industry
Price: Free from website
Country: Austria
Tel: +43 1 71128 7070
Web: www.statistik.at

Rail Statistics

Org: Bureau of Transportation Statistics
Freq: Ad hoc
Type: All
Desc: Wide range of reports and statistics on US and cross border rail travel and the rail industry in the US.
Price: On application
Country: USA
Tel: +1 800 853 1351
Web: www.bts.gov

Rail Transport

Org: Statistisches Bundesamt
Freq: Monthly
Type: Passenger and freight
Desc: Federal and regional results on rail transport.
Price: Free online
Country: Germany
Tel: +49 611 752 405
Web: www-ec.destatis.de

Rail Transport Annual

Org: Statistisches Bundesamt
Freq: Annual
Type: Passenger and freight
Desc: Annual results on goods and passenger transport, infrastructure and accidents on the railways.
Price: Free online
Country: Germany
Tel: +49 611 752 405
Web: www-ec.destatis.de

Rail Transport (Bantrafik)

Org: Swedish Institute for Transport And Communications (SIKA)
Freq: Annual
Desc: Describe developments in the rail transport sector with regard to operators, infrastructure, vehicles, traffic and transport and accidents.
Price: Free on website
Contact: Jan Östlund
Country: Sweden
Tel: +46 63 140 022
Web: www.sika-institute.se

Rail Transport

Org: INE
Freq: Annual
Type: Passengers and freight
Price: Free on website via INEBase
Country: Spain
Tel: +34 91 583 9100
Web: www.ine.es

Road

Bike/Pedestrian Statistics

Org: Bureau of Transportation Statistics
Freq: Ad hoc
Type: All
Desc: Wide range of reports and statistics on US and cross border bike and pedestrian traffic, including accident data.
Price: On application
Country: USA
Tel: +1 800 853 1351
Web: www.bts.gov

Bus and Trolley Bus Statistics

Org: American Public Transport Association
Freq: Annual
Type: Passenger
Desc: Report of revenue vehicles by fleet characteristics
Price: Free on website
Country: USA
Tel: +1 202 496 4800
Web: www.apta.com

European Road Statistics

Org: European Union Road Federation
Freq: Annual
Desc: Analysis of European motorway networks covering the network, infrastructure financing, freight and passenger movments etc.
Price: Free on website
Country: Belgium
Tel: + 32 2 644 5877
Web: www.erf.be

Finnish Road Statistics

Org: Finnish National Road Administration
Freq: Annual
Type: Passenger
Desc: Times series of road traffic statistics
Price: Free on website
Contact: Heikki Heinio
Country: Finland
Tel: +358 2042 2150
Web: www.tiehallinto.fi

The Global Truck Report

Org: Truck and Bus Builder Publishing Ltd
Freq: Annual
Desc: Factual information about bus and coach manufacturing
Price: £820
Contact: Form on website
Country: World
Tel: +44 (0) 1984 639301
Web: www.truckandbusbuilder.com

Goods traffic on the Road: Structural Data, 2006

Org: Statistik Austria
Freq: Annual
Type: Freight
Desc: Freight traffic on Austrian roads
Price: ATS 7.20 or free via website
Contact: Order on website
Country: Austria
Tel: +43 1 71128 7070
Web: www.statistik.at

Index Figures of Traffic Density

Org: Statistics Netherlands
Freq: Monthly
Type: Passengers and Freight
Desc: Data on traffic density
Price: Free - only on website and downloadable from http//:statline.cbs.nl
Country: Netherlands
Tel: +31 0900 0227
Web: www.cbs.nl

Kba Statistische

Org: Kraftfahrt-Bundesamt
Freq: Monthly / Annual
Type: Passenger and Freight
Desc: Series of publications on different aspects of road transport in Germany, including vehicle registrations, traffic data etc.
Price: Free on website
Country: Germany
Tel: +49 4 613 16 0
Web: www.kba.de

Les Transports routiers de marchandises

Org: Institut National de Statistique
Freq: Annual
Type: Freight
Desc: Statistics on Belgian goods transport
Price: Free on website
Country: Belgium
Tel: 32 2 277 5504
Web: www.statbel.fgov.be

Market observation goods traffic, annual report 2006

Org: Bundesamt Für Güterverkehr
Freq: Annual
Type: Freight
Desc: Summarised data on road freight traffic from the BAG's annual report.
Price: Free on website
Country: Germany
Tel: +49 221 57760
Web: www.bag.bund.de

Mercato del nuovo e dell'usato. I numeri di aprile 2007

Org: Ministero delle Infrastrutture e dei Trasporti
Freq: Monthly
Type: Passenger and freight
Desc: Data on new and used car sales in Italy.
Price: Free on website
Country: Italy
Tel: +39 6 590 83290
Web: www.infrastrutturetrasporti.it

Motor vehicle permission statistics

Org: Statistik Austria
Freq: Annual
Type: Passenger and Freight
Desc: Austrian vehicle licensing statistics roads
Price: Free on website
Contact: Order on website
Country: Austria
Tel: +43 1 71128 7070
Web: www.statistik.at

Statistics Of The Motor Vehicles Existence

Org: Statistik Austria
Freq: Annual
Type: Passenger and Freight
Desc: Austrian vehicle parc statistics
Price: ATS 80
Contact: Order on website
Country: Austria
Tel: +43 1 71128 7070
Web: www.statistik.at

New Registrations

Org: Statistisches Bundesamt
Freq: Annual
Type: Passenger and freight
Desc: New registrations of passenger cars
Country: Germany
Tel: +49-611 75-2405
Web: www.destatis.de

Parc des Véhicules à Moteur

Org: Institut National de Statistique
Freq: Annual
Desc: Statistics on all types of motor vehicles
Price: Free on website
Country: Belgium
Tel: 32 2 277 5504
Web: www.statbel.fgov.be

Prospetti analitici sulle immatricolazioni ed i passaggi di proprietà di autovetture

Org: Ministero delle Infrastrutture e dei Trasporti
Freq: Annual
Type: Passenger and freight
Desc: Annual data on new and used car sales in Italy.
Price: Free on website
Country: Italy
Tel: +39 6 590 83290
Web: www.infrastrutturetrasporti.it

Road control statistics of the BAG

Org: Bundesamt Für Güterverkehr
Freq: Annual
Type: Freight
Price: Free on website
Country: Germany
Tel: +49 221 57760
Web: www.bag.bund.de

Road Passenger Transport

Org: Statistisches Bundesamt
Freq: Quarterly
Type: Passenger
Desc: Federal and regional road passenger transport results
Price: Free online
Country: Germany
Tel: +49 611 752 405
Web: www-ec.destatis.de

Roads network, vehicles, drivers and accidents

Org: INE
Freq: Annual
Type: Passengers
Desc: Four datasets on road passenger transport
Price: Free on website via INEBase
Country: Spain
Tel: +34 91 583 9100
Web: www.ine.es

Roads (other than local)

Org: Statistisches Bundesamt
Freq: Annual
Type: Passenger and freight
Desc: Lengths of roads by type
Country: Germany
Tel: +49-611 75-2405
Web: www.destatis.de

Road Passenger Transport Annual

Org: Statistisches Bundesamt
Freq: Annual
Type: Passenger
Desc: Passenger transport, economic figures and infrastructure data.
Price: € 6.94
Contact: Mr Reim
Country: Germany
Tel: +49 611 752 424
Web: www.destatis.de

Road Traffic Statistics

Org: Statistik Austria
Freq: Varies
Type: Passenger and Frieght
Desc: Series of online tables on road traffic
Price: Free from website
Country: Austria
Tel: +43 1 71128 7070
Web: www.statistik.at

Road Traffic Injuries

Org: Swedish Institute for Transport And
          Communications (SIKA)
Freq: Annual
Desc: Describes the consequences of road
          transport in Sweden in the form of
          accidents and injuries to persons.
Price: Free on website
Contact: Marcus Hugosson
Country: Sweden
Tel: +46 63 140 017
Web: www.sika-institute.se

Statistics of the motor vehicles, new permissions 2007 (annual volume booklet)

Org: Statistik Austria
Freq: Annual
Type: Passenger and Freight
Desc: Austrian vehicle new licensing
          statistics
Price: ATS 51 including CDROM
Contact: Order on website
Country: Austria
Tel: +43 1 71128 7070
Web: www.statistik.at

Statistics of the motor vehicles, new permissions 2007 (monthly magazine)

Org: Statistik Austria
Freq: Monthly
Type: Passenger and Freight
Desc: Monthly Austrian vehicle new
          licensing statistics
Price: ATS 43
Contact: Order on website
Country: Austria
Tel: +43 1 71128 7070
Web: www.statistik.at

Statistics on Road Passenger Transport

Org: Instituto Nacional de Estatistica
Freq: Annual
Type: Passenger and freight
Contact: Download from website
Country: Portugal
Tel: +351 842 6100
Web: www.ine.pt

Statistical Report on Road Accidents

Org: European Conference of Ministers of
          Transport (ECMT)
Freq: Annual
Type: Passenger and freight
Desc: Road accident statistics and analysis
Price: € 23
Country: France
Tel: +33 1 4524 9722
Web: www.oemt.org

Statistical Yearbook

Org: Statistics Netherlands
Freq: Annual
Type: All
Desc: Annual statistical compilation with
          detailed transport statistics.
Price: Free - only on website
Country: Netherlands
Tel: +31 900-0227
Web: www.cbs.nl

Structure of the enterprises of the commercial transportation of goods by road and the works traffic

Org: Bundesamt Für Güterverkehr
Freq: Annual
Type: Freight
Desc: Data on economic activities,
          employees and fleet
Price: € 20
Country: Germany
Tel: +49 221 57760
Web: www.bag.bund.de

Swedish national and international road goods

Org: Swedish Institute for Transport and
          Communications (SIKA)
Freq: Annual
Desc: Traffic and transport by Swedish
          lorries, both within Sweden and
          internationally
Price: Free on website
Contact: Christina Eng
Country: Sweden
Tel: +46 63 140 015
Web: www.sika-institute.se

Traffic Accidents

Org: Statistik Austria
Freq: Annual
Type: Passenger
Desc: Traffic accidents by type
Price: ATS 35 including CDROM
Contact: Order on website
Country: Austria
Tel: +43 1 71128 7070
Web: www.statistik.at

Traffic Accidents

Org: Statistisches Bundesamt
Freq: Monthly
Desc: Federal and regional results on traffic
           accidents.
Price: Free online
Country: Germany
Tel: +49 611 752 405
Web: www-ec.destatis.de

Traffic Accidents Annual

Org: Statistisches Bundesamt
Freq: Annual
Desc: Annual results on traffic accidents.
Price: Free online
Country: Germany
Tel: +49 611 752 405
Web: www-ec.destatis.de

Transportation of goods by road of German load motor vehicles

Org: Bundesamt Für Güterverkehr
Freq: Monthly
Desc: Traffic capacities of German load
           motor vehicles
Type: Freight.
Price: Free on website
Country: Germany
Tel: +49 221 57760
Web: www.bag.bund.de

Traffic Returns: Goods Traffic – Traffic Capacity

Org: Statistik Austria
Freq: Annual
Type: Freight
Price: ATS 10.90 of free if downloaded
           from website
Contact: Order on website
Country: Austria
Tel: +43 1 71128 7070
Web: www.statistik.at

Transit Agency Data

Org: American Public Transport
           Association
Freq: Annual
Type: Passenger
Desc: Report of revenue vehicles by fleet
           characteristics
Price: Free on website
Country: USA
Tel: +1 202 496 4800
Web: www.apta.com

Transport of Goods by Road

Org: INE
Freq: Annual
Type: Freight
Price: Free on website via INEBase
Country: Spain
Tel: +34 91 583 9100
Web: www.ine.es

VDA Annual Report

Org: Verband der Automobilindustrie
Price: Free
Desc: Discusses the events that it considers
           to be the most important over the last
           automotive year and gives its own
           comments on them. In addition, it
           provides useful information
Country: Germany
Web: www.vda.de

VDA Annual Statistics

Org: Verband der Automobilindustrie
Price: Free
Desc: Data on vehicle production, trade,
            vehicles on the road and vehicle cost
            index in Germany
Country: Germany
Web: www.vda.de

VDA Monthly Statistics

Org: Verband der Automobilindustrie
Price: Free
Desc: Monthly registration, production and
            trade statsitics on motor vehicles in
            Germany
Country: Germany
Web: www.vda.de

Vehicle Statistics

Org: Swedish Institute for Transport And
            Communications (SIKA)
Freq: Annual/Quarterly
Desc: Statistics on vehicles are published in
            three different surveys: Vehicles
            according to the Road Traffic
            Register; Vehicles in counties and
            municipalities; and Vehicles at the
            turn of the year.
Price: Free on website
Contact: Anette Myhr
Country: Sweden
Tel: +46 63 140 009
Web: www.sika-institute.se

Véhicules à moteur neufs et d'occasion mis en circulation

Org: Institut National de Statistique
Freq: Annual
Desc: Number of new motor vehicles
            (including motor bikes), put in
            circulation during the year per area
            broken down into province and
            district level.
Price: Free on website
Country: Belgium
Tel: 32 2 277 5504
Web: www.statbel.fgov.be

The World Bus and Coach Manufacturing Industry

Org: Truck and Bus Builder Publishing
            Ltd
Freq: Annual
Desc: Factual information about bus and
            coach manufacturing
Price: £ 995
Contact: Form on website
Country: World
Tel: +44 (0) 1984 639301
Web: www.truckandbusbuilder.com

World Road Statistics

Org: International Road Federation
Freq: Annual
Desc: Data on road networks (km),
            production & export of motor
            vehicles, first registration & import of
            motor vehicles, vehicles in use, road
            traffic, accidents etc.
Price: Book copy: CHF 300; CD-ROM
            (Access and pdf versions): CHF 250;
            Book and CD-ROM: CHF 400; PDF
            electronic version (sent by email):
            CHF 200
Contact: Order on website
Country: World
Tel: + 41 22 306 0260
Web: www.irfnet.org

Maritime

Annuaire de la Marine Marchande

Org: Armateurs de France
Freq: Annual
Type: Passenger and freight
Desc: French Shipowners Directory
            (address, contact, fleet.)
Price: € 100 on web
Country: France
Tel: +33 1 53 89 52 52
Web: www.armateursdefrance.org

Inland Waterway Craft Travel

Org: Statistik Austria
Freq: Varies
Type: Passenger and Freight
Desc: Series of online tables on inland
            waterways
Price: Free from website
Country: Austria
Tel: +43 1 71128 7070
Web: www.statistik.at

Inland Waterways Transport

Org: Statistisches Bundesamt
Freq: Annual
Type: Freight
Desc: Inland waterways transport statistics,
            goods ransport and enterprise data
Price: Free online
Country: Germany
Tel: +49 611 752 405
Web: www-ec.destatis.de

ISL Fleet Data Base

Org: Institute of Shipping Economics and
            Logistics (ISL)
Freq: Quarterly
Type: Freight
Desc: All self-propelled sea-going trading
            ships and passenger ships of 300 gt
            and over. Data provided by LLoyd's
            Register Fairplay.
Price: On application
Contact: Christel Heidelhoff
Country: Germany
Tel: +49 421 22096 32
Web: www.isl.org

ISL Monthly Container Port Monitor

Org: Institute of Shipping Economics and
            Logistics (ISL)
Freq: Monthly
Type: Freight
Desc: Data on container traffic (TEU) of
            the world's major container ports,
            presented in the form of monthly
            indices and quarterly TEU-traffic
            aggregates.
Price: PDF €365.
Contact: Christel Heidelhoff
Country: Germany
Tel: +49 421 22096 32
Web: www.isl.org

ISL New Construction Data Base

Org: Institute of Shipping Economics and
            Logistics (ISL)
Freq: Monthly
Type: Passenger ad Freight
Desc: Orderbook data about all self-
            propelled sea-going trading ships and
            passenger ships of 300 gt and over.
            Data is provided quarterly by Lloyd´s
            Register/Fairplay
Price: On application.
Contact: Christel Heidelhoff
Country: Germany
Tel: +49 421 22096 32
Web: www.isl.org

ISL Port Data Base

Org: Institute of Shipping Economics and
            Logistics (ISL)
Freq: Continuous
Type: Freight
Desc: Structured, comparable data from
            1980 onwards for approximately 400
            leading world ports.
Price: On application
Contact: Christel Heidelhoff
Country: Germany
Tel: +49 421 22096 32
Web: www.isl.org

ISL Shipping Statistics and Market Review

Org: Institute of Shipping Economics and Logistics (ISL)
Freq: Monthly
Type: Freight
Desc: Market analysis of shipping and shipbuilding markets, seaborne trade developments, freight rates and world port traffic.
Price: Online €395. Hard copy €450
Contact: Christel Heidelhoff
Country: Germany
Tel: +49 421 22096 32
Web: www.isl.org

ISL Shipping Statistics Yearbook

Org: Institute of Shipping Economics and Logistics (ISL)
Freq: Monthly
Type: Freight
Desc: Statistics on the shipping market, shipbuilding and port and sea canals.
Price: Online €270. Hard copy €308. Hard copy plus CD €334
Contact: Christel Heidelhoff
Country: Germany
Tel: +49 421 22096 32
Web: www.isl.org

Finnish Merchant Fleet Statistics

Org: Finnish Maritime Administration
Freq: Annual
Type: Passenger and freight
Price: €10
Contact: Statistics Division
Country: Finland
Tel: + 358 20 448 4640
Web: www.fma.fi

The Finnish Merchant Marine

Org: Finnish Maritime Administration
Freq: Annual
Type: Passenger and freight
Price: €15
Contact: Statistics Division
Country: Finland
Tel: + 358 20 448 4640
Web: www.fma.fi

Goods traffic on the Danube

Org: Statistik Austria
Freq: Annual
Type: Freight
Desc: Freight traffic on the Danube
Price: ATS 10.9
Contact: Order on website
Country: Austria
Tel: +43 1 71128 7070
Web: www.statistik.at

La Lettre d'Armateurs de France

Org: Armateurs de France
Freq: Monthly
Type: Passenger and freight
Desc: Maritime information.
Price: Free
Contact: Edouard Berlet
Country: France
Tel: +33 1 53 89 52 52
Web: www.armateursdefrance.org

Le transport maritime français: faits et chiffres (French Maritime Transport: facts and figures)

Org: Armateurs de France
Freq: Ad hoc
Type: Passenger and freight
Desc: Maritime information.
Price: Free on website
Country: France
Tel: +33 1 53 89 52 52
Web: www.armateursdefrance.org

Maritime Statistics

Org: Bureau of Transportation Statistics
Freq: Ad hoc
Type: All
Desc: Wide range of reports and statistics on US maritime industry, including ferries, recreational boating and commodity flows.
Price: On application
Country: USA
Tel: +1 800 853 1351
Web: www.bts.gov

Navigation interieure

Org: Institut National de Statistique
Freq: Annual
Type: Freight
Desc: Statistics on inland waterway freight transport
Price: Free on website
Country: Belgium
Tel: 32 2 277 5504
Web: www.statbel.fgov.be

Navigation maritime

Org: Institut National de Statistique
Freq: Annual
Type: Passenger and Freight
Desc: The number of sea-going ships, tonnage and of their type, number and tonnage of the goods, type of cargo and continent of loading or unloading, number of the passengers.
Price: Free on website
Country: Belgium
Tel: 32 2 277 5504
Web: www.statbel.fgov.be

Rapport annuel 2006 d'Armateurs de France

Org: Armateurs de France
Freq: Annual
Type: Passenger and freight
Desc: Annual report of the association which also include statistics on ship movements etc.
Price: Free on website
Country: France
Tel: +33 1 53 89 52 52
Web: www.armateursdefrance.org

Shipping Goods

Org: Swedish Institute for Transport And Communications (SIKA)
Freq: Quarterly
Desc: Shipping, freight and passenger transport, in Swedish ports and wharves.
Price: Free on website
Country: Sweden
Tel: +46 63 140 015
Web: www.sika-institute.se

Shipping Statistics

Org: Finnish Maritime Administration
Freq: Monthly / Annual
Type: Passenger and freight
Desc: Collections of statistics on the Finnish shipping industry and traffic, including movements between Finland and Foreign Countries, Domestic Waterborne Traffic, Canal Traffic, Merchant Fleet Statistics on shore and inland waterway transport
Price: Free on website
Contact: Statistics Division
Country: Finland
Tel: + 358 20 448 4640
Web: www.fma.fi

Shipping Statistics

Org: National Statistical Service of Greece
Freq: Annual
Type: Passenger and freight
Desc: See title
Price: On application
Contact: data.dissem@statistics.gr
Country: Greece
Tel: +30 1 3289529
Web: www.statistics.gr

Statistics on Domestic Waterborne Traffic in Finland

Org: Finnish Maritime Administration
Freq: Annual
Type: Passenger and freight
Price: €10
Contact: Statistics Division
Country: Finland
Tel: + 358 20 448 4640
Web: www.fma.fi

Statistics on Shipping between Finland and Foreign Countries

Org: Finnish Maritime Administration
Freq: Annual
Type: Passenger and freight
Price: €10
Contact: Statistics Division
Country: Finland
Tel: + 358 20 448 4640
Web: www.fma.fi

Swedish Vessels And Foreign Vessels Chartered From Abroad

Org: Swedish Institute for Transport And
           Communications (SIKA)
Freq: Annual
Desc: The development of the Swedish
           merchant fleet and its composition.
Price: Free on website
Country: Sweden
Tel: +46 63 140 015
Web: www.sika-institute.se

Water Transport

Org: Swedish Institute for Transport And
           Communications (SIKA)
Freq: Annual
Desc: Economic statistics on sea transport
           and other support services for sea
           transport s.
Price: Free on website
Country: Sweden
Tel: +46 63 140 015
Web: www.sika-institute.se

All Modes

Annual Services Survey

Org: INE
Freq: Annual
Type: Passenger
Desc: General passenger statistics for Spain
Price: Free online
Country: Spain
Tel: +34 91 583 9100
Web: www.ine.es

Bulletin Statistique du SES

Org: Service Economique et Statistique
Freq: Quarterly
Type: Passenger and freight
Desc: Economic aspects of freight and
           passengers in France.
Price: Free on website
Country: France
Tel: +33 1 4081 2122
Web: www.statistiques.equipement.gouv.fr

Commodity Flows 2004/05

Org: Swedish Institute for Transport And
           Communications (SIKA)
Freq: Every three years
Desc: The quantity of goods, commodity
           value and the mode of transport.
Price: Free on web
Contact: Fredrik Söderbaum
Country: Sweden
Tel: +46 63-14 00 14
Web: www.sika-institute.se

Compendio statistico sul traffico marittimo e aereo - anno 2006

Org: Ministero delle Infrastrutture e dei
           Trasporti
Freq: Annual
Type: Passenger and freight
Desc: Statistics on marine and air traffic and
           their interconnections with the other
           modalities of transport.
Price: On application
Contact: Paolo Staderini
Country: Italy
Tel: +39 6 590 83290
Web: www.infrastrutturetrasporti.it

Conditions and Performance report

Org: Federal Transit Administration
Freq: Annual
Desc: Status of the US's Highways, Bridges
           and Transit.
Price: Free
Tel: +1 202 366 4043
Web: www.fta.dot.gov

Emerging Tourism Markets: China & India, 2006 Edition

Org: Travel Industry Association of
           America
Type: Passenger
Desc: Outbound travel and travel to the U.S.
           from China and India
Price: Members $300, Non-members $495
Contact: Download from website
Tel: +1 202 408 8422
Web: www.tia.org

Funding Transport Systems: A Comparison among Developed Countries

Org: Elsevier Science Ltd
Freq: Ad hoc
Type: Passenger and freight
Desc: Comprehensive statistical data on transport funding in various countries to 1993
Price: €81.95
Country: Netherlands
Tel: +31 20 485 3757
Web: www.elsevier.com

Les transports en 2006

Org: Service Economique et Statistique
Freq: Annual
Type: Passenger and freight
Desc: Web page that includes data on all aspects of freight and passenger in France.
Price: Free on website
Country: France
Tel: +33 1 4081 2122
Web: www.statistiques.equipement.gouv.fr

Local and regional public transport

Org: Swedish Institute for Transport And Communications (SIKA)
Freq: Annual
Desc: The development of publicly financed public transport in Sweden as a whole and in the respective county.
Price: On application
Contact: Christina Eng
Country: Sweden
Tel: +46 63 140 015
Web: www.sika-institute.se

Memento de Statistiques des Transports

Org: Service Economique et Statistique
Freq: Annual
Type: Passenger and freight
Desc: Statistics on the carriages of goods and passengers (undertaken, infrastructures, materials, traffics and transport, formation, safety) gathered in all modes of transport.
Price: Latest year free online. Earlier years charged at € 26 each.
Country: France
Tel: +33 1 4081 2122
Web: www.statistiques.equipement.gouv.fr

New Cronos database

Org: Eurostat
Type: Passenger and freight
Desc: This is the database at the heart of the Eurostat website offering free access to data on air, rail, road and inland waterway transport in the European Union. It is also available via some third parties like ESDS in the UK. Registered users can gain access to bulk downloads of data.
Price: Free via Eurostat website.
Country: Luxembourg
Web: epp.eurostat.ec.europa.eu/pls/portal

Notes de Synthèse du SES

Org: Service Economique et Statistique
Freq: Bi-monthly
Type: Passenger and freight
Desc: Studies on transport statistics
Price: Free online or €9 each in hard copy.
Country: France
Tel: +33 1 4081 2122
Web: www.statistiques.equipement.gouv.fr

Observatoire social des transports

Org: Service Economique et Statistique
Freq: Various
Type: Freight
Desc: Series of reports on the social aspects of freight transport: includes quarterly social economic situation bulletin; annual social assessment and ad hoc reports.
Price: Free online.
Country: France
Tel: +33 1 4081 2122
Web: www.statistiques.equipement.gouv.fr

Passenger/Goods Transport

Org: Statistisches Bundesamt
Freq: MonthlyAnnual
Type: Passenger and freight
Desc: Domestic transport performance in Germany.
Price: Free online
Country: Germany
Tel: +49-611 75-2405
Web: www.destatis.de

Price and price Indices for Transport

Freq: Monthly
Type: Passengers and Freight
Desc: Prices and indices
Price: Free online
Country: Germany
Tel: +49 611 752 405
Web: www-ec.destatis.de

Public Transportation Fact Book

Org: American Public Transport Association
Freq: Annual
Type: Passenger
Desc: General statistical trends on all aspects of transport in US and Canada
Price: Free on website
Country: USA
Tel: +1 202 496 4800
Web: www.apta.com

SES Infos Rapides Transport

Org: Service Economique et Statistique
Freq: 30 times per year
Type: Passenger and freight
Desc: The principal statistical results in the fields of transport, construction and housing.
Price: € 6.50 each or €90 for annual electronic subscription
Country: France
Tel: +33 1 4081 2122
Web: www.statistiques.equipement.gouv.fr

SES en brief

Org: Service Economique et Statistique
Freq: 30 times per year
Type: Passenger and freight
Desc: Topical statistical information on the fields of transport, construction and housing.
Price: Free on website subscription
Country: France
Tel: +33 1 4081 2122
Web: www.statistiques.equipement.gouv.fr

Short-Term Trends Survey

Org: European Conference of Ministers of Transport (ECMT)
Freq: Quarterly
Type: Passenger and freight
Desc: Intermodal transport statistics, excluding air transport
Price: Free on web site
Contact: Publications service
Country: France
Tel: +33 1 4524 9722
Web: www.cemt.org

Special transport services and national special transport services

Org: Swedish Institute for Transport And Communications (SIKA)
Freq: Annual
Desc: Covers the activity of the municipalities relating to the special transport services and national special transport services ; the number of journeys, the number of granted and used permits, and the finances of the activity.
Price: Free on website
Contact: Christina Eng
Country: Sweden
Tel: +46 63 140 015
Web: www.sika-institute.se

Stock of transport means

Org: Statistisches Bundesamt
Freq: Annual
Type: Passenger and freight
Desc: Number of transport vehicles, including airplanes and water craft in Germany
Price: Free online
Country: Germany
Tel: +49-611 75-2405
Web: www.destatis.de

Statistical Summaries

Org: Federal Transit Administration
Freq: Annual
Desc: Provides the U.S. Dept. of Transportation's recommendations for the allocation of funds and includes data on public transport buses.
Price: Free
Tel: +1 202 366 4043
Web: www.fta.dot.gov

Statistical Yearbook 2006

Org: Statistics Netherlands
Type: Passenger and freight
Desc: Compilation of traffic and transport data in the Netherlands
Price: Free - only on website
Country: Netherlands
Tel: +31 0900-0227 (€ 0,50/min.)
Web: www.cbs.nl

Statistiques mensuelles du transport (Monthly Transport Statistics)

Org: Institut National de Statistique
Freq: Monthly
Type: Passenger and Freight
Desc: Data on all types of transport
Price: Free on website
Country: Belgium
Tel: 32 2 277 5504
Web: www.statbel.fgov.be

Transport and Communication Statistics

Org: National Statistical Service of Greece
Freq: Annual
Type: Passenger and freight
Desc: See title
Price: On application
Contact: data.dissem@statistics.gr
Country: Greece
Tel: +30 1 3289529
Web: www.statistics.gr

Transport of Passenger Statistics

Org: INE
Freq: Monthly
Type: Passenger
Desc: Multi-modal passenger information.
Price: Free on website via INEBase
Country: Spain
Tel: +34 91 583 9100
Web: www.ine.es

Transport Statistics (Estatisticas dos Transportes)

Org: Instituto Nacional de Estatistica
Freq: Annual
Type: Passenger and freight
Contact: Download from website
Country: Portugal
Tel: +351 842 6100
Web: www.ine.pt

Web Magazine

Org: Statistics Netherlands
Freq: Monthly
Type: Passengers and Freight
Desc: Range of transport data published
            online each month.
Price: Free online
Country: Netherlands
Tel: +31 0900 0227
Web: www.cbs.nl

UIRR Transported Volume Statistics

Org: International Union of Combined
            Road-Rail Transport Companies
            (UIRR)
Freq: Annual
Type: Freight
Desc: Volumes of traffic processed by its
            member companies in terms of
            consignments
Tel: +32 2 548 78 90
Web: www.uirr.com

SECTION 5

Educational Establishments

The Chartered Institute of Logistics and Transport in the UK [CILT(UK)]

The grade of **Affiliate** is open to anyone who is interested in logistics or transport and who supports the aims of the Institute but who does not qualify for Membership. This grade includes those studying for qualifications in logistics or transport.

Candidates for election or transfer to the grade of **Member** should hold an approved qualification at level 3 (e.g. NVQ3 /HNC) level 4 (e.g. NVQ4/HND/ordinary degree) and have supervisory or management responsibility in logistics or transport. Candidates for the grade of **Chartered Member** should hold the Institute's **Advanced Diploma** or an exempting qualification (usually an approved degree) and have at least 5 years' relevant experience in logistics or transport, including at least 2 years at a senior level. Alternative routes into both grades are available to experienced logistics or transport professionals who do not meet the standard criteria.

Fellowship is open to Chartered Members who have at least 7 years experience in a position or a series of positions of high responsibility in the management of logistics or transport or who have attained a position of eminence in logistics or transport.

Although the Institute's purpose is to serve the needs of individual professionals, it offers companies and other organisations which support its activities the opportunity to become **Corporate Members of the Institute**. When an organisation becomes a Corporate Member, nominated representatives from within then

organisation will be registered as Affiliates of the Institute thereby gaining access to the many services available for the benefit of themselves and their organisation.

Chartered Membership and Fellowship are granted under the authority of the CIT Royal Charter and thus carry the entitlement to use the designatory letters CMILT or FCILT.

Continuing Professional Development

CPD is the systematic maintenance and improvement of knowledge, skills and competence throughout a professional's working life. All members of CILT(UK) are expected to make a commitment to ensure that the knowledge and skills they gained in qualifying for membership are kept up to date.

The emphasis is on individual members to take responsibility for developing and directing their own careers. However, Institute staff will offer members support, advice and guidance in their CPD. There is also a mentoring scheme for members to enable them to work though professional issues, upgrade membership and direct their professional development

Education and professional development

CILT(UK) offers a flexible range of qualifications providing opportunities for professional development and career enhancement from entry level through to Advanced Diploma level.

The CILT(UK) Level 2 Introductory Certificate in Logistics and Transport – an introduction giving a broad general understanding of the whole topic. For new employees to the profession, career changers and students at secondary or FE level.

The CILT(UK) Level 3 Certificate in Logistics and Transport – a qualification for aspiring or practicing supervisors and first line managers. Candidates take a core Management unit plus an option from a choice of 9 units including Road Passenger Transport, Transport Planning and Community Transport etc. The Transport Co-ordinators Certificate is included as one of the options in this qualification. Road Freight Transport, Road Passenger Transport and Transport Coordinator options offer CPC exemption

The CILT(UK) Level 5 Professional Diploma in Logistics and Transport – a programme addressing operational issues in transport at the middle management level and for graduate entry. There are specialist pathways for Transport Operations and Transport Planning. Candidates complete a core Management unit, either Transport Operations and Transport Planning and then two units from a choice of 11 units including Transport and Society, Road Passenger Transport, Sourcing and Procurement and others. European accreditation is available with some pathways.

The CILT(UK) Level 6 Advanced Diploma in Logistics and Transport – a programme addressing the strategic management of transport, logistics, supply chain management and offering the qualification for entry to Chartered membership when taken with the CILT(UK) Professional Diploma.

Membership benefits and activities

CILT(UK)'s resources include a comprehensive specialist knowledge centre based in Corby with an enquiry/information service. Its conferences seminars and lectures draw leading figures as speakers and attendees and a network of local Branches arrange lectures, visits, workshops, and events throughout the country. Its involvement in contemporary issues is reflected in **Logistics and Transport Focus**, the Institute's journal

and the reports and the weekly electronic Current Awareness Bulletin.

There are four Faculties – Supply Chain, Technology, Transport and Resources, under which exist numerous forums which provide opportunities for networking, knowledge enhancement though research projects and conference and dissemination of best practice.

Information

For further information about CILT(UK) please contact:

The Chartered Institute of Logistics and Transport in the UK
Logistics and Transport Centre
PO Box 5787 Corby Northants
NN17 4XQ

Tel: 01536 740100
Fax: 01536 740101
Email: Enquiry@ciltuk.org.uk
Web: **www.ciltuk.org.uk**

A selected list of colleges offering graduate courses in transport related subjects.

Aston University/Institute of Logistics and Transport

Address: Aston University
Aston Triangle
Birmingham
B4 7ET
Tel: 0121 204 3000
Fax: 0121 204 3696
Email: admissions@aston.ac.uk
Web: www.aston.ac.uk/trans/
Courses: **Undergraduate**
~ BSc: Transport Management
~ BSc: Logistics

Postgraduate
~ MSc: Passenger Transport Management
~ MSc: Logistics

University of Central England in Birmingham

Address: Perry Barr
Birmingham
B42 2SU
Tel: 0121 331 5595
Fax: 0121 331 7994
Email: david.gray@tic.ac.uk
Web: www.uce.ac.uk
Contact: David Gray
Courses: **Undergraduate**
~ BA: Business Studies
~ BSc: Town Planning
~ BSc: Enviromental Planning, Transport and Communications
~ BSc: Tech Marine Technology
Postgraduate
~ MSc: Supply Chain Management
~ MSc: Logistics

University of Brighton

Address: Mithras House
Lewes Road
Brighton BN2 4AT
Tel: 01273 643067
Email: service.management@brighton.as.uk
Web: www.brighton.ac.uk
Courses: **Undergraduate**
~ BA: International Travel Management

University of West of England in Bristol

Address: Coldharbour Lane
Bristol
B16 1QY
Web: www.uwe.ac.uk
Courses: **Undergraduate**
~ BA (Hons) Geography & Transport
~ BA (Hons) Planning with Transport
~ BA (Hons) Environmental Management & Sustainability
~ BA (Hons) Transport & Sustainability
Postgraduate
~ Certificate of Professional Development in Transport
~ MA Transport Planning
~ Master of planning
~ MA Transport Studies
~ MSc / PG Dip Transport Planning

Cardiff University

Address: Cardiff
Wales
CF10 3XQ
Tel: 02920 876 564
Email: Colgan@cardiff.ac.uk
Web: www.cardiff.ac.uk
Contact: Cath Colgan
Courses: Undergraduate
~ BSc Maritime Studies
~ BSc Maritime Technology
~ BSc City & Regional Planning
~ BSc International Transport
Postgraduate
~ MSc: Transport and Planning
~ MSc: International Transport
~ MSc: Urban and regional transport
~ MPhil Transport
~ Post Grad Diploma Port &
Shipping Administration

City University

Address: 106 Bunhill Row
London
EC1Y 8TZ
Tel: 0207 7040 8641
Email: c.a.wolley@city.ac.uk
Web: www.cass.city.ac.uk
Courses: **Postgraduate**
~ MSc: Trade, Transport and
Finance
~ MSc: Logistics, Trade and Finance

*Cranfield University

Address: Cranfield
Bedford
MK43 0AL
Tel: 01234 754 517
Email: m.peters@cranfield.ac.uk
Web: www.som.cranfield.ac.uk
Contact: Melvyn Peters
Courses: **Postgraduate**
~ MSc Transport Studies
~ MSc Logistics & Transportation
~ MSc Post Graduate Diploma
Transportation Management
~ MSc Distribution Management and
Technology
~ MSc Air Transport Management
~ MSc Transportation Management
~ Executive MSc Distribution &
Logistics
~ MSc Logistics and Supply Chain
Management
~ Master of Business Studies
~ MSc Defence Acquisition
Management

University of Glamorgan

Address: Pontypridd
Wales
CF37 1DL
Tel: 01443 480480
Web: www.glam.ac.uk.
Courses: **Undergraduate**
~ BSc (joint Honours) with
Transport Studies
~ CILT Qualification Course

University of Huddersfield

Address: Queensgate
Huddersfield
HD1 3DH
Tel: 01484 473969
Email: admissions@transport.hud.ac.uk
Web: www.hud.ac.uk.
Courses: **Undergraduate**
~ BSc Transport & Distribution &
European Logistics
~ BSc Transport & Distribution
~ BSc Geography
~ BSc Logistics & Supply Chain
Management
~ BSc Logistics
~ BSc European Logistics
Management
~ Certificate in Transport &
Distribution Management
Postgraduate
~ MSc Transport & Logistics

Imperial College London

Address: Centre for Transport Studies,
Department of Civil and
Environmental Engineering,
South Kensington Campus
London SW7 2AZ
Tel: 020 7594 6089
Email: j.polak@ic.ac.uk
Web: www.imperial.ac.uk
Contact Professor John Polak
Courses: **Postgraduate**
~ MSc Transport with Sustainable
Development
~ MSc Transport with Business
Development
~ MSc Transport

*The University of Leeds

Address: Institute for Transport Studies
University of Leeds
Leeds LS2 9JT
Tel: 01133 435 337
Fax: 01133 435 334
Email: C.A.Nash@its.leeds.ac.uk
Web: www.its.leeds.ac.uk
Courses: **Postgraduate**
~ MBA Transport Management
~ MSc Transport Planning &
Engineering
~ MSc Transport Planning
~ MSc Transport Economics

Leeds Metropolitan University

Address: Room 119
Cavendish Hall
Headingley Campus
Beckett Park
Leeds LS2 3QS
Tel: 01138 123 112
Web: www.leedsmet.ac.uk
Courses: **Graduate**
~ BA Business & Supply Chain
Management

University of Lincoln

Address: Brayford Pool
Lincoln
LN6 7TS
Tel: 01522 886 954
Email: lowens@lincoln.ac.uk
Web: www.lincoln.ac.uk
Contact: Jonathan Owens
Courses: **Graduate**
~ BSc Logistics Management
Courses: **Postgraduate**
~ MBA Transport Management
~ MA Transport Economics
~ MBA Transport Planning &
Engineering
~ MBA Transport Planning
~ MSc Logistics Management

Liverpool John Moores University

Address: Student Recruitment
Roscoe Court
4 Rodney Street
Liverpool L1 2TZ
Tel: 0151 231 5090
Fax: 0151 231 3462
Email: recruitment@livjm.ac.uk
Web: www.livjm.ac.uk
Courses **Undergraduate**
~ BSc Maritime Studies
~ BSc Maritime and Intermodal
transport
~ BSc Transport
~ BSc Maritime Business &
Management
~ BSc Managament, Transport &
Logistics
Postgraduate
~ Diploma in Transport Studies
~ DMS
~ Diploma in Transport

London Metropolitan University (formerly University of North London)

Address: 166 – 220 Holloway Road
London
N7 8DB
Tel: 020 7133 4202
Email: admissions@londonmet.ac.uk
Web: www.londonmet.ac.uk
Courses **Undergraduate**
~ BA Tourism & Leisure
~ BA (combined honours) Travel
~ BA Business Studies
Postgraduate
~ Diploma in Professional Studies
(Transport Option)
~ MSc Purchasing and Supply Chain
Management
~ MA Transport Policy &
Management
~ MSc International Trade and
Transport

Loughborough University

Address: Loughborough
Leicestershire LE11 3TU
Tel: 01509 223 781
Email: a.l.bristow@lboro.ac.uk
Web: www.lboro.ac.uk
Courses: **Undergraduate**
~ BSc Transport Management &
Planning
~ BSc Logistics & Transport
Management
~ BSc Airport Management
~ BTEC Transport Management &
Planning
Postgraduate
~ MSc Sustainable Transport &
Travel Planning
~ MSc Transport Policy & Business
Management
~ MSc Airport Planning &
Management

Manchester Metropolitan University

Address: Ayton Street
Manchester M1 3GH
Tel: 0161 247 3894
Email: a.w.carroll@mmu.ac.uk
Web: www.mmu.ac.uk
Courses: **Postgraduate**
~ MSc Logistics & Supply Chain
Management

Napier University

Address: Merchiston Campus
10 Colinton Road
Edinburgh
EH10 5DT
Tel: 0131 455 2210
Email: j.cowie@napier.ac.uk
Web: www.sbe.napier.ac.uk
Contact: Dr Jonathan Cowie
Courses: **Undergraduate**
~ BEng Transportation Engineering
~ BSc Transport Studies
~ BSc Transport Studies and
Information Management
~ BSc Transport Management
Postgraduate
~ MSc Transport Planning and
Engineering
~ PG Dip Transport Planning and
Engineering

Newcastle University

Address: Newcastle upon Tyne
NE1 7RU
Tel: 01912 222 547
Email: ceg.transport@ncl.ac.uk
Web: www.ncl.ac.uk
Contact: Mr Roger Bird
Courses: **Undergraduate**
~ HND Business Studies
~ BA Hons Business Administration
~ BSc/BEng Double degree
~ BA Logistics & Supply Chain
Management
~ BA (Hons) Logistics & Supply
Chain Management
~ BA (Hons) Business Studies
~ BA (Hons) Business Management
Postgraduate
~ MSc Marine Transport with
Management
~ MSc Logistics

Nottingham University

Address: University Park
Nottingham NG7 2RD
Tel: 0115 951 5151
Fax: 0115 951 3666
Email: undergraduate-enquiries@
nottingham.ac.uk
Web: www.nottingham.ac.uk
Courses: **Postgraduate**
~ MSc Transport Engineering

Nottingham Trent University

Address: Burton Street
Nottingham NG1 4BU
Tel: 0115 941 8418
Email: admissions@ntu.ac.uk
Web: www.ntu.ac.uk
Courses: **Postgraduate**
~ MSc European Transportation
~ MSc European Traffic Engineering
~ MSc European Traffic and
Transportation Sciences
~ MSc European Traffic and
Transportation

Oxford Brookes University

Address: Headington Campus
Gipsy Lane
Oxford OX3 0BP
Tel: 01865 483 713
Email: pgt-admin@brookes.ac.uk
Web: www.brookes.ac.uk
Courses: **Undergraduate**
~ BA approved Single Field &
Transport
~ BA Transport
Postgraduate
~ Diploma Planning & Public
Transport
~ MSc: Transport Planning

University of Plymouth
Address: Drake Circus
Plymouth PL4 8AA
Tel: 01752 232 446
Email: j.dinwoodie@plymouth.ac.uk
Web: www.plymouth.ac.uk
Contact: John Dinwoodie
Courses: **Undergraduate**
~ BSc Transport
~ BSc Maritime Business
Postgraduate
~ MSc: International Shipping
~ MSc: International Logistics
~ MSc: Port Management
~ Graduate Membership Shipping
and Logistics Management
~ DPS/DMS Logistics Management
~ DPS/DMS Logistics Management
(European)

University of Salford
Address: Salford
Greater Manchester M5 4WT
Tel: 0161 295 5000
Fax: 0161 295 5999
Email: course-enquiries@salford.ac.uk
Web: www.salford.ac.uk
Courses: **Postgraduate**
~ MSc/Post Graduate
DiplomaTransport Engineering &
Planning
~ MSc Transport & Distribution
Management
~ MSc Transport & Logistics
Management

The University of Sheffield
Address: Western Bank
Sheffield
S10 2TN
UK
Tel: 0114 222 2000
Email: pgtaught@sheffield.ac.uk
Web: www.shef.ac.uk
Courses: **Postgraduate**
~ MSc Transport & Traffic
Engineering

Sheffield Hallam University
Address: City Campus, Howard Street
Sheffield S1 1WB
Tel: 0114 225 5555
e-mail: admissions@shu.ac.uk
Web: www.shu.ac.uk
Courses: **Undergraduate**
~ BA (Hons) Planning Studies
~ Bachelor of Town Planning
~ BA (Hons) Planning Studies +
DTP
~ BA (Hons) Planning & Transport +
DTP
~ Bachelor of Town Planning
Postgraduate
~ MA Planning & Transport
~ MA/MSc Transport Planning and
Management
~ Post Graduate Certificate in
Facilities Management
~ Master in Planning & Transport
~ MA/MSc Urban & Regional
Planning Transport

Southampton Solent University
Address: East Park Terrace
Southampton
Hampshire
SO14 OYN
Tel: 023 8031 9000
Fax: 023 8022 2259
Email: enquiries@solent.ac.uk
Web: www.solent.ac.uk
Courses: **Undergraduate**
~ BSc Transport with Logistics
~ BSc International Transport

University of Southampton

Address: University Road, Highfield
Southampton SO17 1BJ
Tel: 02380 593 705
Fax: 02380 593 131
Email: nbh@soton.ac.uk
Web: www.soton.ac.uk
Contact: Dr Nick Hounsell
Courses: **Graduate**
~ BSc Nautical Studies
Postgraduate
~ MSc Transport Planning &
Engineering
~ MSc Global Logistics Management

University of Stratchclyde in Glasgow

Address: 16 Richmond Street
Glasgow G1 1XQ
Tel: 0141 552 4400
Fax: 0141 552 0775
Web: www.strath.ac.u
Courses: **Postgraduate**
~ MSc Transport & Engineering

Swansea Institute

Address: Mount Pleasant
Swansea SA1 6ED
Tel: 01792 481199
Fax: 01792 546471
Email: terry.lake@sihe.ac.uk
Web: www.sihe.ac.uk
Contact: Terry Lake
Courses: **Undergraduate**
~ BTEC HND Transport Studies
~ BSc Transport Management

University of Ulster at Jordanstown

Address: Shore Road
Newtownabbey
Co. Antrim
BT37 0QB
Tel: 0870 040 0700
Email: registryjn@ulster.ac.uk
Web: www.ulster.ac.uk
Courses: **Undergraduate**
~ BSc Transport & Logistics
~ BSc Transport Technology
~ HND Transport & Distribution
~ BSc Transportation
~ BSc Transport & Supply-Chain
Management

University of Westminster

Address: 35 Marylebone Road
London NW1 5LS
Tel: 020 7911 5000
Email: course-enquiries@wmin.ac.uk
Web: www.wmin.ac.uk
Courses: **Undergraduate**
~ BA Business Studies (Services)
Postgraduate
~ MSc Transport Planning &
Management
~ MSc Transport & Development
~ Diploma Transport & Development

SECTION 6

Directory of Media and Publications

Media

TV and Radio

BBC London 94.9

Address: PO Box 94.9
Marylebone High Street
London W1WA 6FL
Tel: 020 7224 2424
Email: yourlondon@bbc.co.uk
Web: www.bbc.co.uk/London

BBC News 24

Address: Television Centre
Wood Lane, London W12 RJ
Tel: 020 8743 8000
Email: bbcnews24@bbc.co.uk
Web: www.bbc.co.uk/news

95.8 Capital FM

Address: 30 Leicester Square
London WC2H 7LA
Tel: 0871 222 2958
Email: info@capitalradio.com
Web: www.capitalradio.com

Channel 4

Address: 124 Horseferry Road
London SW1P 2TX
Tel: 0845 076 0191
Web: www.channel4.com

GMTV

Address: The London Television Centre
Upper Ground, London SE1 9TT
Tel: 020 7827 7000
Email: newmedia@gm.tv
Web: www.gmtv.co.uk

Independent Radio News

Address: 200 Gray's Inn Road
London WC1X 8XZ
Tel: 020 7430 4090
Email: news@irn.co.uk
Web: www.irn.co.uk

Independent Television News

Address: 200 Gray's Inn Road
London WC1X 8XZ
Tel: 020 7833 3000
Email: itvplanning@itn.co.uk
Web: www.itn.co.uk

LBC News 1152

Address: The Chrysalis Building
13 Bramley Road
London W10 6SP
Tel: 020 7314 7300
Email: newsroom@lbc.co.uk
Web: www.lbc.co.uk

Sky News

Address: Grant Way, off Syon Lane
Isleworth, Middlesex TW7 5QD
Tel: 020 7705 3000
Email: news@sky.com
Web: www.sky.com/news

National Newspapers

Daily Express

Address: The Northern & Shell Building
Number 10 Lower Thames Street
London EC3R 6EN
Tel: 08714 341010
Email: news.desk@express.co.uk
Web: www.express.co.uk

Daily Mail

Address: Northcliffe House
2 Derry Street
South Kensington
London W8 5TT
Tel: 020 7938 6000
Email: letters@dailymail.co.uk
Web: www.dailymail.co.uk

Daily Mirror

Address: 1 Canada Square
Canary Wharf
London E14 5AP
Tel: 020 7293 3000
Email: mirrornews@mgn.co.uk
Web: www.mirror.co.uk

Daily Telegraph

Address: 111 Buckingham Palace Road
London SW1W 0DT
Tel: 020 7538 5000
Email: dtnews@telegraph.co.uk
Web: www.telegraph.co.uk

Evening Standard

Address: Northcliffe House
2 Derry Street, Kensington
London W8 5TT
Tel: 020 7938 6000
Web: www.thisislondon.co.uk

Financial Times

Address: 1 Southwark Bridge
London SE1 9HL
Tel: 020 7873 3000
Web: www.ft.com

Metro (London)

Address: Northcliffe House
2 Derry Street, Kensington
London W8 5TT
Tel: 020 7938 6000
Web: www.metro.co.uk

Sunday Express

Address: The Northern & Shell Building
Number 10 Lower Thames Street
London EC3R 6EN
Tel: 08714 341010
Web: www.express.co.uk

Sunday Telegraph

Address: 111 Buckingham Palace Road
London SW1W 0DT
Tel: 020 7538 5000
Web: www.sundaytelegraph.co.uk

Sunday Times

Address: 1 Pennington Street
London E1 9XN
Tel: 020 7782 5000
Web: www.sunday-times.co.uk

The Guardian

Address: 119 Farringdon Road
London EC1R 3ER
Tel: 020 7278 2332
Email: home@guardian.co.uk
Web: www.theguardian.co.uk

The Independent

Address: Independent House
191 Marsh Wall
London E14 9RS
Tel: 020 7005 2000
Email: newseditor@independent.co.uk
Web: www.independent.co.uk

The Observer

Address: 119 Farringdon Road
London EC1R 3ER
Tel: 020 7278 2332
Web: www.observer.co.uk

The Times

Address: 1 Pennington Street
London E1 9XN
Tel: 020 7782 5000
Email: home.news@thetimes.co.uk
Web: www.timesonline.co.uk

Publications

The publications listed in this section are a useful source of information and frequently provide statistical information on transport and related matters in addition to their main editorial function. If the publication is produced by a publisher (*Pub*), contact details are given in the section that follows. If the publication is produced by an organisation (*Org*) it will be found as an entry in Sections 2 – Government Organisations or Section 3 – Non-Government Organisations.

Air

Air Cargo Week
Pub: A-Z Publications Ltd
Price: £100 per annum
Tel: 01737 645777
Email: info@azfreight.com
Web: www.aircargoweek.com

Air International
Pub: Key Publishing Ltd
Price: £40.70 per annum
Tel: 01780 480404
Email: malcolm.english@keypublishing.com
Web: www.airinternational.com
Editor: Malcolm English

Air Traffic Management
Pub: Euromoney Institutional Investor plc
Freq: Monthly
Price: £349 per annum
Tel: 020 7779 8673
Email: information@euromonetplc.com
Web: www.euromoneyplc.com

Aircraft Illustrated
Pub: Ian Allan Publishing
Freq: Monthly
Desc: Photographs, news and reviews
Price: £45.60
Tel: 01932 266600
Web: www.ianallanpublishing.com
Editor: Allan Burney

Airfinance Annual
Pub: Euromoney Publications plc
Freq: Annual
Price: £155
Tel: 020 7779 8673
Email: information@euromonetplc.com
Web: www.euromoneyplc.com

Airfinance Journal
Pub: Euromoney Publications plc
Freq: Monthly
Price: £590
Tel: 020 7779 8673
Email: information@euromonetplc.com
Web: www.euromoneyplc.com

Airline Business
Pub: Reed Business Information
Freq: Monthly
Price: £89 per annum
Tel: 020 8652 3842
Email: murdo.morrison@flightglobal.com
Web: www.flightglobal.com

Airline Coding Directory

Org: International Air Transport
Association
Price: $330
Tel: 020 7660 0068
Web: www.iata.org

Airport Operator

Org: Airport Operators Association
Freq: Regular
Price: Free for members
Tel: 020 7222 2249
Web: www.aoa.org.uk

Airports International

Pub: Key Publishing Ltd
Freq: 9 per annum
Price: Free
Tel: 01780 755131
Email: tom.allett@keypublishing.com
Web: www.airportsinternational.co.uk

AITO Members List

Org: Association of Independent Tour
Operators
Freq: Ongoing
Price: Free on web
Tel: 020 8744 9280
Email: Infor@aito.co.uk
Web: www.aito.co.uk

Aviation Training Directory

Org: International Civil Aviation
Organisation
Desc: Searchable database of civil aviation
training institutions worldwide
Price: Free on website
Email: icaohq@icao.int
Web: www.icao.int/td/

Aviation Week and Space Technology

Pub: Aviation Week
Freq: Weekly
Desc: Business to business publication
covering business, operations and
technology for civil aviation, military
aerospace and space.
Price: $160 per annum
Email: letters@aviationweek.com
Web: www.aviationweek.com

AWIN Business Aviation

Pub: Aviation Week
Freq: Monthly
Desc: Business to business publication
providing technology and educational
information for owners, operators,
pilots, flight department managers of
business air
Price: Various
Tel: +1 515 237 3682
Email: AWNord@cdsfulfilment.com
Web: www.aviationweek.com

British Business and General Aviation Industry Directory

Org: British Business and General Aviation
Association
Price: Free on website
Tel: 01844 238020
Email: info@bbga.aero
Web: www.bbga.aero

Defence Helicopter

Pub: The Shephard Press Ltd
Freq: Bi-monthly
Price: £80
Tel: 01628 604 311
Email: ad@shepherd.co.uk
Web: www.shephard.co.uk
Editor: Andrew Drwiega

European Regions Airline Association Yearbook

Org: European Regions Airline Association
Freq: Annual
Desc: Reference guide to the industry.
Includes statistics
Price: £85
Tel: 01276 856495
Email: info@eraa.org
Web: www.eraa.org

Flight International

Pub: Reed Business Information
Freq: Weekly
Price: £69 per annum
Tel: 01444 445454
Email: flightinternational.subs@gss-uk.com
Web: www.flightinternational.com

Freight

Org: Associated Society of Locomotive
         Engineers and Firemen
Freq: Six monthly
Price: Free to members
Tel: 020 7317 8600
Email: info@aslef.org.uk
Web: www.aslef.org.uk

Jane's Air Traffic Control

Pub: Jane's Information Group
Freq: Yearbook/CD/Online
Desc: Equipment and services vital to ATC
         systems worldwide online
Price: £375/£900/£980
Tel: 020 8700 3700
Email: customerservices.uk@janes.com
Web: http://jatc.janes.com

Jane's Airport and Handling Agents - Europe

Pub: Jane's Information Group
Freq: Yearbook/CD/Online
Desc: Details of airports in the region and
         their handling agents and fixed-base
         operators
Price: £415/£495/£550
Tel: 020 8700 3700
Email: customerservices.uk@janes.com
Web: http://jaha.janes.com

Jane's Airport Equipment and Services

Pub: Jane's Information Group
Freq: Yearbook/CD/Online
Desc: Guide to world's airport suppliers and
         their products
Price: £410/£950/£1,025
Tel: 020 8700 3700
Email: customerservices.uk@janes.com
Web: http://jaes.janes.com

Jane's Airport Review

Pub: Jane's Information Group
Freq: Monthly/CD/Online
Desc: Issues affecting airport industry.
Price: £155 per annum/£550/£585
Tel: 020 8700 3700
Email: customerservices.uk@janes.com
Web: http://jar.janes.com

Jane's World Airlines

Pub: Jane's Information Group
Freq: Binder/CD/Online
Desc: Information on more than 500 airlines
         and their operations
Price: £920/£1,185/£1,280
Tel: 020 8700 3700
Email: customerservices.uk@janes.com
Web: http://jwa.janes.com

World Aviation Directory & Aerospace Database

Pub: Aviation Week
Freq: Online
Price: On application
Tel: 001 561 862 0005
Email: aw_intelligence@aviationnow.com
Web: www.aviationnow.com

Rail

International Railway Journal

Pub: Simons-Boardman Publishing
         Corporation
Freq: Monthly
Type: Passenger and freight
Desc: News & technical/business articles
         for railway professionals in more than
         130 countries.
Price: $140
Tel: 001 402 346 4740
Web: www.railjournal.com

Jane's World Railways

Pub: Jane's Information Group
Freq: Annual Yearbook/CD/Online
Desc: Detailed information from over 140
         countries
Price: £515/£1,115/£1,200
Tel: 020 8700 3700
Web: http://jwr.janes.com

Locomotive Journal

Org: Associated Society of Locomotive
         Engineers and Firemen
Price: Free to members
Tel: 020 7317 8600
Email: info@aslef.org.uk
Web: www.aslef.org.uk

Locomotive and Carriage Institution Newsletter

Org: Locomotive And Carriage Institution
Freq: Quarterly
Desc: Gives details of institution activities and meeting and occasional articles on railway subjects.
Price: Free for members
Web: www.lococarriage.org.uk

Modern Railways

Pub: Ian Allan Publishing
Freq: Monthly
Desc: News and reviews
Price: £45.40
Tel: 01932 266600
Email: james.abbott3@ntlworld.com
Web: www.ianallanpublishing.com
Editor: James Abbott

Rail

Pub: EMAP plc
Freq: Fortnightly
Tel: 01733 264666
Email: rail@emap.com
Web: www.rail-magazine.com
Editor: Phil Haigh

Rail Business Intelligence

Pub: Reed Business Information (Railway Gazette International)
Freq: Fortnightly
Desc: Business newsletter covering all aspects of Britain's rail industry.
Price: £620 per annum
Tel: 0208 652 3855
Web: www.railwaygazette.com

Railway Directory

Pub: Reed Business Information (Railway Gazette International)
Freq: Annual
Desc: Worldwide directory of railway industry, with all suppliers and manufacturers in all disciplines. Also published on the web
Price: £250/£350 online
Tel: 01371 851 800
Web: www.railwaydirectory.net

Railway Express Magazine

Pub: Foursight Publications Ltd
Freq: Monthly
Price: £38.00 per annum
Tel: 01780 470086
Email: editors@railexpress.co.uk
Web: www.railexpress.co.uk
Editor: Phillip Sutton

Railway Gazette International

Pub: Reed Business Information
Freq: Monthly
Tel: 020 8652 8608
Email: railway.gazette@rbi.co.uk
Web: www.railwaygazette.com

The Railway Magazine

Pub: IPC Country & Leisure Media Ltd
Freq: Monthly
Price: £38.34 per annum
Tel: 020 314 84680
Web: www.ipcmedia.com
Editor: Nick Pigott

Sisters on the Move

Org: Associated Society of Locomotive Engineers and Firemen
Price: Free to members
Tel: 020 7317 8600
Email: info@aslef.org.uk
Web: www.aslef.org.uk

Transit

Pub: Landor Publishing
Freq: Fortnightly
Price: £78 per annum
Tel: 0845 270 7868
Email: ed.transit@landor.co.uk
Web: www.transitmagazine.co.uk
Editor: Robert Jack

Road

Automotive Engineer
Pub: Professional Engineering
            Publishing Ltd
Freq: 11 per year
Price: £329 per annum
Tel: 020 7222 3337
Web: www.pepublishing.com

Automotive News Europe
Pub: Crain Communications
Freq: Fortnightly
Price: £70 per annum
Tel: +49 6123 9238 229
Web: www.autonews.com

Bike Biz
Pub: Intent Media Ltd
Freq: Monthly
Desc: Monthly Trade Magazine
Price: £50 per annum
Tel: 01922 535 646
Web: www.bikebiz.co.uk

Bus User
Org: Bus Users UK
Freq: Quarterly
Desc: Current issues and developments in
            bus travel throughout the UK
Price: Free to members
Contact: Stephen Morris
Tel: 01782 442855
Email: enquiries@bususers.org
Web: www.nfbu.org

Bus and Coach Buyer
Pub: Glen Holland Ltd
Price: Free
Tel: 01775 711777
Email: bcbsales@busandcoachbuyer.com
Web: www.glenholland.co.uk

Buses
Pub: Ian Allan Publishing
Freq: Monthly
Desc: News and reviews
Price: £44.40
Tel: 01932 266600
Email: buseseditor@btconnect.com
Web: www.ianallanpublishing.com
Editor: Alan Millar

BVRLA Directory
Org: British Vehicle Rental and Leasing
            Association
Freq: Online
Desc: List of members
Price: Free online
Tel: 01494 434747
Email: info@bvla.co.uk
Web: www.bvrla.co.uk

Coach and Bus Guide
Pub: Rouncey Media Ltd
Freq: Annual
Desc: Listing of manufacturers and
            suppliers in the coach and bus
            industry
Price: £45
Tel: 01733 293 240
Web: www.cbwonline.com

Coach and Bus Week
Pub: Rouncey Media Ltd
Freq: Weekly
Price: £69 per annum
Tel: 01733 293 240
Email: andrew.sutcliffe@
            rounceymedia.co.uk
Web: www.cbwonline.com
Editor: Andrew Sutcliffe

The Coach Operator's Handbook
Pub: Rouncey Media Ltd
Freq: Annual
Desc: Coach tourism guide to venues in UK
            and Eire
Price: £45
Tel: 01733 293 240
Web: www.cbwonline.com

Commercial Motor
Pub: Reed Business Information
Freq: Weekly
Price: £92 per annum
Tel: 020 8652 3612
Web: www.rbi.co.uk
Editor: Andy Salter

Fleet News
Pub: EMAP plc
Freq: Weekly online
Price: £99 per annum
Tel: 01733 468 000
Web: www.fleetnewsnet.co.uk

Fleet World
Price: Free
Pub: Stag Publications ltd
Freq: Monthly
Tel: 01727 739160
Web: www.fleetworld.net
Editor: Ken Rogers

Fleet World Supplier Directory
Price: Free
Pub: Stag Publications ltd
Tel: 01727 739160
Web: www.fleetworld.net
Editor: Ken Rogers

Freight
Org: Freight Transport Association
Freq: Monthly
Price: Free to members
Tel: 08717112222
Web: www.fta.co.uk

International Freighting Weekly
Pub: Informa plc
Freq: Weekly/Online
Tel: 020 7017 4659
Web: www.ifw-net.com
Editor: Chris Lewis

IRF Bulletin
Org: International Road Federation
Freq: Online
Price: Free to members and old editions on web
Tel: +32 2 644 58 77
Email: info@erf.be
Web: www.irfnet.org

Little Red Book
Pub: Ian Allan Publishing
Freq: Annual
Desc: Directory of road passenger transport industry
Price: £35
Tel: 01932 266600
Web: www.ianallanpublishing.com

Local Transport Today
Pub: Landor Publishing
Freq: Fortnightly
Desc: Contains a regular 'Statistics Monitor' section
Tel: 0845 270 7953
Web: www.lttonline.co.uk

Logistics and Transport Focus
Org: Institute of Logistics and Transport
Freq: 10 issues per year
Desc: Journal to members
Price: Free to members
Tel: 01536 740 100
Web: www.ciltuk.org.uk

Motor Transport
Pub: Reed Business Information
Freq: Weekly
Price: £99 per annum
Tel: 020 8652 3285
Web: www.rbi.co.uk
Editor: Andrew Brown

MSA Newslink
Org: Motor Schools Association of Great Britain
Freq: Online
Price: Free
Tel: 0161 429 9669
Email: mail@msagb.co.uk
Web: www.msagb.co.uk

NGV News

Org:	Natural Gas Vehicle Association
Freq:	Six Monthly
Desc:	Newsletter online
Price:	Free
Tel:	01926 462900
Email:	info@ngva.co.uk
Web:	www.ngva.co.uk
Editor:	Caroline Haine

Park and Ride Great Britain

Org:	TAS Publications
Freq:	Annual
Desc:	e-report case studies of transport plans
Price:	£49
Tel:	01729 840756
Web:	www.tas.uk.net

Roadway

Org:	Road Haulage Association
Freq:	Monthly
Price:	Free to members
Tel:	01932 841515
Web:	www.roadway.co.uk
Editor:	Peter Shakespeare

Scottish Transport Matters

Org:	Scottish Association for Public Transport
Freq:	Quarterly
Price:	Free online
Email:	mail@sapt.org.uk
Web:	www.sapt.org.uk

Together

Org:	The Institution of Highways and Transportation
Freq:	10x per year
Desc:	Electronic Newsletter
Price:	Free to members
Tel:	020 7387 2525
Email:	info@iht.org.uk
Web:	www.iht.org.uk

Transport Engineer

Pub:	Aztec Media Services Ltd
Freq:	Monthly
Tel:	01428 714278
Email:	info@aztecxpress.com
Web:	www.transportengineer.co.uk

Transport News

Pub:	KAV Publicity Ltd
Freq:	Monthly
Price:	£22 per annum
Tel:	01355 279 077
Email:	Info@transportnews.co.uk
Web:	www.transportnews.co.uk
Contact:	Alistair Vallance

Transport News Digest

Pub:	Transport Press Services
Freq:	Monthly
Des:	Monthly summary of road-freight developments, primary in the UK
Price:	£28 per annum, £50 for two years
Tel:	020 7727 0253

Truck and Bus Builder

Pub:	Truck and Bus Builder Publishing Ltd
Freq:	Monthly
Desc:	Facts and Figures about trucks and Bus industry
Price:	£180
Tel:	01984 639300
Email:	info@truckandbusbuilder.com

Truck & Driver

Pub:	Reed Business Information
Freq:	Monthly
Price:	£31 per annum
Tel:	020 8652 3303
Web:	www.rbi.co.uk
Editor:	Brian Weatherley

Trucking

Pub:	Future Publishing Company
Freq:	Monthly
Price:	£28 per annum
Tel:	0870 8374 773
Web:	www.myfavouritemagazines.co.uk

UK Motor Industry Directory

Org:	Society of Motor Manufacturers and Traders
Freq:	Annual
Price:	£60 non-members £40 members. Free online.
Tel:	020 7235 7000
Web:	www.smmt.co.uk

Wheels Magazine

Org: United Road Transport Union
Freq: Six per year
Price: Free to members
Tel: 0161 882 2703
Email: info@urtu.com
Web: www.urtu.com

World Highways Magazine/Web site

Pub: Route One Publishing
Freq: Ten times per year
Price: £80
Tel: 01322 612055
Email: apaterson@ropl.com
Web: www.worldhighways.com
Editor: Alan Peterson

Maritime

British Marine Equipment Council - Directory of Members

Org: British Marine Equipment Council
Freq: Online
Desc: Directory of members products and services
Price: Free
Tel: 020 7928 9199
Email: info@maritimeindustries.org.uk
Web: www.maritimeindustries.org.uk

British Marine News

Org: British Marine Federation
Freq: Monthly or email news weekly
Price: Free
Tel: 01784 473377
Email: info@britishmarine.co.uk
Web: www.britishmarine.co.uk

Cargo Systems

Pub: Informa Maritime & Transport
Freq: Monthly
Price: £210
Tel: 020 7017 4187
Email: mt.enquiries@Informa.com
Web: www.cargosystems.net

Cargo World

Org: ICHCA - International Cargo Handling Co-ordination Association
Tel: 01708 735 225
Email: publications@ichcainternational.co.uk
Web: www.ichcainternational.co.uk

Containerisation International Magazine

Pub: Informa Maritime & Transport
Freq: Monthly
Price: £199
Tel: 020 7017 4187
Web: www.lloydsmiu.com

Cruise International

Pub: Informa Maritime & Transport
Freq: Bi Monthly
Price: £160
Tel: 020 7017 4187
Email: enquiries@lloydsmiu.com
Web: www.lloydscruise.com

Electric Boat News

Org: Electric Boat Association
Freq: Quarterly
Desc: Quarterly journal to promote electric boating
Price: Free to members
Tel: 01491 681449
Email: barbara@eboat.org.uk
Web: www.electric-boat-association.org.uk

Fairplay

Pub: Fairplay Publications Ltd
Freq: Weekly
Price: £415
Tel: 01737 379000
Email: Info@fairplay.co.uk
Web: www.fairplay.co.uk

Inland Waterways Association Bulletin

Org: Inland Waterways Association
Freq: Monthly
Price: Free online
Tel: 01923 711 114
Email: iwa@waterways.org.uk
Web: www.waterways.org.uk

The ISSA Ship Stores Catalogue

Org: International Ship Suppliers
            Association
Freq: Annual
Desc: Comprehensive catalogue of ship
            products
Price: On application
Contact: Spencer Eade
Tel: 020 7626 6236
Web: www.shipsupply.org

Lloyd's Casualty Week

Pub: Lloyd's Marine Intelligence Unit
Freq: Weekly pdf email
Price: £475
Tel: 020 7017 4482
Email: Enquiries@lloydsmiu.com
Web: www.lloydsmiu.com

Lloyd's Confidential Index

Pub: Lloyd's Marine Intelligence Unit
Freq: Every six months
Desc: Physical characteristics of 42,000
            vessels for insurance, legal and
            banking professionals.
Price: £2,400
Tel: 020 7017 4482
Email: Enquiries@lloydsmiu.com
Web: www.lloydsmiu.com

Lloyd's Maritime Directory

Pub: Lloyd's Marine Intelligence Unit
Freq: Annual
Desc: Hard copy and CD Rom of ship
            owners, managers, operators and
            shipping services
Price: £353
Tel: 020 7017 4482
Email: Enquiries@lloydsmiu.com
Web: www.lloydsmiu.com

Lloyd's List Ports of the World

Pub: Lloyd's Marine Intelligence Unit
Freq: Annual
Desc: Directory of 2,400 ports
Price: £277
Tel: 020 7017 4482
Email: Enquiries@lloydsmiu.com
Web: www.lloydsmiu.com

Lloyd's List

Pub: Informa Group
Freq: Daily
Desc: Newspaper for shipping
Price: £676 per annum
Tel: 020 7017 5531
Web: www.lloydslist.com
Editor: Julian Bray

Lloyd's Shipping Index

Pub: Lloyd's Marine Intelligence Unit
Freq: Annual
Desc: All current positions and details of
            the world's commercial fleet
Price: £1,700
Email: Enquiries@lloydsmiu.com
Web: www.lloydsmiu.com

Lloyd's Shipping Information Database

Pub: Lloyd's Marine Intelligence Unit
Freq: Online
Desc: Marine database of vessels and
            companies
Price: £1,173.83
Email: Enquiries@lloydsmiu.com
Web: www.lloydsmiu.com

Lloyd's Ship Manager

Pub: Informa Maritime & Transport
Freq: Monthly
Price: £255
Tel: 020 7017 4187
Email: mt.enquiries@Informa.com
Web: www.infomaritime.com

Lloyd's Shipping Econmist

Pub: Informa Maritime & Transport
Freq: Monthly
Price: £839
Tel: 020 7017 4187
Email: mt.enquiries@Informa.com
Web: www.infomaritime.com

Ports Online

Pub: Lloyd's Marine Intelligence Unit
Freq: Online
Desc: Details on 2,800 ports
Price: £387.75
Email: Enquiries@lloydsmiu.com
Web: www.lloydsmiu.com

Maritime Journal

Pub: Mercator Media Ltd
Freq: Monthly
Price: £61.25 per annum
Tel: 01329 825 335
Email: editor@maritime-journal.com
Web: www.maritimejournal.com
Editor: Larz Bourne

Ship and Boat International

Org: Royal Institution of Naval Architects
Freq: Six times per year
Price: £84 per annum
Tel: 020 7235 4622
Email: publications@rina.org.uk
Web: www.rina.org.uk
Editor: Cheryl Saponia

The Ship Supplier

Org: International Ship Suppliers
           Association
Freq: Quarterly
Desc: News and views on ship supply in 80
           countries
Price: Free to members
Contact: Spencer Eade
Tel: 020 7626 6236
Web: www.shipsupply.org

Shipping Finance Annual

Pub: Euromoney Publications plc
Freq: Annual
Price: £155
Tel: 020 7779 8999
Email: hotline@euromoneyplc.com
Web: www.euromoney-yearbooks.com

Who's Who in the Bus and Coach Industry

Pub: Yandell Publishing Ltd
Freq: Annual
Desc: UK bus and coach operators
           alphabetical listing by traffic area
Price: £36.50k
Tel: 01908 613 323
Email: editorial@yandelmedia.com
Web: www.yandellmediagroup.com

General

AITO Members Directory

Org: Association of Independent Tour
           Operators
Freq: Online
Price: Free
Tel: 020 8744 9280
Email: info@aito.co.uk
Web: www.aito.co.uk

CTA Journal

Org: Community Transport Association
Freq: 6 times per annum
Desc: News and feature articles on all
           aspects of voluntary and community
           transport across the UK
Price: Free to members
Tel: 08707 743586
Email: info@ctauk.org
Web: www.communitytransport.com

TSUG Newsletter

Org: Transport Statistics Users Group
           (TSUG)
Freq: 4-6 times per annum
Desc: Newsletter containing news, seminar
           reports and reviews of matters
           relating to transport statistics.
Price: Free to members
Tel: 01722 422 169
Email: liswoods@aol.com
Web: www.tsug.org.uk
Contact: James Woods

T&G Record

Org: Transport & General Workers Union
Freq: Six times a year
Desc: Industrial news, campaigning
           Information and features about The
           T&G's activities
Price: Free to members/content online
Tel: 020 7611 2500
Fax: 020 7611 2555
Email: tgwu@tgwu.org.uk
Web: www.tgwu.org.uk

Travel Weekly

Pub:	Reed Business Information
Freq:	Weekly
Price:	Free or paid for
Tel:	020 8652 8230
Email:	martin.couzins@rbi.co.uk
Web:	www.travelweekly.co.uk
Editor:	Martin Couzins

Publishers

A-Z Publications Ltd

Address:	Darby House
	Betchingley Road
	Merstham
	Surrey RH1 3TT
Tel:	01737 645777
Email:	info@azfreight.com
Web:	www.azfreight.com

Aviation Week

Address:	1200 G Street
	Washington
	DC 20005
	USA
Tel:	001 515 237 3682
Email:	letters@aviationweek.com
Web:	www.aviatioweek.com

Aztec Media Services Ltd

Address:	Hilltop, Beech Hill, Headley Down
	Hampshire GU35 8BD
Tel:	01428 714278
Email:	info@aztecxpress.com
Web:	www.aztec-media.co.uk

Crain Communications

Address:	3rd Floor
	21 St Thomas Street
	London SE1 9RY
Tel:	020 7457 1400
Email:	info@crain.com
Web:	www.crain.co.uk

Elsevier Limited

Address:	Norwich House
	Knoll Road
	Camberley
	Surrey GU15 3PR
Email:	nlinfo-f@elsevier.com
Tel:	01276 701 500
Web:	www.elsevier.com

EMAP plc

Address:	Bretton Court
	Bretton PE3 8DZ
Tel:	01733 465232
Email:	rail@emap.com
Web:	www.emap.com

Euromoney Publications plc/Euromoney Institutional Investors plc

Address:	Nestor House, Playhouse Yard
	London EC4V 5EX
Tel:	020 7779 8888
Web:	www.euromoney.com

Fairplay Publications Ltd

Address:	Lombard House, 3 Princess Way
	Redhill, Surrey RH1 1UP
Tel:	01737 379000
Email:	info@fairplay.co.uk
Web:	www.fairplay.co.uk

Foursight Publications Ltd

Address:	20 Park Street
	Kings Cliffe
	Peterborough PE8 6XN
Tel:	01780 470086
Email:	editors@railexpress.co.uk
Web:	www.railexpress.co.uk

Glen Holland Ltd

Address:	The Publishing Centre
	1 Woolram Wygate
	Spalding PE11 1NU
Tel:	01775 711777
Web:	www.glen-holland.co.uk

Ian Allan Publishing Ltd

Address: Riverdene Business Park
Molesey Road, Hersham
Surrey KT12 4RG
Tel: 01932 266600
Email: info@midlandcounties.com
Web: www.ianallanpublishing.com

Informa plc

Address: Mortimer House
37-41 Mortimer Street
London W1T 3JH
Tel: 020 7017 5000
Web: www.informa.com

Intent Media Ltd

Address: 6a St. Andrew Street
Hertford
Hertfordshire S14 1JA
Tel: 01992 535 648
Web: www.bikebiz.co.uk

IPC Country & Leisure Media Ltd

Address: King's Reach Tower
Stamford Street
London SE1 9LS
Tel: 020 7261 5533
Web: www.ipcmedia.com

Jane's Information Group

Address: Sentinel House
163 Brighton Road
Coulsdon CR5 2YH
Tel: 020 8700 3700
Email: info@janes.com
Web: www.janes.com

KAV Publicity Ltd

Wheatsheaf House
Montgomery Street
The Village, East Kilbride
Glasgow G74 4JS
Tel: 01355 279 077
Fax: 01355 279 088
Web: www.transportnews.co.uk

Key Publishing Ltd

Address: PO Box 100
Stamford PE9 1XQ
Tel: 01780 755 131
Web: www.keypublishing.com

Landor Publishing Ltd

Address: Quadrant House
250 Kennington Lane
London SE11 5RD
Tel: 0845 270 7950
Fax: 020 7587 7960
Web: www.landor.co.uk

Lloyd's Marine Intelligence Unit

Address: Telephone House
69-77 Paul Street
London EC2A 4LQ
Tel: 020 7017 4482
Fax: 020 7017 5007
Web: www.lloydsmiu.com

Mercator Media Ltd

Address: The Old Mill, Lower Quay
Fareham PO16 0RA
Tel: 01329 825 335
Web: www.maritimejournal.com

Professional Engineering Publishing

Address: 1 Birdcage Walk
London SW1H 9JJ
Tel: 020 7973 1300
Web: www.pepublishing.com

Route One Publishing

Address: Horizon House
Azalea Drive
Swanley BR8 8JR
Kent
Tel: 01322 612055
Email: media@ropl.com
Web: www.ropl.com

Reed Business Information

Address: Quadrant House, The Quadrant
Sutton SM2 5AS
Tel: 020 8652 3500
Web: www.reedbusiness.co.uk

The Shephard Press Ltd

Address: 111 High Street
Burnham SL1 7JZ
Tel: 01628 604 311
Email: ad@shephard.co.uk
Web: www.shephard.co.uk

Simons-Boardman Publishing Corporation

Address: 1809 Capitol Avenue
         Omaha, NE 6810-4972
         USA
Tel: 001-402-346 4300
Web: www.railjournal.com

SPG Media Group plc

Address: Brunel House
         55-57 North Wharf Road
         London W2 1LA
Tel: 020 7915 9660
Email: info@spgmedia.com
Web: www.spgmedia.com

Stag Publications Ltd

Address: 18 Alban Park, Hatfield Road
         St Albans AL4 0JJ
Tel: 01707 739160
Web: www.fleetworld.net

Transport Press Services

Address: 38 Portabello Road
         London, W11 3DH
Tel: 020 7727 0253
Fax: 020 7229 5909
Email: jds@transportpressservices.com
Web: www.uktpl.com

UK Transport Press Ltd

Address: Bank House, High Street
         Cuckfield, West Sussex
         RH17 5EN
Tel: 01444 414 293
Web: www.uktpl.com

Yandell Media Group Ltd

Address: PO Box 5116
         Milton Keynes MK15 8ZQ
Tel: 01908 613 323
Email: editorial@yandellmedia.com
Web: www.yandellmedia.com

Research Companies

*BRL Shipping Consultants Ltd

Address: One Plumstead Road
         Wooolwich, London
         SE18 7BZ
Tel: 020 8316 2005
Fax: 020 8854 4917
Email: brlshpg@btconnext.com
Web: www.brldata.com

*Datamonitor

Address: Charles House
         108-110 Finchley Road
         London, NW3 5JJ
Tel: 020 7675 7000
Fax: 020 7675 7500
Email: euroinfo@datamonitor.com
Web: www.datamonitor.com

*Drewry Shipping Consultants Ltd

Address: Drewry House
         Meridian Gate – South Gate
         213 Marsh Wall
         London, E14 9FJ
Tel: 020 7538 0191
Fax: 020 7987 9396
Web: www.drewry.co.uk

*Fleet Audits Ltd

Address: Rivendell House
         Winton Road
         Petersfield
         GU2 3LL
Tel: 0201730 266666
Email: info@fleet-audits.com
Web: www.fleet-audits.com

*GP Wild International Ltd

Address: 15 Gander Hill
         Haywards Heath
         West Sussex, RH16 1QU
Tel: 01444 413931
Web: www.gpwild.com

*IRN Research

Address: Concorde House
Trinity Park
Solihull, Birmingham
B37 7UQ
Tel: 0121 635 5210
Email: info@irn-research.com
Web: www.irn-research.com

*MDS Transmodal Ltd

Address: 5-6 Hunters Walk
Canal Street
Chester, Cheshire
CH1 4EB
Tel: 01244 348301
Web: www.mdst.co.uk

*PRB Associates Limited

Address: Royal Dock Chambers
Flour Square, Grimsby
North East Lincolnshire
DN31 3LW
Tel: 01472 353532
Fax: 01472 351112
Email: peter.baker@prbassociates.co.uk
Web: www.prbassociates.co.uk

*SSY Consultancy And Research Ltd

Address: Lloyds Chambers
1 Portstoken Street
London
E1 8PH
Tel: 020 7977 7404
Email: research@ssy.co.uk
Web: www.ssyonline.com

*The TAS Partnership Ltd

Address: Ross Holme
West End
Long Preston, Skipton
BD23 4QL
Tel: 01729 840756
Web: www.tas-part.co.uk

*Topflight Research Ltd

Address: Hurst House
157-169 Walton Road
East Molesey
Surrey, KT8 0DX
Tel: 020 7193 4145
Email: info@topflight.co.uk
Web: www.topflight.co.uk

*Trend Tracker Ltd

Address: the CIL Building
Corsley, Warminster
Wiltshire, BA12 7QE
Tel: 0870 421 4350
Email: info@trendtracker.co.uk
Web: www.trendtracker.co.uk

SECTION 7

Index of Organisations

(listed in Sections 2, 3 and 4)